ANCIENT LIFE IN MEXICO AND CENTRAL AMERICA

A Quirigua Design

ANCIENT LIFE IN MEXICO AND CENTRAL AMERICA

By EDGAR L. HEWETT, *D.Soc., LLD., LHD.*

*President of the Schools of American Research
of the Archæological Institute of America
Professor of Archæology, University
of New Mexico and University
of Southern California.*

Author of *Ancient Life in the
American Southwest*

ILLUSTRATED

THE BOBBS-MERRILL COMPANY
PUBLISHERS
INDIANAPOLIS   NEW YORK

Printed in the United States of America

PRINTED AND BOUND BY
BRAUNWORTH & CO., INC.
BUILDERS OF BOOKS
BRIDGEPORT, CONN.

To

THE STUDENTS WHO IN CAMP AND
CLASSROOM HAVE WITH ME EXPLORED
OUR AMERICA AND TRIED TO
UNDERSTAND ITS ANCIENT LIFE

CONTENTS

CONTENTS—*Continued*

CONTENTS—*Continued*

ILLUSTRATIONS

ILLUSTRATIONS (Continued)

FOREWORD

WHEN the book, *Ancient Life in the American Southwest,* was published in 1930 it was understood that its reception would determine whether or not there should be written at a later date a similar one on Mexico and Central America. In the opinion of the publishers, the book has had a satisfactory circulation and has been found readable and useful. That settles it so far as I am concerned. I shall put together the results of twenty-five years' study of Mexico and Central America, including many field trips into that ancient world; explorations extending from Chihuahua to Honduras; personal contact with the principal surviving tribes; and first-hand knowledge of most of the important ruins. There have been five excavating seasons of my own for the institution that I have directed for a quarter of a century (The School of American Research of the Archæological Institute of America), observation of most of the excavations made by others, direction of the Middle American studies of many university students, and the reading of all the literature, good, bad, and worse, that anyone has any business to read on that part of the world.

I have had some concern about the character of this second work on ancient America. Should it be a more rigidly scientific organization of the material, following the method of textbooks designed for university students, or should it endeavor to meet this need to some extent and at the same time be useful to a reading public that cannot be reached through college textbooks and scientific reports? To help me out, the publishers kindly sent me a bundle of clippings, newspaper and magazine reviews of the preceding publication. Unless ninety-five per cent of these are wrong, the way is clearly indicated. I detect among the reviewers the student, the college professor, the philosopher, the banker, the archæologist, the writer, the artist, the lover of science, and the lover of literature. While they are too generous, I conclude that they represent fairly the intelligence of the country and reflect the reaction of a large reading public to the work. Therefore, the more popular style of book has it.

Though it will deal with vanished people who have left only the débris of culture to work on, I shall try to make this a living picture of ancient life. That calls for some imagination, some artistry, some enthusiasm—essentials in the equipment of an archæologist, for no people has ever left more than a fragmentary record. This book will be made up mainly of descriptions that are verifiable or the contrary according as my observations have been accurate or not and my inferences sound or otherwise. There will be occasional allusions to vagaries which pass for knowledge, but this is not to be a critical history. I shall not annoy readers of a book of this kind with footnotes and tedious documentation. The facts speak for themselves and usually I let it go at that. Readers of this book will want to know what this writer has seen and thought and has to say, and will not care for controversial matters. I shall trouble them with diverse opinions only when it seems important for them to consider opposing conclusions. At the same time I am very desirous that this work shall convey to its readers the soundest information obtainable concerning Middle America. I shall therefore quote at considerable length the statements of those who have written dependable archæological history.

In the reviews of the previous book above referred to, there was almost no criticism of the facts and conclusions presented, but some faults of omission were pointed out. There was some displeasure expressed with my commendation of the veteran archæologists and explorers of the Southwest and my silence concerning recent work of alleged excellence. The same fault will be found with this book. I shall of necessity omit reference to much that deserves credit. I shall probably again give unstinted praise to the veterans who did their work when tropical exploration was serious business. Their contributions, seasoned by time, give us foundations of everlasting rock. Twenty-five years from now I may be proclaiming the great work of the present decade with equal fervor. We shall know by that time what was worth doing and how well it was done. It matters little who says the first word in science or the last word. It is the enduring word that counts.

For the assistance of those who have failed to comprehend what I have set out to do in these studies and publications on ancient life in America, let me say that I have conceived my part in American archæology to be an endeavor to understand the genius of the native American race and make it better known—to help establish it in the culture history of the world. Libraries have been printed on Old World cultures. Every phase of life in classic lands has been thought worthy of study and exposition. American research has consisted largely in investigation of isolated phases of Indian culture. Out of the débris of its past and survivals of its achievements I should like to produce an integrated view of this race as evolved when it was unmolested, and of its future place in the civilization of America.

During more than a quarter of a century, much of it in the saddle; following the trails of peoples who have passed into the shadows; sitting at campfires in council with those who have been left behind, I have derived my picture of ancient life in America. To present that picture as a whole, as impressed upon my own mind, is now attempted as a modest contribution to the history of the human race. I shall develop it in about the order in which I have proceeded in personal exploration. All political boundaries are erased. The most important seats of culture are described as I have personally explored them, and from the literature on each, authoritative extracts have been selected for reproduction.

The history of any people that has occupied the stage for a time and passed into the shadows is essentially a drama. It embraces all the elements: human aspirations, strivings, successes, failures. It has its time of exuberance, depression, victory, defeat, decline, and, normally, of tragic ending. To resurrect the past of Middle America, to portray the domestic, esthetic and religious life of that ancient world, calls for a vivid impression of what survives of it in the old environment, in the midst of the ruin of what the ancients created, supplemented by the records of eyewitnesses to any part of the action that are available. A situation in which all these factors are preserved for the hand of the historian does not exist. However, in Mexico and Guatemala that ideal condition is approximated.

In a work on America that must be largely archæological there is constant temptation to use too much of the wealth of material that is at hand and to present it in such detail as to discourage readers excepting those professionally interested. That tendency, I shall resist. This will not be a catalogue of ruined towns nor an archæological survey, nor a study of linguistics and physical characteristics, nor a critical exposition of documentary sources. The purpose of this work can best be accomplished by presentation of typical examples from each region, chosen from those that I can describe from personal study on the ground, supplemented by eyewitness testimony where possible. The study embraces two great regions, Mexico and Central America, lying between the Tropic of Cancer on the north and latitude 15° on the south, all on the main continental axis and for the most part rugged, mountainous countries of high elevation. Exceptions will be noted in the proper time and place.

It is especially significant that of the four regions of the New World in which exceptionally high cultures arose, namely, the American Southwest, the Mexican plateau, the Guatemalan highlands (omitting the Caribbean region for the present), and the Andean valleys of South America, three are within the torrid zone, all in high altitudes—the three tropical regions being at such altitudes (five thousand to twelve thousand feet) that they enjoy climatic conditions comparable to temperate and sub-tropical zones. It is interesting too to note how much the peoples of all these regions had in common—the sedentary mode of life, community organization, representative government, modest industrial achievement, rich esthetic life, sound moral codes, ancestor veneration, naturalistic religion, dependence upon deific powers for the well-being of the group. In fact, the Pueblos of New Mexico and the Maya-Quiché of Guatemala could have exchanged places, and the

Aztecs of Mexico with the Quechuas of Peru, without serious inconvenience. A few minor adjustments and life would have gone on in the old placid way, though not the way of "civilization," for that had not come to the American Indians. They had no science, no nationalism, no church; but they had the fine culture values of religion, of community spirit, of confidence in nature. It is in no sense of disparagement of the great peoples of ancient America that one speaks of them as not being in the state of "civilization." They had what was, for them, infinitely better, namely, a cultural life that they could not have been induced to surrender. Why exchange faith for skepticism? known for unknown? certainty for doubt? serenity for perplexity? is the way the Indian would have considered it if left a free agent. Looking at the wreckage in our civilization there is something to be said for the Indian's point of view.

This work will follow the general pattern of *Ancient Life in the American Southwest.* Parts One and Two of that book should be read before starting this one. That will save me the trouble of a lot of restatement of facts essential to the understanding of American life in any part of the New World.

PART ONE

ON THE WRITING OF ANCIENT AMERICAN HISTORY

"The moving finger writes,
and, having writ, moves on."
—OMAR KHAYYAM

Ancient Life in Mexico and Central America

—◆—

PART ONE

ON THE WRITING OF ANCIENT AMERICAN HISTORY

WE HAVE in ancient culture centers of America—the Southwest, Mexico, Central America, Peru—an aboriginal people of numerous languages and general similarity in culture type and somatic character, surviving from what must seem to them in retrospect a Golden Age. They are so non-mechanically minded as to be considered a "backward race" by their masters. They actually possess as mature a culture of the esthetic-religious type as the world has produced, and, though stunned by the impact of a ruthless and barbaric conqueror, the European, they are holding on in the face of appalling disaster, stolidly keeping alive their sacred fires from which the soul of a race may possibly be rekindled; unconsciously living the heroic life. In the Southwest we lump these survivors under the name, Pueblo Indians,—only a few thousand of them, living in twenty-seven ancient villages and half a dozen farming communities of recent origin. In Mexico and Central America we have these survivors of a better age to describe under the names, Aztec, Tarascan, Totonac, Zapotec, Mixtec, Quiché, Cakchiquel, and Maya, with tribes of lesser note constituting from seventy-five to eighty per cent of the total population. The Indian race in Mexico and Central America probably numbers today from fifteen to sixteen millions.

The life that these people are living, as seen by the casual observer, does not give the exact picture of the ancient life though close study reveals much in the way of culture survival. Even now the world has but little actual knowledge of the American Indian race. The point of view is mostly traditional. Thinking about Indians in the United States is still dominated by Fenimore Cooper; in Mexico, by Prescott. Hence, this book and the one that preceded it. Interpreting a human race, especially one that has been so wrecked by adverse forces, is work for both scientist and philosopher. It is the business of specialists in culture history to recover the fragments and reassemble them and see the race and enable others to see it in its pristine state. The Americanist is fortunate in having such a wealth of living material before his eyes—actually *ancient life*—held over from a far past. The student of early America, be he ethnologist, historian, or archæologist, overlooks his best source if he fails to associate himself with the surviving people and gain from living minds the actual knowledge of race and life that lingers on, generation after generation, even under the most adverse conditions. There is no master key to the inner life of a people, but language unlocks a vast treasure house. Words never cease to reflect racial feeling and experience. Therefore, so long as the fragments of an archaic language remain in use, you have access to a record that is priceless.

Likewise, so long as primitive arts and industries are practiced, so long as deific powers are invoked in ritual and dramatic ceremonials, the door to knowledge of ancient mind is accessible, but it cannot be

entered by way of laboratories and museums and class-
rooms and afternoon teas on comfortable verandas.
You have to live and "take it rough" with the people.
I have often taken occasion to express my dissatis-
faction with much recent work in American archæology,
and while my good-natured banter has for the most
part been cheerfully received, the situation is not yet
such as to cause great elation. A generation has been
wasted on unworkable nomenclatures, and the subject
has been messed up with new cultures for every change
of diet or habitat: Corn complex, Salmon culture,
Basket Makers, Pit House people, Slab House people,
Fumarole people! Why not in recent American history
the Baked Bean culture, the Pot Likker people, the
Great American Pie culture, the Sod House people, the
Frame Shack people, the Tin Lizzie Age? Devising
mathematical, astronomical, engineering, and various
scientific achievements for the ancient Americans is
among the diversions which can be carried on almost
anywhere; but the study of *life as it is* as the way to
an understanding of life *as it has been,* means, among
other things, desert dust and jungle fever in order to
be among men who speak and work and worship and
impersonate and look out upon their world in the ways
of old. Archæologists of no other field have such incomparable opportunities as do the Americanists, though
students of the ancient civilizations of the Old World
are not limited to the digging up of ruin-mounds.
Berbers, Arabs, Kurds, Kirghiz, and Mongols still
exist in hordes, and in their languages, arts, rituals,
folklore, music, occupations, the cultural achievements
of antiquity survive.

However, there are countless places in America, once
well populated, that are covered with ruin-mounds with

not an inhabitant left that can claim descent from the original people. Here the archæologist is deprived of the inestimable privilege of learning from the living, or "catching his archæology alive" (Lummis). What happened? is the inquiry of everyone who sees these noble ruins. Sometimes the pressure of an enemy has forced an exodus. Disease has destroyed populations. Sometimes in human experience food supply has failed or water become inadequate, and suddenly or gradually, as the situation compelled, the people disintegrated and drifted away to other locations. Sometimes hard living conditions have become unbearable and a tribe has fled in a body. Such was the exodus from Egypt of the Children of Israel, who were forty years in getting to their Promised Land, not so very far away. There have been instances when a horde of people without any good reason have packed up, bag and baggage, cleared out, and kept going in spite of every conceivable hindrance until a predetermined destination was reached. Such was the flight of the Kalmuck Mongols from the Volga plain in Russia when, in 1771, they suddenly started for an ancestral home on the farther side of Asia. History records nothing to compare with this trek of thousands of miles by a people harassed by relentless enemies, freezing to death on Siberian steppes, burning to death on Mongolian deserts; starvation, thirst, and exhaustion taking toll by hundreds every day, but going on and on as though driven by furies, to stop only when their destination, the Chinese Empire, was reached; that is, by a fraction of the number that started. That migration trail must have been marked by hundreds of thousands of human skeletons and who knows how much camp refuse.

So human migrations are hard to account for. When the urge to move is on, hardship is no hindrance and distance cuts no figure. When the Aztecs appeared in the Valley of Anahuac, they claimed to have been wandering many generations since leaving their Land of the Seven Caves. One asks of the great stone monuments of the Southwestern desert which bear evidence of abrupt abandonment, questions of whence and whither that numerous and virile people? Up to now the answer is—silence. But the quest goes on. Distance need not limit the search. If they went clear to Yucatan they would not have equaled that memorable trek of the Kalmucks. Columbus's trip from Spain to the West Indies has always been considered quite an adventure, but he had three comfortable (for that time) caravels, propelled by the winds. Polynesian navigators of the South Seas beat him for distance twice over, traveling in little open boats propelled by man power.

The archæologist has the ruins of ancient homes, even whole cities (in America mainly towns), and the débris, cultural and physical, left along old migration trails, as his material for study. Upon his interpretation of these remains, spectacular, mute, mysterious, the general public relies for its beliefs. It is a heavy responsibility, for once a reputed archæologist says so, that settles it. He is quoted with childlike confidence. Before offering any interpretation at all, he should know the mind of the Indian. We have in America too many pyramided errors that writers of our mechanically minded race have erected by reading into ancient phenomena scientific and mechanical achievements unthinkable to the mystically minded Indian. What disillusionment if we could call up the spirits of ancient Indian priests and get some real information! I have often imagined the hilarity of the ancients in Wenima (the dwelling place of ancestral spirits) as they discuss the pronouncements of writers on ancient America. Interpretation calls for sober judgment, understatement, often frank admission that it is largely guesswork. Half-baked special writers and unbaked field lecturers hand out to an uninformed public with absolute finality the information that certain important things are so and so, the only evidence being that some other uninformed person has said so. The misinformation is entirely satisfactory to the multitude. The near-scientist is too often more concerned about getting his opinion accepted than in finding out what is true.

However, the archæologist is not always to blame. The multitude has been educated to want thrills and the newspaper must reflect the minds of its readers. I have in a lecture modestly spoken of examining ancient buildings *four* to *five* stories high, and the next morning the cub reporter had it, "Archæologist discovers building *forty-five* stories high." I have described old Indian trails worn hip deep in the rock by people who *did not* wear hobnailed boots, and incautiously in the same lecture referred to dinosaur remains. The newspaper had it, "Scientist discovers hobnailed dinosaurs in New Mexico." It is certainly true that people like to be humbugged. Readers on Central America are never going to give up Ignatius Donnelly and LePlongeon, nor Lost Atlantis and the Continent of Mu. The lucubrations of fakers and fourflushers make exciting reading, while the modest statement of hard-won facts by honest-to-goodness dirt archæologists fails to register.

Nevertheless, it is to the dirt archæologist that we must turn for recovery of the uncorrupted culture of a people. He knows cultural material when he sees it and knows its value. If he has approached his science by way of tireless ethnological study, he tries to see with the eyes and reason with the mind of the Indian. If he can put aside his own way of thinking, he can read what is interpretable with some assurance, can see vestiges of survivals where they exist, and refuse to see the non-existent. He knows the limitations of his subject, avoids the brash finality of the amateur, refuses to commit himself on problems that are unknowable, has the patience of Job derived from contemplation of the long procession of the ages, has boundless faith in and admiration for his remote ancestors, and believes that man learns mainly by experience. As his whole occupation is that of investigating human life, he is likely to be much interested in everything that is important to man. He has little use for the forward-looking person who does not know his past. He believes that the true progressive is one who knows what has and has not worked in human experience and is guided thereby. He views every "new deal" with a critical eye, for history has been largely a succession of new deals. That is what gives the archæologists so much to do. Russia, Italy, Germany, China, all are getting new deals at the present time. Archæologists look forward eagerly to their future opportunities there. The American Indians got a new deal when Columbus landed on these shores.

In our day it is said that "names make news." It is probably true enough. Looking over front-page headlines, we shall probably admit that the names, Roosevelt, Wilson, Foch, Hindenburg, Hoover, Lenin, Mussolini, Hitler, represent the world's taste for news in the first third of the twentieth century, and that what

is written in connection with these names fairly reflects
our capacity for admiration, adulation, appreciation,
anathema, faith, hope, and hysteria. In a like sense
it may be said that names make history. Try Alexander, Cæsar, Charlemagne, Genghis Khan, Cromwell,
Washington, Lincoln, and imagine our world without
them. Names make philosophy, too; witness Plato,
Aristotle, Buddha, Confucius, Jesus, Mahomet, Bacon.
Just plain thinking seems to have been quite as potent
as action in human history; but note that in all the
above we are thinking of Old World life, Old World
thought, Old World civilization; of the humanity of
Europe, Asia, and Africa. (The Americans named
above were all of Old World genesis.) Screened off
from that world where all of our history was enacted,
separated from it by seas and skies that isolated it
through the ages, as completely as space divides us from
Mars, was another world. When we found it we called
it the New World, also, America, because we did not
know what else to do about it. Its own inhabitants,
distributed from Arctic Ocean to Antarctic, gave us
no name for it, in which respect they were like the people of other continents. Europe, Asia, Africa, were
named by outsiders. For all purposes except conjectural romances and vagaries the seclusion of this vast
land between the oceans was complete. How life got
started on it is not a matter of inquiry here. It had a
vast natural history of its own and a human race of
its own, which, whatever may have been its origin, had
no consciousness of any other world or any other human
life. It had a long past, as shown by its monuments,
but with this race names did not make history. They
had history, centuries of it, but it was made by the
people, and, in culture history, individuals do not count.

At least, no notice was taken of them in the long record of the race. They lived and exercised all the human attributes. The European chroniclers noticed among the Indians strong individuals and heard of others of former generations and made them historic, made of them kings, queens, leaders, etc., but native chroniclers never bothered their heads about such matters. They were concerned about the group. In all the history of ancient America, legendary or otherwise, there is no indisputable record that any human individual ever ruled a nation, commanded an army, built or destroyed a city, invented a machine, made a scientific discovery, wrote a book, painted a picture, designed a temple. Of deities there were plenty, and of late laborious efforts have been made to make inventors, scientists, and teachers of some of them. But so far, all attempts to take Quetzalcoatl, plumed serpent deity of the entire continent, out of his mythic world and make an ordinary astronomer or teacher of agriculture out of him have been as pathetic as were the efforts of government to teach the Hopi how to farm by the scientific methods of Washington. We have learned some things *about* Indians and are even finding out that we can learn much *from* them. We go to them now to learn how to raise crops in the desert sand. Our Ph. D.'s sit humbly at the feet of Pueblo potters and Navaho weavers. The knowledge we get out of those old Indian artists we use in making more Ph. D.'s. They have become the teachers. If some fairhaired individual appeared, as we are told, among the Maya of Yucatan and proceeded to teach them how to raise corn, they probably found it necessary to teach him to get in out of the rain.

In the light of the above observations, it will be clear

that I consider the writing of ancient American history after the Old World pattern to be rank nonsense. Old World history is built about names, personalities, and arranged on a chronological pattern. New World history rests upon cultural evolution, is built about group achievement, and refuses to be cramped into a chronological scheme. There are time sequences, to be sure, as, for example, that demonstrated by the ingenious tree ring calendar that has enabled us, tentatively, to date Southwestern sites, and the Maya hieroglyphic calendar, partly agreed upon by Americanists, whereby we place in time the temple ruins of the Maya. These are interesting and useful, but not of such importance as a sure understanding of ancient Mexican social structure including such facts of culture as the land tenure system. Upon the latter depends the future success and happiness of a nation of millions of people, probably of all the nations of Middle America that are still predominantly Indian. Some of the mathematical problems of ancient America afford a certain intellectual satisfaction. So does a jigsaw puzzle.

I can see little reason for devoting precious time to study of small, isolated phenomena when the greatest problems of human life invite attention. From the débris of ancient American culture we may rescue and perhaps revive the genius of a race. In a clear understanding of ancient Mexico lies the future of American nations and the way toward the solution of world affairs. When the ruling powers of Middle America grasp the fact that their populations are primarily Indian, can understand that these peoples through ages of cultural evolution achieved the fundamentals of a good life, that no other life than their own can ever insure their well-being; then we may look for happy, tranquil nations south of the Rio Grande. Otherwise, the sordid story of suppression, enslavement, revolution, must go on for more centuries. The unlettered Indian of desert and mountain and jungle can teach us the principles of good government, the essentials of the good life—for him.

Some years ago when my present job was assigned to me I was requested to prepare a platform on which to base the archæological work that would fall to us to do. Archæology was not a very definite science in those days; perhaps is not yet, but the statement presented was approved by the committee that examined it (Alice Fletcher, W. H. Holmes, J. Walter Fewkes), and so I have followed it as a general scheme. Recently it has been critically examined by a group of young Americanists, and they report that the tendencies in American archæology today are substantially along this line. Accordingly, that platform is here put down with the suggestion that those who are interested only in the more popular aspects of the subject pass it over.

In American archæology, man in the cultural process is the unit of investigation. This establishes the limits of the science. Its subject matter lies mainly in the prehistoric period, but this must be studied in the light of auxiliary sciences which have for their field of investigation the living people. It necessitates the study of all phenomena that will add to our knowledge of the intellectual attainments of the native American race or illustrate the evolution of its culture. It aims at a reconstruction and interpretation of the order of civilization existing in America before the Caucasian occupancy.

Nowhere had the race attained to the art of literary expression, though in Central America certain tribes were verging on it. The record of their progress must be sought, first, in the remains of their material possessions; second, in survivals of their intellectual achievements written and unwritten; and, third, in the recorded observations of eyewitnesses to scenes and events of the historic period. Their arts afforded a means of lasting self-portraiture. These display the common abilities and common beliefs of the people and reflect the racial progress. They illustrate the gradual conquest of mind over natural forces and materials. Architectural and industrial remains illustrate the evolution of the social order. Sculptural and pictorial remains display the stages of development of the esthetic sense, and, through the symbolism in which they are expressed, embody the common conceptions of things spiritual, the early phases of the upreach of mind, efforts to enlist the aid of supernatural beings—in short, all the primitive methods of attacking the fundamental problems of existence. In primitive arts we have the mirror of the racial mind. There are also recoverable remains of the intellectual possessions of the ancient Americans in the form of survivals of archaic ceremonies, rituals, and traditions of living tribes. These are vital to the understanding of the life and history of the people.

The history of any surviving group of native American people may be divided broadly into two epochs. The first represents a reach of time during which the autochthonic character of the race unfolded, a period of racial isolation, of unadulterated culture. The second begins when the group is touched by outside racial influences. This represents at most a period of four centuries, its beginning depending upon the time when Caucasian influence penetrated the group in question.

Until the racial isolation was broken by the coming of the Spaniards, bringing in new industrial methods, new incitements to activity, and new ideals of achievement, the simple ethnic mind had not been an object of contemplation to itself. Unconscious of its limitations or of its status in culture, because ignorant of any other, its expressions in the form of arts, ceremonies, and symbolism were perfectly naïve.

With the coming of the Spaniards a period of racial self-consciousness began. The simple process of unfoldment of culture gave place to the complex phenomena of ethnic mind acted upon for the first time by external stimuli of a most violent sort, and thus suddenly aroused to consciousness of its own operations and limitations. There was immediate selection of esthetic, industrial, societary, and religious elements from the conquering race. Arts, industries, and social conditions underwent vital modifications. The ancient social and religious order was broken down and reorganized along new lines. Ceremonies disintegrated with the passing of the clans in which they were developed. Primitive ritual took on numerous aspects of Christian worship which resulted in the corruption of symbolism. The term acculturation, an adding to culture, describes the process that resulted in the present condition of the American aborigines.

The study of the phenomena of this epoch is more complex than that of the earlier period. The process of separating the recently acquired from autochthonous elements is laborious, and the chances of error numerous. Traditionary episodes, ceremonies, rituals, and symbolism must be subjected to critical analysis. However, there is a valuable residuum of facts of archaic culture resulting from the sifting.

The study of prehistoric archæology presents less complexity. Definite external surroundings give rise to definite efforts of the human mind to utilize, to overcome, and to account for them. The result is certain activities, the dynamic expression of the cultural process. The study of this process in the stage prior to the intrusion of any foreign elements, in the light of facts which ethnology lends to the interpretation of archaic phenomena, is a field comparatively free from the necessity of conjecture. The service which prehistoric archæology is capable of rendering to anthropolgy is comparable with that which paleontology renders to biology.

In the study of the historical development of the native American race, it becomes necessary to eradicate all political divisions and to find cultural limits instead. These coincide to some extent with natural boundaries giving rise to "culture areas." This term is used to designate a region in which some dominant type of cultural phenomena prevails to the subordination of other types. Such an area is the so-called Pueblo region of the southwestern part of the United States. Numerous areas of this character are more or less clearly defined from Alaska to South America.

All information that we possess at the present time tends to establish the fundamental unity of the American race and points to an evolution from lower to higher civilization. The time element in this process is by no means constant. The gap between the lowest and highest ethnic groups might have been closed by a generation or two of influence under favorable surroundings, or it might have required many centuries in the absence of such stimuli. In the flowing of populations that prevailed in ancient as in recent times, groups were segregated from parent stocks, carrying with them the ancient traditions, and as a result of isolation new and distinct seats of population arose, flourished, swarmed, and degenerated. While there were no means of storing up knowledge such as we possess, yet in the form of tradition it was transferred, replanted, and engrafted to such an extent that it may reasonably be doubted if any vital possession of the ancient races of America has passed into total oblivion.

It is necessary to investigate the fundamental causes of these specializations in culture, to ascertain and follow the direction of waves that flowed out to occupy new localities and influence other communities. The determination of affinities between widely separated regions requires long and laborious study of fixed remains in the field as well as of the movable antiquities to be found in the museums of the world, together with the investigation of religious and social traditions which survived the shock of the Conquest, and calls for the correlated efforts of many students and institutions.

Another important line of research in American archæology is archive work. The records of those who had the opportunity to observe the native people at the beginning of the contact with the intrusive race are of great service. Voluminous as has been the publication of historical works on aboriginal America, there are yet archives of great extent in Mexico and Spain which have not passed under the eye of the historian. It cannot be doubted that much valuable material relating to the early historic period awaits discovery. There is great need for re-examination, in the light of present-day ethnological knowledge and by the critical methods of modern historical research, of source material that has been much used in the past. It is not sufficient that the archives be explored and unpublished documents copied and given to the public. Discriminating analysis is necessary if the truth about ancient America is ever to be recorded. It must be remembered that these are not the records of trained scholars seeking only to make known actual facts. They are in many cases the accounts of untrained observers biased by the excitement of conquest and moved to exaggeration by the desire to influence royal and ecclesiastical action at home.

The first task of the archæologist is to rescue the material and intellectual remains of the people whose history he is seeking to restore. It can never be hoped that a continuous record will be recovered, but the greater the amount of material secured the more nearly complete can it be made. But archæological research is more than the recovery and study of material. As history is not only a recital of events but an inquiry into their genesis, it is imperative to investigate and describe all phenomena upon which such events are conditioned. Therefore, physiographic conditions are essentially correlative with facts of culture, and physical and psychic causes are to be held in the closest possible relation if we are to interpret correctly the intellectual remains of the native race of America, whether in the form of myth, ritual, and symbolism of plains and desert tribes, or in architectural, sculptural, pictorial, and glyphic remains of the Mexican and Central American civilizations.

The foregoing dissertation was not written for the purpose of airing my views on certain subjects not germane to the subsequent text. It was mainly for the reason that the American people are beginning to realize that the New World has its ancient history, but do not clearly see the character of it. The native race of America was working out the problems of life in its own way for ages before the Europeans came. The human drama was far advanced. Through ages of striving with their surroundings for life and comfort, with one another for material possessions, with mythic beings which were supposed to rule their destinies, the ancient Americans had risen in several centers far above the stage of savagery. They had achieved great material works, had developed and matured a complex religious and social order, had become a thinking people.

The history of the human race records no greater tragedy than the overwhelming of the entire cultural structure of the "red" race by the white, in the sixteenth century. Few stop to think what it means to shatter completely the culture which millions of people have been patiently building up through ages of time, peremptorily upsetting their mode of life. That is precisely what happened with the discovery and conquest of America. Here, as in the early ages of the Old World, humanity had divided into tribes, some of which remained in savagery while others built permanent settlements, founded confederacies, strove toward a place in the sun, suffered extermination by conquest and absorption, and made way for others. The record of this constitutes the ancient history of America. That it is not recorded in the way to which we are accustomed, makes it all the more fascinating. We can read man's thoughts in the buildings which he erects, the forms which he carves in stone, the symbols with which he decorates the articles of domestic and ceremonial use, even better than when expressed in literary characters. What men say or write is full of affectation. What they build for the protection of their families or in honor of their deities, what they carve in stone or picture in color for the gratification of religious or esthetic sense, is true and unaffected.

The dim past of the native American race becomes vivid as we read its history in the archæological remains left behind. In the cliff and pueblo ruins of the Southwest, the pyramids of Mexico, and temple precincts of Central America, we have the best achievements of the ancient people. These are America's classic lands. The cliff-dwellers and Pueblos of the American Southwest excelled all others in domestic architecture. The cliff ruins, rock citadels, and community houses scattered over southern Colorado and Utah, the whole of New Mexico and Arizona, tell the story of a peaceful, industrious people who relied upon defense rather than aggression. They were skilled in pottery making and in simple industrial pursuits. Their picture writing was of the crudest sort. Their religion, while full of weird ritual, was free from inhuman practices. Their culture reached its climax before the coming of the white race.

The ancient Mexicans were the strong people of the high plateau where the City of Mexico now stands. Their architecture took the form of massive pyramids of earth and stone, surmounted by temples, embellished by sculptures and carvings representing their deities. Their religion was marked by rites of extreme barbarity, among which was that of human sacrifice. They had a system of picture writing in which they expressed their ideas of the calendar, the names and attributes of their gods, and depicted place names.

The people of Central America attained to the highest culture, in some respects, of any native Americans. Their architecture, as seen in the ruins of their temples, was substantial and imposing, and beautifully embellished in stucco and mosaic. Their sculpture, ceramic and textile arts were as fine and strong as those of Oriental peoples, and their hieroglyphic writing was verging upon literary characters. Their culture had run its course and was on the decline before the coming of the Spaniards.

The fundamental unity of the race is conceded and an evolution in culture from lower to higher levels, with subsequent decline. What I most desire to impress is that culture in ancient America had reached, in most places, a plane of sustained value. It was no childlike piling up of earth and stone and aimless embellishment. It was the product of disciplined, directed skill, sustained by profound appreciation of esthetic values, and, underlying it, a philosophy of life which promises rich reward for painstaking study.

Finally, let it always be kept in mind that in writing on ancient America the objective is not *history of civilization,* but *culture history;* that what is aimed at here is an interpretation of the Indian race, not in terms of *European civilization,* but in terms of *Indian culture.*

PART TWO

THE NORTHERN THRESHOLD
OF ANAHUAC

"Four are the Hills of the Life of Man,
Four are the steps of Earth's terraced Bowl,
Its corners are keyed with Heaven above,
Its Pattern of old was made whole—
    in that Land where man walketh in Beauty,
    in that Land where man dreameth in Beauty!"

—HARTLEY BURR ALEXANDER

PART TWO

THE NORTHERN THRESHOLD
OF ANAHUAC

I. THE PLAINS INDIANS

IT HAS perhaps been made clear already that in what
we have undertaken here we are dealing with the
débris of an ancient world. Tribes and communities
are broken up; their culture is a confused record; their
abodes and sanctuaries are ruin-mounds. How a beneficent nature prepared a continent for the use of man
is a fascinating story—a tale of mountain making, coast
formation, drainage establishment, furnishing with
plant and animal life, finally guiding humanity to its
boundless opportunties. How man made use of it
is the story that archæology has to tell. As the Indian
race spread over the continent there was wide choice
of habitat. Why some bands developed preference for
the inhospitable Arctic, some for the restricted Pacific
coast, some for the parched intermountain Southwest,
some for the northeast forests and lakes, others for
the wind-swept plains, and still others for tropic jungles,
we can never know. The quest for food, shelter, clothing, material needed for domestic use, found guidance
in climatic and other geographic conditions. Choice
is unaccountable.

Before the coming of the European, the great plains
east of the Rocky Mountains of northern America
attracted and maintained in comparative abundance and
security a mobile population which developed into a

definite physical and cultural type—the Plains Indians. Those vast grassy steppes were ideal grazing lands, and the animal that possessed them, the American bison, or buffalo, largest of American ruminants, was ideally adapted to that spacious environment. It bred in vast numbers and roamed in uncountable herds over a territory five hundred miles wide, a thousand miles in latitude. To the Plains Indian it was food, clothing, shelter. With the addition of an amount of plant food, as maize (Indian corn), man's living was assured. True, there were ups and downs in the life of the Plains Indian, but on the whole, taking it year in and year out, he was about as certain of his living as man could hope to be. He could not settle down to a permanent home and develop a building culture; he must follow his service of supply. The conservation of these gifts of nature—the buffalo, the corn—the ordering of life in harmony with the mighty powers that gave and governed all existence, these were the duties of the tribe. Out of these conditions grew the tribal culture—immaterial, orderly, spiritual. Out of such conditions real men emerged. Sioux, Omaha, Cherokee, Pawnee, Comanche; these are some of the tribal names that pertain to that ample region, that genuine culture. It was not "progressive" to our way of thinking; it had to disappear utterly when civilization came. It had no substantial material remains to endure. It could not exist without the buffalo, the wide spaces, the voices of nature. What it would have amounted to, if unmolested for another thousand years, is worth thinking about. Fortunate that it had an Alice Fletcher and its own Francis La Flesche to record and interpret it.

II. THE COAST PEOPLE

FOR the bands which adhered to the Pacific coast of
America there was abundant food supply in the gifts
of the sea.   There was nothing of the spacious life of
the plains or the desert to expand the cultural horizon.
Between the ocean and mountains was a narrow world.
Sea food afforded the essential supply, as did the buffalo on the plains. With the acorn of the foothills to
take the place of corn, there was comparative security
in subsistence.   There was constant seasonal migration
from seashore to lower mountain slopes, always within
a narrow range of climatic and geographic conditions.
This was reflected consistently in the culture of the
coastal people.   There was nothing conducive to home
building.   The climate did not demand warmth and
shelter and clothing.   Domestic needs were met with
stone and shell for utensils, with fiber for basketry and
other equipment for carrying and storing.   We miss
the deep philosophy of the Plains tribes, the rich esthetic
and ceremonial life of the desert. In artistic basket
making, however, they reached the top. The peculiar
domestic life called for unbreakable carrying utensils,
and nature supplied in abundance the finest grasses to
meet the need.   One wonders if ancient California
weavers, drifting desertward for trade, may not have
carried to the San Juan drainage of Utah the art that
was destined to give name to an archaic people, the
"Basket Makers" of Southwestern archæologists. The
Northwest Coast people added artistic carving on wood,
bone, and ivory to their accomplishments. The coastal
people were about the least resistant to disintegrating
influences of any of the regional populations.   They

gave way with surprising suddenness when the industries and religion of the Spaniards were brought to them. So rapid has been the decline of the California Indians that Harrington, Kroeber, and others, who have labored so zealously and effectively in recording their culture, have in many cases considered it rare good fortune if a single survivor could be found of once numerous language groups.

There has been approximately ninety per cent decline in the Indian population of California since the white race undertook its guardianship. In many places formerly well populated, the decline long since reached one hundred per cent—virtually extinction. This vast decline has not been due to absorption into the white population except in small part. The cold stark fact is, the population has died at an abnormally high rate. Moreover, this decline set in and proceeded along with the benevolent and perfectly intelligent work of the Franciscans, the missionization of the Indians. One finds nothing to criticize in the methods and work of the *padres*. The missionization of the Pueblo Indians of New Mexico carried on in substantially the same manner was attended by no such mortality. The general treatment of the Indians of California by the white people was not such as would bring on an abnormally high death rate. It was practically the same as in New Mexico and in Old Mexico south to the Aztec country.

The Indians of Southern California developed a culture comparatively unstable and easily disintegrated. There was among many groups seasonal migration between coast and back country, following the food supply. At times the estuaries of the coast swarmed with rafts of *tule,* the shores teemed with a camp population, enjoying for a time an aquatic life. With the change of season, this was transferred to the hill country, and the acorn became the staple food, approaching in importance the corn of the Southwest and Mexico. House-life was of the simplest and most fragile sort. There was lack of the permanent, substantial building culture that characterized the areas described above. We note the absence of the deeply matured ritualistic life so potent in shaping social structure. In the arts characteristic of the Indian race generally, the Indians of Southern California were pre-eminent only in basket making. This they have clung to most tenaciously, but it must disappear with the destruction of the material which made it possible. The teaching of crafts and trades in the missions failed to meet the cultural necessities of the Indian. The culture that he had was doubtless precious to the California Indian, but it lacked the essentials of stability and permanence. As material for his future education it is inadequate even if it could be revived.

So the California Indian was without the sustaining influence of a stable, integrated culture to help him withstand the advance of civilization. The potency of tradition cannot be overestimated in culture history. What we call the spirit of man, the genius of a people, is the reflection of those culture traits that are the human heritage from a formative past. Therein lie joy in life, stability of character, continuity of purpose, hope of survival. Humanity craves always the opportunity to live, holds existence in any state preferable to nonexistence, finds happiness in creative achievement, however small, and delights in the practice of those activities which have spiritually enriched the race. This is a heritage of which no people can justly be deprived.

In the process of saving souls the spirit of man has sometimes been terribly broken and his physical survival defeated.

The California Indians were not constituted to withstand the impact of the European civilization, their inferiority of endowment being both cultural and physical. The Pueblo and Navaho of the Southwest suffered temporary decline, recovered, and have attained an assured survival through firm cultural resistance and the recovery, before it was too late, of their cultural virility when it was on the decline. The Indians of California, deficient in cultural background, defeated in the struggle for survival, present a less hopeful picture. Never having attained to a firm, integrated culture, they were lacking in resistance, and rapidly broke down under the pressure of white civilization. They show little promise of recuperation. They well illustrate the principle that no people can survive the destruction of its culture whether it be high or low. The use of its own endowment is the only assurance of survival that any race can have.

III. THE DESERT COMMUNITIES

WHEN one begins to write of the ancient Pueblos and cliff-dwellers, the real work on Mexico and Central America, to some extent also on the Andean people, has commenced. It is a far cry from the southern limit of the Pueblos to the plateau where Toltec cultures arose and flourished, farther still by some hundreds of miles to the lands of the Maya and Incas. Yet one cannot travel the Mexican plateau or the Guatemalan and Andean highlands without being conscious on every hand of shadows from the great Southwest. The Pueblo region proper ends in southern Chihuahua, roughly with the Conchos Valley.

In the Southwest, human conditions were shaped and controlled by the semi-desert environment. Existence was primarily dependent on one factor—water; secondarily, upon conditions subordinate to the major factor. Population was limited by proximity to springs and streams and the adequacy and permanence of the water supply. Human life was dependent on the products of the soil. The sociological result was the Pueblo communities; later, in modified form, the Navaho groups. Society was anchored to the soil, preoccupied with a food quest that was relatively sure and simple. Agriculture was the main business of life, supplemented in a small way by hunting. To insure the fruits of the soil and of the hunt, the Indian of the Southwest sought to understand his world, to enlist all the forces of the cosmos in his struggle for existence. He had the advantage of vast spaces, of time for contemplation, of comparative freedom from the pressure of enemies from without, at least in the early stages. He acquired a clear, natural, reasonable view of life. These cosmic forces meant everything to him. They were deified. A culture dominated by ceremony and ritual which, once established, was invariable, was the result. Nowhere else in the world, to my knowledge, do we find so clear an example of a philosophy of life, in this case essentially a religious philosophy, so coercive as to dominate every phase of culture.

The Indian of the Southwest mastered the few industrial processes necessary to his welfare. There was little to induce improvement. The dry farming of the Hopi of a thousand years ago was as efficient as it is today. Our government experts have not improved upon the procedure. The principal accessory was the planting stick for depositing the seeds deep down below the surface where moisture is retained even in the desert sands. It still beats the white man's corn planter. Friends of the Indian, official and unofficial, have long sought to instruct him in the elements of our system of planned economics. They have proved unattractive, though appealing to his subtle sense of humor.

Equally significant among the culture traits of the Indians of the Southwest were such arts as pottery making, basketry, weaving in various forms. These were their cultural possessions from earliest times, and passed far beyond the realm of useful arts. They were esthetic achievements of the highest order, unquestionably affording to the Indian profound satisfaction in an environment that to us seems hard and a life that we would consider devoid of most of the necessities of existence. In their esthetics they are as obtuse as in their industries. They resist the power loom, the potter's wheel, quantity production in every form. The struggle between stark utility and inherent love of beauty in their lives is pathetic, but in the conflict between the tin lard pail from the trading post and the clay water jar, shaped with infinite love and embellished in color and design that expresses both the individual and racial spirit, the latter has it when given half a chance. In religion the Southwestern Indian is only apparently pliable. His esoteric life is not susceptible to profound conversion. His ancient rituals minister to his actual, spiritual needs. He may take on something from Catholicism, something from Protestantism, but it is medicine of secondary importance, not to be depended on. The white man's deity, the church's saints, arouse no antagonism, but unfailing potency resides in Tan Sendo (the Sun Father), and in the Plumed Serpent.

In matters physical, the superb endowment of the Southwestern Indian, supported by a coercive social system, has served him extraordinarily well. Grave as have been the consequences of his acquisition from the whites of whisky and venereal disease, he has survived their devastation and is holding his own against them now at least as well as the white man is.

In one Rio Grande pueblo, by an experiment extending over twenty years, now influencing the entire Pueblo population, we have demonstrated that the fine old arts and crafts, such as pottery making, painting, lapidary, leather, and bead work, which had sadly degenerated and in some communities entirely disappeared, were simply dormant, could be revived, successfully practiced in spite of the pressure of modern progress, to the great joy and profit of the Indians. It is with much satisfaction that we note that our system of Indian education has for some years past been in process of revision and is being made to conform to some sound principles of ethnic psychology.

IV. Between Pueblo and Aztec Lands

1. Tarahumaras, Tepahuanas, Migration Routes

The gap of a thousand miles between Pueblo and Aztec lands is lacking in the conspicuous remains of houses and house-life and of the characteristic religious edifices of the north and south. But it is not without archæological interest. It is a transition ground of the highest importance in the study of the population movements that were guided by the Continental Divide. The space can be covered by any one of three natural routes. It is possible to follow the west coast from the head of the California Gulf; probably small bands of migrating Indians did so. On the east side of Mexico is the Rio Grande Valley, a natural migration trail from the heart of the Pueblo country to the northern confines of Aztec land, by way of such tributaries as the Conchos. Spanish expeditions, as Oñate's, found this a feasible route to the north, but it is as yet relatively unknown. The central route, that along the eastern base of the Sierra Madre, is one of the most inviting of migration trails connecting two great centers of population that I have been able to discover anywhere. It has been my good fortune to traverse practically every mile of it, on horseback or on foot, from the Arizona line to Mexico City. From one end to the other, it lies in high altitudes, five thousand to nine thousand feet, except for a few canyon and valley crossings. The magnificent pine forests of the eastern slope are continuous for hundreds of miles. One may ride on the very crest of the range, but if one tries to diverge to the west there are encountered *barrancas* of nearly a mile in depth, where a day's travel may find one still in sight of the morning camp. But these are off the north-south trail. Open grassy parks abound in the forests of the Sierra; it is needless to speak of the abundance of wild game. Fertile valleys are crossed toward the headwaters of the important rivers, suitable to high altitude crops, with and without irrigation. Rainfall is abundant and in its season incessant. My field notes record a period of thirty days in which my camp bedding was never dry. Another note on torrential rains recounts an enforced detour of two hundred and fifty miles to get to a point less than five miles away, beyond a swollen river.

These high, well watered slopes give down in places to plateaus and valleys that approximate, in aridity, the mesa lands of New Mexico. But, on the whole, the country is much better covered with vegetation than are the regions of similar elevations and contours farther north. Terracing of mountain- and hillsides for the purpose of maintaining small patches for farming, by the simplest of irrigation methods, was extensively practiced here by an ancient people. There are literally hundreds of miles of these narrow shelves on the eastern slope of the divide, many of them barely discernible in the forested areas. They are numerous in places now wholly without population. One cannot avoid the conviction that ancient people, perhaps unconsciously, thereby did modern Mexico a vast service. These terraces have retained cones and other seeds, held moisture, supported ground cover, and kept whole mountainsides forested. If these old terrace builders had tarried a while in southern Arizona and New Mexico, that might today be a different-looking country.

As stated before, this was an inviting migration route,

whether for passing bands on the move to some distant
goal, or for the slow drift of tribes and settlements
toward regions that called them, as the American West
did its white settlers a generation or two ago.

In all large population movements, some find what
they want and remain in lands that are traversed.
Northern Mexico, upper Chihuahua, is largely archæological ground. Tribes have clung to the western
slopes of the Sierra Madre—Pima, Yaqui, Seri, and
others—but the Chihuahua side, its valleys and plains
covered with ruin-mounds, its canyon walls sheltering
numerous cliff-dwellings, has been long uninhabited
until we reach the range of the Tarahumara. Probably
the most numerous of all the tribes in Mexico that
have not disintegrated with the changing conditions,
the Tarahumara belong ideally to the environment
above described. Essentially a forest people, they love
the open parks of the Sierra for farming, and the
barrancas of the western slope for winter protection.
Much food is carried with them in the annual trek to
the sunny western valleys, to supplement what nature
affords there. Early spring finds them back in their
mountain parks. They have few industries, few arts,
few religious ceremonies, as compared with the Pueblos. They have almost too perfectly adapted themselves
to a happy environment. Physically fine, lithe of
build, fleet footed, of incredible endurance in traveling,
not in carrying or in heavy labor, they are ideal guides,
but get desperately homesick if taken too far from their
native forests. They love the trail and in long-distance
travel outlast your best horse. The community race,
village against village, starting with many runners on
a side, continuing over the forest circuit of five to fifteen
miles for an unbelievable time (eighteen hours was

Example of the Legendary Caves, Chihuahua, Mexico

Tarahumara Musicians, Chihuahua, Mexico

Yaqui Dancers, Sonora, Mexico

asserted to be the record) until the final struggle, one on each side, is the most remarkable endurance test that has ever come to my notice.

They are rather indifferent hunters, caring little for meat food. *Pinole,* powdered parched corn (small ears and grains like popcorn), mixed with a little native, brown sugar (*pinoche*) from the west coast, is the principal article of diet. It is eaten by mixing about a tablespoonful at a time in a gourd of water. Your guide can carry a week's rations in the pouch at his belt. I found them caring little for coffee, beans, bacon,— our camp staples,—usually declining them when offered, but favorable to the Mexican *tortilla*. In my sojourns among them, I heard no traditions of wars, famines, and epidemics, and saw little disease of any kind. My earliest visits to the Tarahumara country were thirty years ago, when their seasonal migrations were kept up consistently, when many valleys had hardly known a white man, and their contacts with civilization were infrequent and of short duration, mainly brief pilgrimages to Chihuahua City for trade. In later years the marginal communities have been more or less influenced by the railroad, lumbering, mining, and other interests which have offered employment, and along with it, contributed epidemics of influenza and other accompaniments of civilization. It is noticeable, however, that the Tarahumara have rather well resisted these encroachments and have remained a comparatively sober and healthy people with a strong tendency toward isolation. They have cared little for the schools that have been offered them by the government, have been only slightly Christianized, have retained their liking for the simple, primitive life, and kept their blood unmixed to a degree not found elsewhere in Mexico. White man's food, clothing, and houses would mean their rapid decline. One would like to see the primeval habitat of this fine stock set aside as a human game preserve, just to see what would come of one uncontaminated American Indian stock.

There are no conspicuous archæological remains in the Tarahumara country. Except where ancient Pueblo culture extends into it, there are no house remains of consequence. There are small mounds here and there, and, in places, the terraced slopes above mentioned. In cave archæology, however, the region is extremely rich. These caves apparently have little to tell of the Tarahumara ancestry, neither do they suggest Pueblo occupation. They would seem to pertain to a culture that antedates the advent of the Tarahumara; consequently, there may be here débris of one of the very early migrations over this transition land. If the Tarahumara have any archæological history it has not yet been found.

South of the Tarahumara are the strong Tepahuana people. Their habitat is largely the state of Durango, but Tepahuanas may be found in scattered groups in the adjacent states of Chihuahua, Sinaloa, Jalisco, Zacatecas, and Coahuila. Their home country is still fairly well forested in certain zones, but there are broad valleys, fertile, well-watered plains suitable for farming on a large scale. The country has attracted modern Mexican population with attendant race mixture to the extent that aboriginal Tepahuana stock is becoming comparatively rare. There are, however, some settlements of fairly pure blood and uncorrupted language. The native culture is fast on the decline, the ceremonies obscured with Christian elements; the houses and houselife Mexicanized.

The Tepahuanas are of stocky, muscular build, capable of carrying loads, adapted to heavy labor. That they should lose their primitive characteristics was under the circumstances inevitable. Their archæological history is yet to be studied. Material for it is abundant. House building was of the "jacal" type (vertical poles for walls, with thatched roof). There are numerous small mounds that have not yet been plowed under. The hills, in addition to being in places terraced for farming, are in many instances furnished with strong fortifications of stone. Among these are structures that suggest religious purposes, but the fortification idea is unmistakable. Here then is evidence of warfare, well supported by Tepahuana tradition. There is no better example than the fortified mountain of Zapé one hundred and twenty miles northwest of the city of Durango. This is still, as far as I know, the best center for the study of Tepahuana archæology. In this region, not many miles from the present town of Zapé, one encounters for the first time in southward bound exploration, stone monuments that begin to forecast the monumental remains of the Mexican plateau. These consist of small monoliths of from one to four feet in height, some anthropomorphic, some of phallic motive. As they are set in the valleys, or at least allowed to remain there by the present farmers who regard them with superstitious respect, one suspects a connection with the fructification and growth ceremonials. The Indians neither affirm nor deny this significance. North and west of the town of Tepahuana, two or three days' ride, are ancient village sites where many mortars and metates are to be seen, and stone idols in animal and human form also found in the fields. In this section are many caves containing human bones.

Disintegrated as their culture is, the Tepahuanas

form an important link in the chain of native populations between the American Southwest and the Aztec
plateau, being linguistically of a numerous Southwestern stock, the Piman. They seem more likely than
the Tarahumaras to have been hold-overs from a very
ancient migration that resulted in permanent settlement. Their archæological history may yield some
significant evidence.

2. *The Country of the Chichimecos*

On reaching the country south of the Tepahuanas'
range, especially after crossing the Tropic of Cancer,
in which latitude is the modern city of Zacatecas, the
northern margin of the great Middle American cultures is entered. North of this are the open north and
south migration arteries: first, the narrow, scantily
populated Pacific coast plain; second, the populous
Sierra country, to which special attention has just been
paid; and, third, the Rio Grande Valley, sparsely settled at any time, but an essential migration route. Between the Sierra and Rio Grande Valley lay a broad
expanse of hilly, forbidding, desert land that remained
almost without occupation until recent times.

Below the tropic, the two coasts have always been
open roads for population movements; the Rio Grande
Valley artery on nearing the gulf coast being joined
by an equally important branch from the east, following the gulf coast naturally from the Mississippi Valley. The migration map printed as an end paper is
submitted as a logical scheme, based on the major topo-
graphic features of that part of North America, to
account for the natural flow of population from the
broad valleys and plains of the north into the suddenly

narrowing confines of Mexico and Central America. These must not be thought of as definite lines of travel, but as the ample geographic ways over which populations could flow, and probably did, in waves ranging from small independent bands to large tribes; moving in a continuous trek in some cases, but for the most part drifting, as peoples civilized and uncivilized have done, pushing their frontiers forward during long periods of years. These movements may have continued for several centuries, beginning with the earliest flow of people in large or small bands from the far north and the ultimate Asiatic source. That might be five thousands years ago, or fifty thousand. It is all guesswork as yet. It may be considered an unwarranted assumption to use the expression "from the far north and the ultimate Asiatic source." It is used because, as to the peopling of North America, it expresses the only theory that has any logic in it; the only one that brings the populating of North America from any outside source within the range of possibility. Admitting that this is a plausible theory, it would appear that through four main routes from the broad north region, population poured into the narrowing confines of Middle America. The neck of the bottle, fifty miles in diameter, is reached at Panama, but a more northern isthmus, Tehuantepec, two hundred miles wide, would constrict a flow of population from Mexico into Central America into very narrow limits. It is suggested that the migration map be carefully considered at this point. Given time between movements; considering the prior cultural conditions of the successive waves of immigrants, and the varying environmental situations arrived at in the south, the outstanding Mexican and Central American cultures, namely the indefinite, undifferentiated archaic, the Toltec-Aztec of Mexico, the Maya-Quiché of Central America, and the minor stocks subsidiary to them, they logically have developed into just what we find them to be.

The plateau country south of the Tropic of Cancer, lying between the Sierra Madre Mountains on the west and the broken ranges on the east side, is rough hill country, arid in places, but of great variability as to rainfall and temperature, verging upon the sub-tropical. It is not favorable to concentration of population, but rather would compel a scattering in small bands for subsistence. The flow of immigrants, by way of the Sierra and Rio Grande arteries, would of necessity break up in this region, those which remained settling in disintegrated bands. The country was not conducive to high culture in any respect. Houses were of the "jacal" type, built in small, straggling villages, with cave shelters in use in many places. Subsistence was rather scanty; industries only the essential ones for the simplest of farming and fruit production. It is not a first-rate corn country, still that was the premier food crop. Cacti and agave in many species predominate in the vegetation, all affording food of sorts. Game was fairly plentiful.

Under such conditions, neither close community nor integrated tribal life would flourish. Numerous language groups exist, and there can be a rough grouping into tribes, but the most satisfactory disposition to make of this heterogeneous population is to lump them all under the name "Chichimecos," a term having no ethnic significance, meaning simply "barbarians," or, as some would have it, "wild hunting people." The name is very well chosen. As compared to the high cultures to the south, they would indeed seem a barbarous lot.

However, out of this wild region came the wandering bands that made ancient American history—Toltecs, Aztecs, and the numerous relatives of the latter, who preceded them to the historic Valley of Anahuac. The tribe of especial note is the Otomi. They still exist, numbering about two hundred and fifty thousand souls. Their language is Otomian. It seems likely that somewhere in this indefinitely bounded Chichimec region should be found the original roots of the Nahuatl tongue, the language that, with its principal focus in the Anahuac Valley, around the Lake of Texcoco, was of amazing extent: to the south as far as Costa Rica, eight hundred to one thousand miles away, where it spread from coast to coast; and north, basic in the vast Uto-Aztecan and Shoshonean stock, several thousand miles, embracing California and Northwest Coast tribes, and even penetrating the Southwestern desert. The most virile language of Mexico, this may denote a vast ancient migration movement. If unmolested for some centuries more, Nahuatl might have become the common speech of Mexico, thus eliminating the handicap which, more than any other, has stood in the way of national advancement in that country. Several million people of scores of languages, with no common means of communication other than signs, could hardly be expected to attain to the unity essential to the making of a nation.

The country of the Otomi, within the Chichimec boundaries, including parts of the modern Mexican states of Zacatecas, Aguas Calientes, Guanajuato, Queretaro, Hidalgo, is for the most part rough and only moderately productive, but from the time of the Conquest it has supplied a fairly large and industrious population. Their contributions to the great culture of the Anahuac Valley will be considered farther on. The archæological remains of the region are not conspicuous, the notable exception, aside from caves and simple mounds, being the ruins of La Quemada, thirty-five miles southwest of the city Zacatecas. Here the mountainside is covered with stone walls, terraces, platforms, culminating in the temple ruins of La Quemada proper. This remarkable structure is the first encountered in southward exploration, in which the column is a true architectural element. The round columns of La Quemada are not monolithic, but are built up of small blocks, laid in a friable mortar, and probably originally covered with stucco. If roofed, the building embraced numerous cloister-like halls or porches. That "if" is used advisedly; in many ceremonial precincts in Mexico columns did not support roofs or superstructures of any kind. La Quemada may have been of this sort.

Not far from these ruins are many cave shelters of ancient use. In this region ornaments and fetishes of *chalchihuitl* are found, also an unusually fine quality of pottery. La Quemada is "the farthest north" of the great temple ruins of Mexico. It can hardly be Aztec or Toltec, possibly early Otomi; possibly ancient Tarascan.

PART THREE

DÉBRIS OF AN ANCIENT WORLD: MEXICO

"Are these men come out of the silence
to walk beside me?
Are these gods who flit with invisible
wings?"

—HARTLEY BURR ALEXANDER

PART THREE

DÉBRIS OF AN ANCIENT WORLD: MEXICO

I. THE ANCIENT AZTEC-TOLTEC LAND

1. The Land and Its Legends

i. THE AZTECS

WE GIVE this country the name Aztec Mexico because, though the latest of all its cultures, the Aztecs gave it a place in history. There is an indeterminate level at the bottom of the cultural stratification of the Valley of Mexico, well named by the Mexican archæologists, the "archaic." Above this is the exuberant Toltec stratum, marking doubtless a golden age in prehistoric Mexico. Like the Phœnicians of the Old World, the Toltecs lurk in the shadows of time, baffling, illusive, mythical, but magnificent in their identifiable architectural achievements. The third, or latest, the Aztecs, have held the stage for four historic centuries, with several hundred years of antecedent tradition. The writings about them fill libraries. In twentieth-century language, the Aztecs have had, since the discovery, a most efficient press service. Certainly no people in all history have been more brilliantly written up or persistently glorified. As with modern propaganda, there has been effective playing up of what they were not and persistent ignoring of what they actually were. This commenced with the Conquest, for reasons that are readily understandable. But there is no excuse for perpetually handing on the glamorous, fantastic picture of Aztec life that every archæologist knows to be misleading. Those attributes of European civilization—kings, counts, lords, palaces—were unknown to aboriginal America. The first European witnesses of the spectacular ceremonies of the Indians wrote of them in terms with which they were familiar, terms of European civilization. If for those we substitute chiefs, councils, headmen, pueblos, we have a fairly accurate nomenclature in terms of Indian culture history. On this subject, I wish to quote the late Professor Marshall Saville, from an article published by the Heye Foundation, Museum of the American Indian:

"It may be stated at the outset that the use of the term 'king' is inappropirate in connection with the rulers of Mexico, or indeed of any part of aboriginal America. Among the Aztecs the term used was *tlatoani,* defined as meaning great or chief lord, or overlord or speaker. The Haitian word *cacique* was extensively used by early chroniclers to designate the priest-chiefs of the mainland throughout America, and it has been incorporated into the Castilian language with this significance. The word *tlatoani,* referring to Mexican 'chief lords,' is much to be preferred, as it more nearly expresses the true function of a ruler in this part of ancient America. Usage is so strong, however, that it has become customary to use the term 'king,' as was done by the early English writers on the American colonies; but there were never kings or emperors in America, in the sense in which those terms were used in the Old World. Similarly misleading is the term 'empire' which has come into general usage to designate the native governments of ancient Middle and South America."

In sober truth, the "kingdoms" around the Lake of Texcoco, at the time of the Conquest, would probably have matched the half-dozen adobe towns of pre-historic Zuñi (Cibola), or Hopi (Tusayan), except for their more pretentious plazas or temple precincts. The houses of Tenochtitlan were more numerous, perhaps more commodious, than those of New Mexico's Taos—probably quite similar in their multiple stories and broad terraces. Nowhere in the Toltec-Aztec country were such substantial residences ever built as in the Chaco Canyon of New Mexico, nor as in the less well-built pueblos of the Rio Grande Valley. The great houses of the American Southwest have endured through centuries even of abandonment. Not even foundations of comparable structures remain in Mexico or Central America, though the cultures were contemporaneous, and all have been equally subjected to the ravages of time and civilization. In short, religious life, exhibited in temple building for spectacular ceremonies, was the outstanding factor in Toltec-Aztec culture, as it was also with Central and South American peoples.

That there was colossal misrepresentation of the political and civic status of Mexico is supported by other than archæological evidence. In the matter of population, there was the same over-statement of fact, probably for similar reasons. It was quite as natural to falsify cultural conditions as to exaggerate population. All went to intensify the glamour of the Conquest and to augment the favor of government and the church. As a basis for examining the population estimates of the Conquest period, note the results of recent studies by trained investigators. Dr. Karl Sapper, German geographer, University of Marburg, figuring from subsistence and other geographical evidence, estimated the entire indigenous population of the American continent in 1492 at a maximum of from 40,000,000 to 50,000,000. Dr. A. L. Kroeber, University of California, places it at 8,400,000. Various others arrive between these extremes. I am impressed with the method and results of Professor Angel Rosenblatt's recent study of the problem. He approaches it from the economic standpoint and arrives at the estimate of 13,385,000, for the entire continent of America. After considering the procedure and results of all who have attempted the problem, I am disposed to adhere to Rosenblatt's figures. Consider now the estimates of the Conquest period. Father Las Casas, staunch protagonist for the Indians, declared that 4,000,000 were exterminated during the twelve years following the invasion by Cortéz— an incredible slaughter, nearly one-third of all the Indians on the entire continent, from Alaska to Patagonia. Clavigero claims that 6,000,000 (nearly one-half the population of the continent!) assembled to witness the dedication of the great temple of Mexico, in 1486. Cortéz wrote the King of Spain about the defeat in battle of 149,000 Tlaxcalans by his 400 soldiers—a bit over 370 to the man. Then comes Juan Diaz de la Calle with 43,000,000 Indians baptized in Mexico by the Franciscans—more than three times the entire population of America at that time. These are fair examples of unreliable population estimates. In the face of this, it is not hard to believe that the magnificence of life depicted at the same time was even more luridly colored.

The difficulty of sifting the documentary accounts concerning ancient America has long been recognized. Nearly fifty years ago, Adolph Bandelier wrote:

"Not only the history of ancient Mexico, but the true condition and degree of culture of its aboriginal inhabitants, are yet but imperfectly known. Nearly all architectural remains have disappeared; the descendants of the former aborigines have modified their plan of life, and we are almost exclusively reduced, for our knowledge of Mexican antiquities, to the printed and written testimony of those who saw Indian society in Mexico either at the time of, or not too long after, its downfall. But these authors, whether eye-witnesses of the conquest, like Cortes, Bernal Diaz del Castillo, Andres de Tapia, and others; or missionaries sent to New Spain at an early date,—as Toribio of Benavente (Motolinia), Sahagun, or (towards the close of the 16th century, or beginning of the 17th century) Acosta, Davila, Mendieta and Torquemada,—they are sometimes, on many questions, in direct opposition to each other. Thus the uncertainty is still increased, and the most difficult critical labor heaped upon the student. Furthermore, to magnify the task, we are placed in presence of several Indian writers of the 16th and 17th centuries (like Duran, Tezozomoc, and Ixtlilxochitl), who disagree with each other on the most important questions, quite as much as the Spanish authors themselves. It may appear presumptuous, while knowing of the existence of such difficulties, to attempt the description of even a single feature of life of Mexico's former Indian society."

The Valley of Mexico, anciently known as Anahuac, has probably as rich a cultural history as any spot of equal area on the globe. It varies from seventy-five hundred to nine thousand feet in altitude, and is completely surrounded by mountains. On the southeast rim of the basin is the Sierra Nevada, with the great volcanoes, Popocatepetl, always active, always threatening, and his mate Ixtaccihuatl (White Woman), dormant since some remote age, when one of the greatest explosions in geologic time blew off the entire upper part of the mountain and folded it back into its present romantic aspect, that of the white, sleeping woman. Never without their caps of snow, are Popocatepetl and Ixtaccihuatl; never without its puffs of white smoke, the former. What the mystically minded Indians of the valleys about their bases and on their slopes have been thinking about these two sacred mountains during the past two or three millenniums, would make marvelous reading if it could be captured. Lesser volcanic peaks lie to the south and southwest, in the Serrania de Ajusco and Sierra de las Cruces. From cones in this quarter came the eruptions of recent geologic time that covered that side of the valley with the ash and basalt of the *pedregal;* settling one point for the American archæologist, namely, that in at least one place on the American continent human remains, both physical and cultural, are under volcanic deposits. Unhappily, the geologists give us a range of guesses of from three thousand to thirty thousand years for the eruptions that swamped a primitive population here. So the problem of man's age on the continent is not helped a particle. Other ranges that help to complete the inclosure of the Vale of Anahuac are, on the west, the Sierra de Monte Alto, and, on the north and northeast, the Serrania de Pachuca.

Figuring dramatically in both the history and prehistory of the Valley of Mexico, was the beautiful Lake of Texcoco, near the center. Upon its shores were built the towns ("kingdoms") such as Texcoco, Atzcapotzalco, Ixtapalapan, Coyoacan, Tacuba. Upon its swampy island grew up the Aztec pueblo ("capital") of Tenochtitlan, destined to become the paramount community of the valley in pre-Spanish times; to be the scene of the mighty efforts of Hernando Cortéz and his adventures; to become, in our time, the seat of government of a great nation—a city of one million inhabitants. The once ample lake has shrunk to a shallow pool of a few inches in depth during the rainy season; during the greater part of the year a dusty desert.

The tribe that was marked for such a dramatic destiny was a feeble, straggling band that came out of the Chichimec country and gained a precarious position in the swamps, in about the year 1325 A.D. They were the weakest of all the bands in the Mexican Valley, but they steadily increased in number and strength. In less than a century they dominated the valley, and were exacting tribute from towns beyond the confines of Anahuac. In another hundred years, their history as a strong, independent people came suddenly to an end, with the advent of the Spaniards into the valley that for several centuries had been the nurse of virile cultures, but of a type that Europeans could not understand; a type that modern Americans even yet fail to appreciate.

Such, in broad outline, is the dependable history of the Aztecs. It may be considered documentary from 1325 on, by way of their picture manuscripts and the Spanish archives. But their traditional history is well worth knowing. It begins with their coming out of their mythic Aztlan, far to the north, in the year of the Aztec calendar, 1 *tecpatl* (one stone knife), which Joyce makes out to have been 1168 of the Christian era. This event is depicted in one of their picture manuscripts known as the Boturini codex, part of which is shown.

This codex will serve to illustrate Aztec picture

writing. Their Aztlan, in the "land of the seven caves," is represented as being on an island in the center of a lake. The Aztec is seen crossing the water in a boat. The date, 1 *tecpatl,* next appears. Their trek is to Colhuacan—footsteps show the route—where they receive their deity Huitzilopochtli. They join with eight related tribes, shown to the right with their glyphs; these are the Matlazinca, Tepanec, Chichimec, Malinalca, Cuitlauaca, Xochimilca, Chalca, and Uexotzinca, all of the same Nahuan stock. Such is the reading of their simple pictorial record. Following their traditions further, they account for about one and a half centuries of wandering, which I must believe was merely a shifting about in the wild Chichimec country. The eight kindred tribes moved on, the Aztecs remaining behind in a wild state. Arriving at last in the Valley of Mexico, a small vagabond crew, they rejoined their former associates, who had preceded them to the south, and who had pre-empted all the desirable lands around the lake. Strong towns had been built at Atzcapotzalco, Texcoco, Ixtapalapan and other places. The feeble Aztecs had no choice. The swampy island was all that was available—"no place to live in, but a good place to die in." So Tenochtitlan was founded in 1324 or 1325, with the results above stated. On the founding of Tenochtitlan, we have the interesting account in the codex Mendoza:

"In the year 1324 the Mexican people first arrived at the place called the City of Mexico. The locality pleased them after their journeying for many years from place to place, sometimes stopping a number of years in the course of their travels. Not being content, however, with the places where they had stopped, they continued

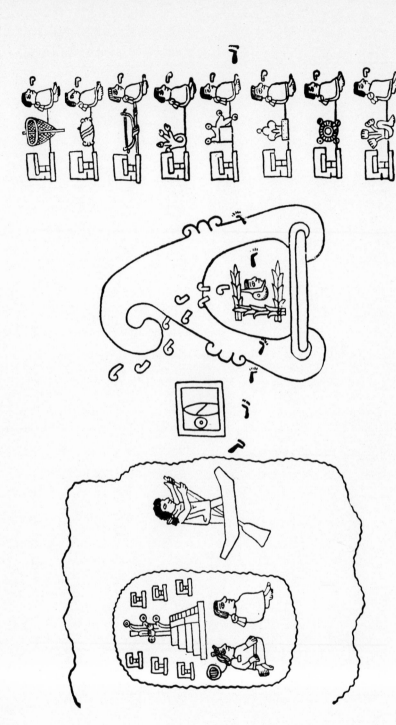

Aztec Picture Writing (from Codex Boturini)—Legendary Migration of the Aztecs

Map of Tenochtitlan, by "The Anonymous Conqueror"

(See page 87)

until they finally came to the site of Mexico, at a time when it was a complete marsh, overgrown with briars, and rushes called *tule,* and full of very tall flags, reed grass, making it resemble a thicket. Throughout the area of the place there flowed a spring and stream of clear water which was free from sedges and bushes, which stream also went through it crosswise like the cross of Saint Andrew. . . . And in about the middle of the place of the stream of water, the Mexicans found a great rock, and growing on it was a great reed or bush called *tunal,* upon which a great eagle had her abode and place for food, as shown by the scattered bones and feathers of various birds, and fowl of divers colors. After exploring the country in all directions they found it fertile, supplied with ample game, birds, and fish, and likewise those products found in swampy lands upon which they could sustain themselves; and they felt that it also afforded them a means of livelihood through trade with the neighboring pueblos. The security afforded by the water, which their neighbors could under no circumstances ever cut off, together with other motives and reasons, induced them to go no farther in their travels. Having therefore made up their minds upon this point, they strengthened their position by utilizing the waters and clumps of *tule* and reed grass for their walls and bulwarks. Having thus laid the foundation for their settlement and nation, they decided to give a name to the place, calling it Tenochtitlan, on account of the *tunal* growing on the stone, for Tenochtitlan, interpreted in the Castilian language, means, the *tunal* growing upon a rock."

For fifty years, according to their tradition, the Aztecs slowly grew in power. They were governed, as most Indian tribes always have been, by a council, until in 1375 they elected a "king." From now on we will use the term "chief," so as to bring our narrative into literal Indian tradition. This chief, Acamapichtli, who ruled in peace for twenty-one years, was reputed to be a decendant of the Toltecs, that once potent stock of the Valley of Mexico, which at this time had been moribund for several generations. From this time on the Aztecs had a succession of chiefs of sufficient authenticity to warrant their being recorded in history. Huitzilhuitl, something of a warrior, was chief for twenty-one years; Chimalpopoca for ten years. Itzcoatl was the wise chief for thirteen years, under whom the Aztecs annexed Atzcapotzalco and Xochimilco, and in less than one hundred years from their feeble settlement in the swamps, became the dominant tribe of Anahuac. With Montezuma I, a great name comes into history, not through his own, but through a successor's career. The first Montezuma, however, was a great chief in his own right. In his time the Aztecs flourished materially, having wars with Chalca, Cuernavaca, and distant Guatemala. A ten-mile causeway was built across the lake, from Atzacoalco to Ixtapalapan. In this twenty-nine years Tenochtitlan gained ascendancy at considerable distances from home. Axayacatl, who laid many towns tribute, came next, for twelve years; then his brother, Tizoc, chief for only five rather peaceful years, followed by Ahuitzotl, another warrior chief who in sixteen years conquered many towns. The Aztecs had now been under eight chiefs, for a total period of one hundred twenty-seven years. Then, in 1502, there came to the chieftaincy, the warrior-priest, Montezuma II, son of a former chief, Axayacatl. We have now come to the most tragic figure in Indian history, whose name has gone further than that of any other man of his race. Leader of his people for eighteen years, it was through no fault or policy of his own that this hapless chief gained the spotlight in Aztec history. He was the victim of one of the most dramatic events in history, the Conquest of the New World. We look upon it from our European standpoint as one of the great landmarks in human progress—the event that opened to our race the opportunities of a new world; that carried our religion around the globe; that made possible all that America has added to civilization.

Can we now view it from the standpoint of the "red" race, whose type of mind and culture I hope have been made clear? It was a race of some millions of thinking men and women, working out its problems in another way; traveling another road toward its place in the sun. It was far on its way in Mexico, Guatemala, Peru, and the American Southwest. Who knows whether or not its apogee had been reached under the Aztec Confederacy of Montezuma? Who knows what America might have brought forth in another thousand unmolested years? That they were a people of high aspirations cannot be doubted. The temples of Middle America still stand. The ruins that will be shown and described later speak for the Aztecs, Toltecs, Maya, and contemporaries of lesser note. It was a potent race that erected these sanctuaries to their deities; that put into imperishable art and architecture these records of how they were thinking out the problems of human life here and hereafter. Egypt, Mesopotamia, China did no better. They were absolutely unconscious of any other world or people. What burst upon them could be compared with a sudden attack upon us from another planet, with weapons of which we have never dreamed.

The Aztecs received the brunt of this attack. They had a representative form of government. Montezuma II was their chief. No leader known to history, no superman, could have withstood the impact. We can conceive of a time when moral will successfully cope with physical force. That time had not arrived at the beginning of the sixteenth century. It is perhaps foreshadowed in the twentieth. Montezuma II, bewildered chieftain of a bewildered people, left nothing undone that could have done more than postpone for a while the destruction of his country.

Other towns than those of the Aztecs, in the Mexican Valley, produced leaders worthy of mention. Xolotl, the Chichimec, of the second half of the twelfth century, is purely legendary. The name of another Chichimec, Ixtlilxochitl, appears about the year 1400, as chief of Texcoco. Out of the same virile northern stock, came the wise Nezahualcóyotl, contemporary of Montezuma I, head of the strong town of Texcoco for forty-one years. In the Indian way, he was a promoter of the arts, a builder of temples, a maker of laws and government, who would have been an ornament to any race. Tezozomoc, the Tepanec, made Atzcapotzalco a town to be reckoned with, and for a time ruled Texcoco also. Nowhere else in the valley, however, do we find such a strong, unbroken line of chiefs as the nine rulers of the Aztecs. The line does not quite end with the death of Montezuma. His brother, Cuitlahuac, chief of Ixtapalapan, carried on for forty days. Then came the unfortunate Cuauhtémoc, true hero of the losing fight against the Spaniards; a warrior who would have given a good account of himself alongside any of the heroes of history. Last of the *tzins,* or chiefs, of the Aztecs, he in some ways overshadows Montezuma, for he preferred to go down fighting. One would like to slur over the almost unbelievable story of the torture of Cuauhtémoc by the Spaniards, and finally his brutal murder by Cortéz. But something more must be said on this subject later on.

We have previously put down the leading points in the legendary history of the Aztecs, from their coming out of their traditional Aztlan (1168), to the death of Cuauhtémoc, roughly three hundred and fifty years; the first one hundred and fifty purely legendary, two hundred in the domain of history. It is unlikely, though within the realm of possibility, that anything more definite will ever known about their origin. Atzlan may be as mythical as Atlantis. On the other hand, there are elements of verisimilitude in the story. The traditions of primitive people, even though dim in the mists of time, often have a basis in fact. If Atzlan was an actual place of abode, I would be inclined to place it in northern Chihuahua, in the region of the inland, almost always dry, Guzman lakes. Here may have been a body of water as large as Lake Texcoco at the time of the reputed settlement. Here might well have been an island large enough to accommodate a considerable band of people. It is in the midst of a rich archæological district, on the natural line of population movements, described earlier in this work; a trail that would lead directly into the Chichimec country, where the Aztecs wandered for many years as hunters, and out of which they came into the Valley of Anahuac, to settle in 1325. A brief chapter on this subject, "Anahuac and Aztlan," may be read in my *Ancient Life in the American Southwest*. A few interesting facts may be pointed out here, without any implication of relationship. The great communities of Chaco Canyon, New Mexico, were abandoned, according to tree ring dating, during the first half of the twelfth century. Atzlan was aban-

doned in the second half of that century—legendary
date 1168. Tula (Tollan), ancient Toltec stronghold,
fifty miles northwest of Lake Texcoco, was abandoned
in 1064, and occupied by the Aztecs at some period on
their southward migration. Here they gained, from the
inhabitants who had overspread the abandoned region,
an abundant legendry of the people who preceded them
and who built the great edifices, among the ruins of
which they were living. This great pre-Aztecan site I
explored years ago, when endeavoring to pick up the
trails of the ancient migrants who came out of the
north to people Anahuac.

ii.   THE LEGENDARY TOLTECS

Aztec and Maya-Quiché tradition, as recorded by
writers of the Conquest period, supplemented by archæological evidence, is our main reliance in trying to
bring the Toltecs out of their obscurity. We get their
own traditions of three centuries of pre-eminence in
the Valley of Mexico, with Tollan (the present Tula)
as the main focus of their culture. We have shadowy
traditions of Tula in the Maya country, mainly among
the Xius, who are reputed to have built Uxmal in
Yucatan, and the Quichés of Guatemala. These bands
that gave Tula, or Tulan, as the place from which they
migrated, may or may not have referred to the ancient
Toltec country. Father Sahagun, besides being a great
priest and historian, would have been considered a
first-rate anthropologist, if anthropologists had existed
in his time. He gathered his information about the Toltecs when their disintegration was not so far in the past
as to have made their traditions utterly apocryphal;
therefore is our best witness concerning them. Based

on both the legendary and historic evidence, we may sift
the Toltecs down to something like the following, to be
taken with all our usual cautions. They were a pre-
Aztecan people, inhabiting the Valley of Mexico for
several centuries. They spoke the same language as the
Aztecs and all the other bands that succeeded them in
the valley, namely Nahua. They were under priest-
chiefs, a comparatively peace-loving lot, devoted to
agriculture and religion. The principal deity was Quetzalcoatl, represented by the flying or feathered serpent,
which was as it should be, for this was the most prevalent conception of deific power among the higher cultures of ancient America. Their traditions, embodied in
the *Annals of Cuauhtitlan,* mention some half-dozen
chiefs between 752 and 1064. They were the greatest
builders that ever inhabited the Valley of Mexico, and
more advanced in their culture than any later tribes, as
will be seen when we describe their archæological remains. A people that could build Tula, Teotihuacan,
Atzcapotzalco, Xochicalco, and Cholula, deserves to
rank with the greatest that aboriginal America brought
forth. Their early decline was probably due to the pressure of incoming tribes of more warlike disposition, from
the barbarous Chichimec north. They do not disappear
from Mexican tradition by sudden, wholesale migration after the destruction of Tulan in 1064, but gradually disintegrate among the more virile tribes in the
valley. For more than three centuries, after the tribal
dissolution, they are looked upon by the ruder peoples
as a sort of nobility. To be of Toltec blood was high
honor, as witness the choosing of Acamapichtli, a Toltec, to be the first chief of the Aztecs, after their settling
in the Valley of Mexico. It is unlikely that any considerable number of the Toltecs ever emigrated from

Anahuac. Small bands may have gone out to Yucatan, to Guatemala, even farther, but the stock was doubtless absorbed into the new population and has probably made an important contribution to the blood of modern Mexico.

Much has been written, almost entirely speculative, as to the probable origin of the Toltecs. The laborious efforts to trace them through many migrations have been futile. Since they were Nahuatl in language, as were all the later comers in the Valley of Mexico, I am disposed to ascribe to them the line of least resistance, and to believe that they were simply the earliest to come out of that fecund motherland to the north, the rugged Chichimec country, and that through stimulation by a new environment of some potential culture-trait, they went to a plane of accomplishment that their successors never reached.

The Toltecs were not the first people in the Valley of Anahuac. Centuries before, a primitive culture was planted there, which the Mexican archæologists have appropriately called the "archaic." People of this culture do not appear in the domain of history or even of tradition. As we have only testimony of archæology concerning them, they must be considered in a later chapter. They may have seen the ancestors of the Toltecs.

2. The Archæology of Anahuac

i. AZTEC RUINS

While it reverses the process of history making, it seems best in an archæological study to begin with the topmost stratum of remains, obviously that of the latest people, and work back toward the beginning. Therefore, in the study of the archæology of Anahuac,

Great Pyramid of Teotihuacan after Excavation

Façade of Temple of Quetzalcoatl, Teotihuacan, Mexico

we shall first hunt out what remains of the Aztecs and their contemporaries. In pursuit of this objective, I, years ago, undertook an exploration that was designed to cover every square mile of the Valley of Mexico, to be followed by a study of the antiquities of the region that have been collected and placed in museums. Of these latter, the treasure houses are, the National Museum in Mexico City; the National Museum in Washington; the American Museum of Natural History and the Museum of the American Indian, New York City; the British Museum of London; the Ethnographic Museums of Berlin and Paris. Many other museums and universities are rich in collections from Mexico. To study them all thoroughly would require several lives. However, from these sources, one gains a clear picture of the most substantial achievements of the peoples who have made the culture history of this valley. It will be possible, within the limits of this work, to review only a few of them. Exploration in the Valley of Mexico is a fascinating job. There are few regions in which archæology squares so well with tradition and history. It must be admitted at the outset, that there is no infallible way of telling the difference between Aztec and Toltec antiquities, nor of positively identifying remains of the other great cultures of Mexico and Central America, such as Maya, Zapotec, Tarascan, Totonac, etc. However, the general features of the Aztec temple differentiate it from the Toltec, and the same may be said of the arts of the two great stocks. As between the closely related, contemporary Nahua groups that occupied the towns around the Lake of Texcoco, there was not sufficient differentiation in culture to warrant any absolute identification of their productions.

The natural starting place for the exploration of the architectural remains of the valley is at the *zocolo,* or great plaza of Mexico City. Here on the island, Tenochtitlan was built; here stood the great *teocalli* of Huitzilopochtli, the war god. The tradition of the building of a great temple to the war deity runs through the entire story of the Aztecs. From their earliest settlement they were attempting it. This is almost universal Indian tradition. A place sacred to the deific powers was the first concern of the plains and desert Indians of northern America. The great *teocalli,* as first seen by Cortéz and his men, was one of the wonders of this strange new world. Just when, or under what chiefs, that identical structure was started cannot be stated, but we know that it grew by successive accretions, as probably most of the American pyramids did. Large additions to it were made by Montezuma I, still more by Tizoc. That it was finished in 1487, by Ahuitzotl, is quite certain. It had grown into a vast compound, embracing not only the pyramid proper, but many additional structures. Such an excellent description of it has been written by Doctor Saville, based on Maudslay's details and Sahagun's records, that I take the liberty of quoting this by permission of the Museum of the American Indian, Heye Foundation, rather than attempt a new account of it:

"We have referred several times to the great temple compound, that dominated the city of Tenochtitlan, on which the final work of enlargement was undertaken by Tizoc and was completed shortly after his death by Ahuitzotl.

"A number of early writers render more or less information respecting the size of the great temple. In a recent note on the position and extent of the temple enclosure of Tenochtitlan, and the position,

structure, and orientation of the *teocalli* of Huitzilopochtli, Maudslay has brought together statements of the most important authorities, and in the
light of modern archæological discoveries in different portions of the site of the compound in the
vicinity of the cathedral he has attempted to de-
limit the location of the *teocalli* and to indicate its
juxtaposition to various groups of edifices that
surround it. It seems clearly evident that the temple completed in 1487 occupied the most commanding position on the summit of the substructure
which constituted what was known as the great
temple. There can be no doubt that the temple
was composed in much the same manner as in the
Main Structure of Copan; the Temple or Great
Palace of Palenque; and the enormous complex of
the temple of Comalcalco; namely, as a gradually
increasing aggregation of buildings. At Copan we
find that the great structure ultimately contained
more than twenty small buildings, with two main
courts, the houses and towers being built on at
least three different levels. The temple enclosure
of Tenochtitlan was surrounded by a high masonry
wall, and reconciling the measurements of the compound as given by various writers we find that it
must have been fully one thousand feet square,
somewhat larger than the main structure of Copan, but about the size of the temple group of
Comalcalco. It was one of the two largest temples
of ancient Middle America. Sahagun mentions
seventy-eight buildings in connection with the great
temple, but, as Maudslay observed, it is almost
certain that these were not all within the temple
enclosure.

"The structure begun by Tizoc and completed
by Ahuitzotl was the culmination of the growth in
size of the great compound. It was undoubtedly
the pyramid dominating the whole group and was
surmounted by two edifices. It was indeed what

has been called the great *teocalli*. After a study and comparison of the various statements made by the old writers in regard to it, Maudslay came to the conclusion that it measured about three hundred feet square at the base, being a solid quadrangular edifice in the form of a truncated stepped pyramid. It was probably about a hundred and fifty feet in height (if we consider that it was ascended by more than a hundred steps) from the elevated part of the great substructure upon which it was placed, and allowing for the height of the two houses on its summit. Moreover, to this we must add the height of the substructure platforms upon which the other numerous buildings of the thousand-foot-square compound had been erected."

This may be taken as the greatest achievement of the Aztec people. Its location is perfectly well known, but the excavation of its remains will probably never be accomplished, since the great cathedral of Mexico and many important public and private buildings stand upon its ruins. Portions of it, however, have been laid bare, within a short distance from the *zocolo,* where a vacant lot permitted some excavations by the Department of Antiquities of Mexico a few years ago. The massive foundations, walls, platforms, and sculptures identify this as an imposing section of the compound, probably a portion of one of the minor structures, rather than of the great *teocalli*. It is hoped that the Mexican Government will, as modern buildings become dilapidated and ready for demolition, reserve every square yard of space so vacated, and dedicate it to the reclamation of whatever remains buried of this crowning glory of their ancient history. The recent excavations in the heart of Rome demonstrate the possibilities of rescuing the works of a glorious past, not to the detriment, but to the honor of modern civilization.

The "city"—I prefer to call it "pueblo"—of Tenochtitlan probably consisted largely of its great *teocalli* and other temples devoted to community affairs, mainly religious. Father Bernardino de Sahagun, the Franciscan monk, scholar, ethnologist, historian, who knew it well in the generation following the Conquest, describes seventy-eight edifices, or temples, pertaining to this great establishment. They must have occupied the major part of the island. This is quite conceivable. The common people lived in huts, the counterpart of which may be seen today all over the Valley of Mexico. Their fields and gardens were mostly the built-up swamp lands of the lagoon, the survival of which is to be seen in the "floating gardens" of Xochimilco, a suburb of the modern city of Mexico. I have an idea that the map here shown of the pueblo and lagoon which comes to us from the "Anonymous Conqueror," probably a companion in arms of Cortéz, is exceptionally good for its time; that the edifices shown thereon surrounding the great square represent the seventy-eight described by Sahagun.

Mexico City, which overlies the ancient Tenochtitlan, is on what is now the southwest margin of Lake Texcoco, so far has the lake receded in the last four centuries. Taking the broad street of the modern city, which leads out of the south, probably following one of the ancient causeways, the old shore line of Coyoacan is reached, and Ixtapalapan, both towns of note in pre-Conquest times. Of the former, little remains except a few old walls, encountered in the laying of sewer and water mains. The latter, Ixtapalapan, has much of interest to be seen. Such of its ruins as are preserved occupy the romantic "Hill of the Star," on the former south margin of the lake, an elevation from which one of the most magnificent views in the Valley of Mexico is to be had. It must have been possible to see over every one of the traditionary "seven kingdoms" from here. Of this town, was the chief, Cuitlahuac, successor of the ill-fated Montezuma II, destined to a short chieftaincy of but forty days, when stricken with the new disease, just from the Old World, smallpox. Nothing is to be found in the way of ruins of the "palaces" described by Bernal Diaz, of stonework and cedar and other sweet scented woods, with great rooms and courts and awnings. But *calzadas* of stone lead up the hill from the modern village of Ixtapalapan, with ruined shrines along the way. On the top are vestiges of ancient construction, possibly of a small *teocalli,* but of unusual interest, for it was at this shrine, according to tradition, that at the end of every fifty-two year cycle, when all fires had been allowed to die, and all utensils, especially pottery, broken up, the new fire was struck from the flint by the fire priest, and by messengers carried to all towns of the valley, for the kindling of the new fire that marked the beginning of a new cycle and the renewal of their cultural life.

Passing around to the east side of the lake, the modern town of Texcoco is entered. It is built, in part, over the site of the ancient Texcoco, one of the strong communities of pre-Conquest days. The lake has receded quite far from the present town, but the ancient shore line is well known. Traditionally founded for the Acolhua band that long preceded the Aztecs out of the Chichimec country to settle in Anahuac Valley, the fame of prehistoric Texcoco rests largely on the career of one remarkable chief, the sage, Nezahualcóyotl. True, Texcoco emerges in tradition somewhat earlier, because of its strife with Atzcapotzalco, on the other side of the lake, for supremacy in the valley. Its native chief, Ixtlilxochitl, 1400 A.D., was of some note in this conflict, but seems to have been worsted about the year 1418, and his successor, destined to become the wise chief above referred to, was driven out by Atzcapotzalco's Tepanec warrior, Tezozomoc, who became for a time ruler of both towns; a short time only, however, for both were on the wane under the increasing ascendancy of the Aztecs of the island of Tenochtitlan. Their strong chief, Itzcoatl, (1427), followed by Montezuma I (1440), consolidated that supremacy, and it was held until the cataclysm came. Texcoco, meanwhile, passed back to the chieftaincy of its greatest son, Nezahualcóyotl.

There is a charm in the study of Texcoco that is exceptional even in Mexico. There is something reminiscent of the reverential philosophy of the Plains Indians; of the art and religion of the Southwestern Pueblos; something to bring to mind ancient Babylon's law-maker, Hammurabi. To sum it all up, there is in the character of the pagan chief, Nezahualcóyotl, something which brings to mind another pagan who was ages ahead of his time, Akhnaton of Egypt. Like the latter, Nezahualcóyotl was neither politian nor warrior. He was willing that others should have those glories, that he might live in a world of the spirit. Making all due allowance for the defects of the evidence of that age, we may place to his credit the following achievements. He was a builder of temples and gardens. He improved the laws of his people to the extent that his code for Texcoco was used as a pattern by surrounding towns. He was against human sacrifice, either practiced as religion or as a means of liquidating opposition.

89

In the Indian way, poetry (primitive philosophy), music, painting, virtually all the fine arts, flourished in his time, and under his encouragement Texcoco became an outstanding "culture center." He was a valued counselor. On his advice, Montezuma I built the dyke across the lake, from Atzacoalco to Ixtapalapan, which was no mean engineering feat for its time. It was ten miles long, furnished with flood-gates to control inundations, and must have been a public achievement of great service to all the surrounding towns, for it created of the west part of the lake a basin of fresh water for fish and wild fowl. He must have had about forty years for his work. He died in 1472. A master mind, a maker of culture history, Nezahualcóyotl would have been an honor to any race or people.

Besides tradition, enough remains of the substantial culture of Texcoco to keep the explorer busy for a long time. No remains of the "palace" have been found, but we have its ground plan in the Humboldt manuscript, in Berlin. A simple structure, which could have been perfectly Indian in every respect, if we cut out the palatial idea of European writers. Climbing about, over the hills around the present Texcoco, one finds minor antiquities everywhere, and numerous larger remains. On the slopes of Tezcotzingo are long, beautifully made stairways of stone. The entire mountain is rich in *calzadas,* terraces, platforms, shrines, in excellent state of preservation because cut in the living rock. The remains of the sanctuaries on the four sides, near the top, are reminiscent of the four world quarters of the American Southwest.

If one were willing to accept all the manufactured glamour of it as valid, one could, standing on the summit of Tezcotzingo with the magnificent view of the whole Mexican Valley spread before one, and the panorama of human life through the ages animated again, easily think oneself upon an American Acropolis with a New World Athens at one's feet. Not without reason have antiquity-loving Mexicans been wont to speak of Texcoco as "the Athens of America."

Coming down to the cold facts of history, Texcoco was an important base for the army of Cortéz during the campaign of the Conquest. It was from here that he launched his flotilla that gave him a means of attack from the east upon the island town. From here most of his forays were sent out to complete the mopping up of the Aztec towns and fighting bands that continued the hopeless struggle up to the final conquest of Mexico, in August, 1521.

Atzcapotzalco lay on the west side of the lake, straight across from Texcoco. It is now several miles inland, but was originally a shore town. The traditionary founders were Tepanecas, of the lot who came out of the Chichimec country some generations ahead of the Aztecs. However, rubbish heaps of the ruin area, about forty feet deep, yield cultural material that is clearly Toltec. This would indicate that the newcomers, the Tepanecas, occupied and built upon the ruins of an ancient Toltec settlement of many years' duration. The name best known in its history is Tezozomoc, chief during a period when warfare with Texcoco was endemic. As stated before, he became, for a time, master of both towns. They were not to exceed thirty miles apart, in an airline across the lake, perhaps forty by the land route. He lived to an advanced age, and has little to his credit as compared with his great contemporary, Nezahualcóyotl of Texcoco, or Itzcoatl of Tenochtitlan. The community was badly divided after his death. One of his sons, Maxtla, became chief by the assassination route. He was a turbulent character and reckless. He attacked Tenochtitlan without provocation, was badly whipped by the forces of Itzcoatl, driven to his own stronghold and there besieged and killed. It was a heavy penalty to pay for the rashness of a leader, for from then on the Tepanecas were a subordinate people. The Aztecs were then top dog until the cataclysm came.

The ruins of ancient Atzcapotzalco lie in the midst of a populous district. The most conspicuous object was the *teocalli* which has been destroyed by the railway. There is much to be excavated at this site, the superposition of a town of the late period upon an early Toltec settlement affording an exceptional opportunity for study in comparative culture history. Its near neighbor to the north, Tenayuca, has proved to be one of the most interesting ruins in Mexico. When I first knew the place it was an overgrown hill, looking like so many others in Mexico that have to be dug into before identified as natural or artificial. A masterly work of excavation by Señor Reygadas-Vertiz, archæological engineer and head of the Department of Antiquities in Mexico for several years, has uncovered this superb *teocalli* and made of the place a Mecca for students of the archæology of Mexico.

Tenayuca is a typical Aztec temple, upon an ancient Chichimec settlement. It has the severe plan that characterizes the religious structures of that people, though in one respect it is embellished in a more striking manner than any of its contemporaries. The great pyramidal base on which it rests extends as a platform from under the pyramid, and upon this, extending around the wall, is a succession of enormous serpents very crudely sculptured, it is true, but nevertheless forming a setting of singular strength and impressiveness. The walls of the temple rise in terraces from this platform, the front being furnished with a double stairway. What may have rested upon the apex of the pyramid in the way of cells or shrines cannot now be determined. The excavator performed a great service to students of the pyramid when he tunneled the interior and lighted the passageways so that one can explore at will the inner structure. It is by this means that a characteristic of Aztec temples, which has heretofore only been imperfectly realized, is made clear. There is invariably a central core around and upon which the pyramid has grown by successive layers, these enlargements taking place at intervals unknown to us and for reasons that are not yet understood. Of most Aztec pyramids only the outer shell is known. This one has been thoroughly dissected and its construction made clear. Enough red color is preserved in protected places on the surface stucco to demonstrate that the building was originally painted. The same was doubtless true of the great serpent platform decoration. Partly owing to the friendly protection of earth and humus that preserved this noble building, partly to the intelligent work of the excavator, one is inclined to rank Tenayuca as the finest extant example of an Aztec temple.

In the lovely vale of Cuernavaca, over the volcanic rim that borders the Valley of Mexico on the south, and some two thousand feet lower in altitude, is the ancient home of an Aztec tribe known as the Tlahuica. This valley is rich in remains of the ancient Aztecs. Numerous pieces of their sculpture are to be found in and about the present city of Cuernavaca, and sculptured idols in great numbers have been collected here for public and private museums. In the outskirts of the city is the temple of Teopanzolco. This also, when I first knew it, was apparently a natural hill. Its true character became known only a few years ago, whereupon it was excavated and put in repair.

It proved to be a typical Aztec structure, almost without embellishment, consisting of successive layers resting upon the customary pyramidal base. Two stairways ascend from the basal platform to the top, where the remains of two shrines or cells are still to be seen. Within the cells are benches against the walls, reminding one of those in the kivas of the American Southwest. Teopanzolco is perhaps the least artistic of all the known Aztec temples.

On the rim of the vale of Tepoztlan, some twelve or thirteen miles away, rises a roughly cylindrical mountain to a height of twelve hundred feet above the valley, on the top of which is the ruined temple that I have long been accustomed to point out as the type specimen of the religious architecture of the Aztec people. It is known as the pyramid of Tepozteco, receiving its name from the deity of rather undesirable repute, long worshiped by the Tlahuica tribe, namely the Tepoztecatl, god of *pulque* or drunkenness, a sort of Aztec Dionysos.

The situation of the temple on the top of this vertical precipice makes it almost impregnable, quite so to the ancient enemies of the builders, and now to be reached only by way of the substantial iron stairways erected by the Mexican Government. The sloping sides of the pyramid rise in three plain terraces, resting upon a platform about sixty-six feet square, according to my measurements of many years ago. The shrine on the top is reached by way of the typical Aztec stairway of very narrow treads. Inside are benches such as those described in the pyramid of Teopanzolco, but these in the temple of Tepozteco are embellished with hieroglyphics. The entire structure is built of the basaltic lava of the mountain on which it rests. The temple would be quite unimpressive were it not for its remarkable situation which makes it the most picturesque of all ancient Aztec sites, the stupendous mountain scenery surrounding the vale of Tepoztlan forming an indescribable setting for the ruin.

It was long the custom of the Indians of the village of Tepoztlan to ascend to this ruined temple on the night of September eighth, and there enact their drama of the Tepoztecatl. Hearing of this, I proceeded to the summit of the mountain, some days in advance of the ceremony, and pitched my small tent at the base of the ruin, with the intention of witnessing the ceremony. I was rewarded by one of the most dramatic spectacles that it has ever been my good fortune to see. The Indians arrived after dusk, somewhat startled to find a stranger occupying a front seat, but refrained from tossing me over the cliff, thanks to the good offices of their revered mentor, Señor Mariano Rojas, true Aztec sage and, ever since, my fast friend.

After dark, and it was a coal black night, the Indians lighted huge bonfires on the ruined walls, and thereupon enacted their stirring drama, the performers in striking costume standing between the bonfires on the temple walls, and shouting their parts out into the black depths of the night. Such a stage and setting are almost beyond human imagination.

At intervals between the acts, while the Indians gathered around, I brought my phonograph into action, the first they had ever heard, and gave them an entertainment of negro and Indian melodies from the North that was probably as weird to them as their dramatic performance had been to me. At last, some of their performers, with much shaking of the knees, ventured to sing their songs into the mysterious instrument, and were amazed upon hearing them repeated back from inside the machine. Here again, I was indebted to the wisdom of their old counselor, Señor Rojas, who assured them, "Why, it is now possible that even the sound of our voices may be heard by those who come after us many, many years from now." Not many white men, I think, were ever permitted to view this weird ceremony, performed in its primitive manner and setting on the summit of Tepoztlan Mountain. But, on the following day, in the plaza of the village below, in a small temple constructed for the purpose, the ceremony was repeated for the benefit of all the people, the occasion being partly in the nature of a religious festival, a curious illustration of the mingling of pagan and Christian ritual.

For the most part this drama consists of a glorification of the culture hero, Tepoztecatl. That in one variation he is portrayed as the god of inebrity is true, but I suspect here is a derivative variant not found in the original story, for Tepoztecatl is a semi-deified hero singularly analogous to 'Ahayutah of the Southwestern hero twins, only there is but one of him. He was born, of a devout virgin and was a model of goodness as well as an intellectual prodigy. His first heroic act, performed as a young boy, was the slaying of the giant who terrorized the valley, eating the children, of whom a certain number were required of every village. The boy Tepoztecatl offered himself among the number taken from his town. Providing himself with flint blades, he allowed himself to be swallowed by the giant, then "boring from within" cut the giant in pieces and calmly returned to his home to be thenceforth acclaimed a mighty hero. This myth is astonishingly reminiscent of the tale of the killing of the giant, Tsaviyo, by the twin war gods in the Rio Grande Valley—in fact, is in many particulars identical. (See my *Ancient Life in the American Southwest*.)

The drama especially glorifies Tepoztecatl as a warrior. Homeric battle scenes are enacted with alternate defeats and victories over legions of his enemies, in which one detects almost every phase of Indian warfare. In the grand finale, from the walls of his impregnable fortress (the mountain temple above described), Tepoztecatl shouts defiance to his raging foes, while his exulting warriors execute a war dance quite in the spirit of the Comanche scalp ceremony. In one version, the coming of the Spaniards is dramatized.

ii. TOLTEC RUINS

The examples above described will suffice to show the present condition of the principal architectural remains of the valleys of Mexico and Cuernavaca that belong to the late period, that is, the time leading up to the great cataclysm that brought to a close the culture evolution of the Aztecs and related peoples. Since all these had come under the domination of the Aztecs, were of the same linguistic stock, and have, since the Conquest, become so completely amalgamated, it will be well to call this the "Aztec Period." The older, higher, culture that flourished in the same region for several preceding centuries, which was supplanted by the later, ruder, "barbarians" from the north and largely absorbed by them, can have no more fitting name than "Toltec."

97

Nebulous as their traditions are, they must be given, as shown heretofore, an actual place in the archæological history of Mexico. Their language was virtually the same as that of the northern invaders, but their culture was far superior. As builders, their works were stupendous, the greatest on the American continent, rivaling those of ancient Egypt. While in ground area at least two of the Toltec pyramids were in the class of the Egyptians, they lacked the impressive height of the latter, and the vast amount of dimensioned stone in their construction. But the hearting of rubble and earth was sheathed in dressed stone facing. Because of the great stairways, terraces, and sculptural embellishment, they were far in advance of the Egyptians as examples of artistic architecture. In other fine arts, notably sculpture, their superiority was equally marked, while in the less material factors of culture, such as religion, they attained to exalted heights. They lacked the war spirit, and in the larger aspects of their history we see a repetition of Old World experience—creative, esthetic, even spiritual endowment, overwhelmed by organized force.

In this superposition in the Valley of Mexico, of a later, cruder culture, upon an older, more refined one, we note an interesting parallel in the great ruins of the American Southwest. In the excavation of Chetro Ketl (see my *Chaco Canyon and Its Monuments*), it has been shown that the late occupation, which terminated probably in the twelfth century A.D. (the same period that marks the decline of the Toltecs), was superimposed upon the work of a group of master builders who preceded them in time and overshadowed them in culture. We give to the name Toltec no ethnic significance. Tulan, Teotihuacan, old Atzcapotzalco, Xochicalco, Cholula, may have been, probably were, the homes of communities of about the same degree of relationship as Aztec, Tepanec, etc. So from now on, we will let the term Toltec include all those related peoples of the early period, and Aztec embrace all those of the late period, without restricting either to exact ethnic significance. It is convenient and correct to bring Aztec and Toltec together under the term "Mexican," that is, late Mexican and early Mexican.

The ruins of the legendary Tulan lie about fifty miles to the north of Mexico City, not within the Valley of Mexico. The hill country in which this early Toltec community settled was on the southern margin of the Chichimec country. It probably marks the first decisive step in the transition of the Toltecs from the "barbarian" stage to the condition of enlightened culture to which they attained. The settlement never reached the vast extent of the later Teotihuacan and Cholula, but further exploration and excavation may extend its limits far beyond what is apparent on the surface at the present time. It lacks the enormous pyramids of the above mentioned sites, but was built in the standard form, with a sacred precinct of impressive proportions. An Aztec ball court is indicated. Father Sahagun wrote concerning Tula that one of its temples was composed of four buildings, the one on the east being ornamented with gold, the one on the north with red jasper, that on the west with turquoise, and the one on the south with silver and white shells. He further states that another temple was similar, but that the interior of the buildings was decorated with yellow, red, blue, and white feathers. Some of its buildings were furnished with the serpent columns that link Mexican and Maya architecture under a common motive. Its ceramic art, as seen on the surface, is clearly

Aztecan. It would be an excellent place for further excavation for pre-Toltecan or ruins of the archaic age. It is possible that Tulan was a mother center, from which bands went out to what must have been the world's end of those times; that the traditions of Yucatan and the Guatemalan highlands are valid. On this possibility, I would venture the suggestion that it is the site of all Mexico that calls for intensive study. The excavations that have been made there are not definitive. It must be admitted that the ruins of Tula, as seen today, do not measure up to what is expected of the legendary Tula. It is not impressive as compared with other Toltec ruins. The conclusions of the distinguished Mexican archæologist, Dr. Manuel Gamio, require us to consider the whole problem from a new angle, that furnished by his excavation of Teotihuacan.

The glory of the Toltec age, of Mexican archæology, as we see it today, is Teotihuacan. Situated within easy distance, about twenty-five miles, of Mexico City, it is the most visited of all Mexican ruins. Indeed, no one can fully sense the achievements of ancient America without seeing Teotihuacan. It is what the pyramid group of Gizeh is to Egypt. Yet, in the legendry of Mexico, Teotihuacan is all but unknown. The excavation of this great sacred precinct, a true "holy city," if the term were admissible in Indian culture, though less than half completed, is a monument to the genius of Dr. Manuel Gamio. The work on the "Pyramid of the Sun," before his time, was not efficiently done, but, since irremediable, it will not be further criticized. Doctor Gamio's work squares with the highest standards of archæological science in any country. This judgment is pronounced upon the practical work of excavation that he has conducted. His pre-eminence, however, does not rest with this excavation alone, but upon the comprehensive anthropological study of which this was a part. Since he is the recognized authority on Teotihuacan, I am taking the liberty of using his description of that great site instead of what I could so less well write. The account is slightly abbreviated from his English digest of the Report on the Valley of Teotihuacan.

"This archaic metropolis was built on a gently sloping plain irrigated in part by crystalline springs and protected from the icy north winds by the extinct volcano of Cerro Gordo, the lava of which in fragments or volcanic shells is very abundant in the immediate surroundings and afforded material for the construction of magnificent monuments. The soil consists of hard and impermeable *tepetate* which made the laying of foundations unnecessary and prevented the destruction of buildings by humidity. Another reason for the selection of this spot for building a town consisted in the large deposits of obsidian at the northeast of the valley furnishing raw material for the fashioning of arrowpoints, knives and other arms, as well as of jewelry and other ornaments. In those deposits or quarries a fabulous amount of shavings and splinters of obsidian are found.

"Toward the south and southwest at that time there stretched the lakes of Texcoco, Xaltocan and Zumpango, the water of which, besides regulating the climatic conditions of the region, offered fish, aquatic birds and other food as well as plants for industrial use such as *tule* and reed-grass.

"The extension of the city must have been very great because vestiges of it have been discovered within an area of over six kilometers in length by three in width. . . .

"The building material generally used is *adobe,*

tezontle (porous building stone), volcanic tufa or
tepetate and other sedimentary or plutonic rocks
which are found in the region. Pavements are made
with lime, clay, pulverized *tezontle, tlapilli,* etc.
The interior structure is usually of *adobe,* or rubble
work, the latter being made of stone and clay.
The coating of these monuments on some of the
principal buildings consists of big square slabs,
plain or sculptured and almost always painted in
polychrome colours. On other edifices the coating
is of rubble work but of a smoother quality than
on the inside. This rubble work is covered by a
kind of concrete, the surface of which was stuccoed,
polished and generally painted in red ochre. Wood
was profusely used for columns and interior structures as can be seen on the *Temple* of *Quetzalcoatl.*

"The truncated pyramid, with the superposed
quadrangular or rectangular prism, forms the
geometrical bodies from which the forms which
constitute the architecture of Teotihuacan are
principally derived. The system of drainage was
profuse and consisted of subterranean tubes constructed with indigenous concrete and covered with
slabs. It is supposed that these drainage canals
emptied into the ravine which crosses the ancient
city.

"The edifices can be classified in four groups
according to the purpose they served: 1st.—Votive
monuments such as the pyramids of the Sun, the
Moon and of Quetzalcoatl (the ancient *Citadel*).
In such cases the small sanctuaries erected on the
upper terrace of the pyramids were relatively secondary because the immense blocks which supported them signified more eloquently the offering
to their gods of work, pain, blood, and tears by a
people ruled by the theocracy who exploited their
fanaticism. 2nd.—Temples and living quarters of
the clergy. These were spacious and consisted of
numerous apartments built over the foundations of

the pyramids and prisms referred to above. In this case the foundations are of secondary importance in as much as the preeminence was given to the apartments which composed the building. Among this group we call attention to the temple of the god of water, Tlaloc (*Excavations of 1917*), and called such because a great many images of this god were found in the building. In one of the upper apartments of this structure an altar can be seen and two cavities which were possibly used for ritual ceremonies. Other apartments were probably occupied by the priests attached to this cult. 3rd.— Palaces of civil authorities. It has been impossible to identify these until now because the monuments discovered during our activities correspond to the two first named groups. However, we believe that the *Edificios Superpuestos* or *Subterraneos* belong to a palace, for there were no images of deities found in them. 4th.—Popular habitations. We think that in what is comprised in the actual archæological zone there were only structures of the three first named groups. The living quarters of the common people must have been very small and of poor and perishable material such as *adobe,* grass, *maguey* leaves, etc., and have disappeared centuries ago.

"The principal systems of groups of edifices which form the city are the following:

"Pyramid of the Sun and annexes.—The pyramid is sixty-four meters high and measures two hundred fifteen on each side approximately so that it has a base of forty-six thousand two hundred and twenty-five square meters; its dimensions were formerly somewhat larger, but at the time it was discovered and reconstructed in 1905 several exterior coatings were removed which measured several meters in thickness.

"On the front which looks toward the west is the staircase which in this as on almost all of the big monuments, faces the west. On the east side is the entrance of the pyramid which is of *adobe*. This monument is surrounded by three big platforms which were crowned by buildings. Toward the west side of the plaza which was formed by the pyramid and the platforms stretches the so-called *Street of the Dead*.

"Pyramid of the Moon and annexes.—This pyramid measures forty-two meters in height and its base covers eighteen thousand square meters. Here the staircase lies toward the south, an exception to the rule. The inner construction is of *adobe*. The edifices which surround the pyramid form a more complicated system than these around the pyramid of the Sun. This pyramid has been barely explored and only a few portions of its external structure were discovered.

"Street of the Dead.—Opposite the south side of the pyramid is the so-called *Street of the Dead* which is the central road and axle of the city having on either side several mounds which represent as many buildings. According to tradition there were tombs in these buildings and that is why the whole avenue is known by the name of *Street of the Dead*.

"Temple of Tlaloc, god of rain.—This temple consists of a series of apartments superimposed on others of the first epoch, it being worth while to notice specially, the top room which presents an altar and two cavities which probably were used in some ritual ceremony. There are still to be seen the smaller cavities (alveoles) where two wooden pillars were inserted. Among the débris taken out of this apartment numerous plaques of clay were found with the images of Tlaloc in relief.

" 'Superposed Edifices'.—These are erroneously called *Subterranean* by the people. These structures give us more than any others, a clear idea of the architectural remains of the two salient epochs of the architecture of Teotihuacan. Especially worthy of attention is a mural *fresco* representing a Grecian fret in many colors, not at all of the usual Teotihuacan style, but rather resembling the Totonaca culture.

"Temple of Quetzalcoatl.—This is popularly known as *The Citadel.* This cluster is undoubtedly the most interesting one discovered so far in the ancient city. It consists of a spacious quadrangular plaza formed by platforms measuring four hundred meters on each side and raised several meters above the ground. These elevations are bordered on the outside by slopes and aisles while the sides that look towards the plaza are formed by two rows of batters and superimposed panels. On the exterior front towards the west, is a staircase which gives access to the plaza from the outside, while several equi-distant stairs connect the floor of the plaza with the platforms which top the elevations. On each one of these three platforms are four structures showing the typical taluses and their respective panels with the exception of the platform to the east which has only three buildings. At the inter-section of the diagonals of this plaza stand two big structures which formerly bore the appearance of a big mound or natural hill, because they were covered with vegetation. When this hill was ex-plored it was found to consist of two buildings. The first one was a truncated pyramid of four sides of twenty-two meters in height and standing on a foundation covering twenty-five thousand square meters; each one of these sides consists of a talus on which a sculpture of a plumed serpent appears representing Quetzalcoatl and surrounded by sea shells. On this talus rises a rectangular panel on which appear inlaid, by means of long pegs, big serpent's heads emerging from gulas in the shape of flowers which form the ends of plumed bodies ending in rattles and surrounded by sea shells. Towards the middle of each serpent body big heads

105

are noticed which seem to indicate the attribute of the god Tlaloc. On the small rails of the stairway which connects the upper terrace of this pyramid with the floor of the plaza, there appear inlaid from space to space analogous heads of snakes as on the panels with the only difference that there are no plumed serpent's bodies attached to them. On the uppermost terrace six graves were found and six deep shored wells containing six big wooden pillars. These were probably used as frame works furnishing the construction of the pyramid. This monument, the coating of which consists of huge stone slabs with sculptures of above mentioned shapes and profusely colored, corresponds to the first epoch, the epoch of the highest development in architecture at Teotihuacan.

"Dating from the second, or the epoch of decadence, we find built against the west front of this monument, probably with the intention to enlarge it, a second pyramid, its shape following in general outlines and in style the form of the old one. Its four sides consist of taluses surmounted by panels and projecting wall stones. The coating, however, is inferior as far as structure and ornamentation go; it is not made with large sculptured stone slabs, but with rubble work of broken stones and clay and later covered by polished plaster painted in red. On this second pyramid there also were found supports and wooden beams analogous to those mentioned above."

Doctor Gamio, after his excavations at magnificent Teotihuacan, and some study of less imposing Tula, was impressed with the discrepancy between tradition and archæological evidence above noted. He states the problem and cuts the Gordian knot in substance as follows:

The "Citadel": Aztec Quadrangle, Teotihuacan, after Excavation

Plumed Serpent Head on Stairway, Temple of Quetzalcoatl, Teotihuacan, Mexico

"We know the region of Tula. From the nature of the territory and its topography there could not have stood a big city such as the famous Tula of the Chroniclers was supposed to have been. Teotihuacan is given little importance in annals and chronicles. It is therefore beyond doubt that there exists a serious error somewhere in regard to Tula and Teotihuacan. This error must be corrected. We shall try and contribute to this end with our modest opinion. It is our belief that Teotihuacan is the primitive, the magnificent Tula, which must have flourished five or ten centuries before the Christian era."

The research that led Doctor Gamio to this revolutionary conclusion was so thorough that, in writing of Teotihuacan, I wish to emphasize the fact that we may actually be dealing with ancient Tula, and that the ruin which he describes above, under that name, is merely what remains of a Teotihuacan colony. Perhaps it may support my former suggestion that it probably marks the first decisive step in the transition of the Toltecs from the "barbarian" stage to the condition of enlightened culture to which they attained—I may now add, at Teotihuacan.

The other great Toltec center was Cholula, in the broad rich valley, some ninety miles from Teotihuacan. Walter Lehmann, the distinguished German-Americanist, calls it "the Rome of the New World." Teotihuacan, and Cuzco of Peru, would be competitors for that eminent title. In either case, the comparison would be valid only in so far as it would mean a great religious center. Certain it is that American aborigines were never united in a far-flung religious domain with a "pope" or priestly sovereign over all. That there were centers of great religious activity cannot be denied.

The vast Temple of the Sun at Cholula, reputed to have been a *teocalli* of Quetzalcoatl, was in ground area the largest pyramid in the world. Humboldt's measurement in 1806 made it approximately fourteen hundred feet square. I measured it exactly one hundred years later, and found it thirteen hundred feet square. The discrepancy is easily accounted for. Besides being sadly mutilated in every way, the pyramid has been reduced in area, at the ground level, by encroachment of the farms by which it is surrounded. A Christian church has replaced the sanctuary that was on the apex. Modern roads and inclines have been built without regard to the original *calzadas*. It is not until we near the top that we encounter the ancient "grand stairway."

The pyramid was never substantially built. The internal construction is not fully known to us, but it appears that the hearting was of earth and rubble. The indications are that the stone facings were never so complete nor so ornate with sculpture as those at Teotihuacan. Like all the great Toltec, and many of the Aztec temples, it doubtless grew by a series of accretions, which increased its ground area and height from time to time. The Cholula Valley is one of the most beautiful in all Mexico. Magnificent Orizaba dominates the landscape, while mountains of no mean height rim the valley. The area is more ample than that of the Valley of Teotihuacan. The vast Sanctuary of the Sun commanded many subordinate towns. I have personally located ninety ruin-mounds in the Cholula Valley, each one of which marks a settlement with its minor shrines. Upon almost every one a church has been built, this having been, in all lands and times, the favorite way of declaring the triumph of the "true faith" over paganism or infidelity. Standing on the top of Cholula pyramid today, and with a field-glass surveying the entire valley, eliminating in imagination every church that is visible, and substituting a small temple with appropriate minor structures, you have reproduced, in its main aspects, the picture that Cortéz and his army gazed upon in 1520, when they marched up from the gulf coast and occupied the Indian town at the base of the great "Temple of Quetzalcoatl." The *teocalli* was probably a dilapidated, abandoned bulk at that time, held in superstitious awe and to some extent used in ancestral ceremonies by the Tlaxcalans. The temples upon the small mounds of the valley were, on surface evidences, Tlaxcalan and largely in use at the time of the Conquest. More meticulous excavation and study of the ruins of this valley would differentiate the two epochs of occupation, early Toltec and recent Tlaxcalan.

It was here in the Tlaxcalan country that Cortéz learned how to conquer the Aztecs. He discovered the ancient warfare that had existed between these two peoples over the salt deposits. This enabled him to array a great force against Montezuma, without which he would probably have been driven into the sea, if any survived to get that far in retreat. "Divide and conquer."

No eyewitness has told us anything about the great sanctuary at Cholula as it was in the days of its glory, the age of Toltec supremacy, but Bernal Diaz, soldier-historian of the Conquest, wrote of Cholula as he saw it with the army of Cortéz on its march to Tenochtitlan:

"The city of Cholula much resembled Valladolid, being in a fertile plain, very thickly inhabited; it is surrounded by fields of maize, pepper, and maguey. They had an excellent manufacture of earthenware, of three colours, red, black and white, painted in different patterns, with which Mexico and all the neighboring countries were supplied, as Castile is by those of Talavera and Plasencia. The city had at that time above a hundred lofty white towers, which were the temples of their idols, one of which was held in peculiar veneration. The principal temple was higher than that of Mexico, and each of these buildings was placed in a spacious court."

In the account of Aztec temples, I described those in the vale of Cuernavaca, some fifty miles south of Mexico City. In the same valley, twelve miles from the city of Cuernavaca, surrounded by the lovely scenery of this most romantic valley in all Mexico, is the hill of Xochicalco (place of flowers), on which is a group of ruins that has, by most archæologists, been pronounced Toltec. Certainly their lavish decoration takes them out of the Aztec category. The main *teocalli,* in the usual low terraced form, has for its decoration a striking plumed serpent design extending around the four sides of the pyramid. The carving is in strong, high relief. At intervals, under the folds of the serpent, is a seated figure strangely reminiscent in features and costume of the northern warrior. The temple appears to have been covered with stucco, its sculptured design brought out in strong red and yellow earthen colors. Xochicalco, in the days of its glory, must have presented a most brilliant appearance.

The core of the pyramid is of rubble and adobe, the facing being of the native andesite rock of the ridge on which the temple stands. The entire hill is terraced and its artificial shaping preserved by retaining walls of masonry. The hill is honeycombed with subterranean passages, tunnels and shafts—the use of which can only be conjectured, and the antiquity of which might be questioned.

Xochicalco was in ruins when first seen by the Spaniards, this placing it in the pre-Aztecan period. It was first described by Alzate in 1777. It still awaits systematic excavation. Gamio says it is unquestionably Maya. I have here to offer with considerable diffidence the suggestion that the Temple of Xochicalco, in the heart of an Aztecan valley, and the Temple of Quetzalcoatl, built within the great sacred precinct of Toltec Teotihuacan, are both Maya temples; not indicating Maya occupancy of the Valley of Anahuac, but a contribution from the great religious hierarchy of Mayaland—Central America. Both seem utterly foreign to their surroundings.

The foregoing examples will serve to picture the architectural trend of the Toltecs—the inexplicable urge to build beyond everything ever known in their world. They were a nebulous lot historically. Some deny their existence entirely. Some see Toltec influence clear to Guatemala, even in Peru. Some consider them the great mother-culture from which the Maya germed. Some reverse it and make them the offspring of the Maya. Certain it is that there was similarity in many phases of their culture. Which was the hen and which the egg, I do not know, but I am convinced that some such relationship existed between them.

II. The Marginal Cultures

1. The Tarascans

As POINTED out in an earlier chapter, Aztec Mexico appears to have been peopled from the north. The area actually occupied by the Mexican population (Toltecs and Aztecs) was not extensive, but the influence of this virile people extends very far. It cannot be said that they influenced the north; rather, that it was the north that contributed the primitive bands which, in the stimulating environment of the tropical highlands of Mexico, rose to the higher culture levels that we have commenced to discuss. Doubtless an occasional backwash occurred, but for the most part the drift of population was to the south. Unmistakable Mexican culture appears all along the highland region until we reach Nicaragua and Costa Rica. Equally unmistakable is the culture admixture in the low countries of both sea coasts, but the time and directions of these inter-penetrations are very elusive. We shall not attempt to examine the many theories of population movement, back and forth, between Mexico and Central America, but will at this time describe the non-Mexican, marginal cultures that surrounded Aztec land on three sides, east, west, and south.

The Tarascan country embraces the whole state of Michoacan, with some extension into the states of Jalisco, Guerrero, and Guanajuato. It is the most beautiful country in Mexico, a region of magnificent mountains, forests, and lakes. There is no dependable tradition of immigration into Tarasco land. The inhabitants are of an ancient stock, with little idea of an origin outside of their own beautiful lake and mountain world.

Some think they find Tarascan ruins in Zacatecas, believing La Quemada to be Tarascan. I have seen nothing to support this. I found islands in Lake Patzcuaro, completely overgrown with tropical bush, that pass for natural bodies of land which, on examination, prove to be, in whole or part, artificial, being built up with stones from the mainland. One must picture thousands of small dugouts plying back and forth, bringing stones to be dumped on the spot chosen for temple building, until an island rose above the water, on which a superstructure could be erected. There are several of these island temple ruins on the Michoacan lake. They afford rendezvous for uncountable green water snakes that come out and drape themselves over the jungle so thick that you literally see nothing else as you approach. Your Indian boatman is likely to have a keen sense for practical joking—at least my *Mono Chico* had. He loved to row me unexpectedly onto an island shore (he paddles facing the direction in which the boat is going; you sit with your back to the prow), then watch me turn to see what had happened, and see my hair rise as I faced an island of snakes. His wizened old face beamed with delight at my terror; then a rock thrown by him into the mass sent the whole harmless lot scurrying into the water, and I could explore my island without seeing a snake.

The most impressive ruins known to me in the Tarascan country are at Tsintsuntsan, an Indian town on the shore opposite Patzcuaro. Each is a long mound rising in a succession of platforms or terraces, three is the greatest number I have seen, which I think were sufficiently flattened on the top to afford long, narrow edifices for religious purposes. They overlook ample courtyards or plazas, with numerous small mounds grouped about, indicative of shrines, altars, or minor pyramids. Until excavations lay them bare, we shall know little more about Tarascan ruins. The one shown in my photograph is typical; completely overgrown so that not a single, architectural feature is to be seen. Tarascan excavation is about the most to be desired of any in Mexico. Legendary history of the Tarascans is so meager that archæological history becomes doubly important. The late Dr. Nicolas Leon is our leading authority on the Tarascans.

2. *The Totonacs*

To the east, on the gulf coast, and extending up into the hill country, is the land of the Totonacs and their relatives the Huastecs. The latter are clearly archaic Maya; the former, generally conceded to be of related stock. Their range is the low country, *tierra caliente,* from the Panuco Valley on the north, to an indefinite southern boundary, where mixed breed merges into pure Maya. They are the descendants of the Indians first seen by Cortéz, on landing near the present Vera Cruz. They had towns of considerable size, with sacred precincts that bewildered the first Spanish beholders, who reported them to be faced with silver plates, the illusion being caused by the polished concrete surfaces that masked the cobblestones of the walls. The buildings of Cempoalan (see studies of J. Walter Fewkes, *Bureau of American Ethnology, 25th Annual Report*) were placed upon platforms of rubble and concrete. They were of the terraced pyramid type, with balustraded stairways.

The most remarkable Totonac temple, and one of the most beautiful in all Mexico and Central America, is that at Papantla. It is a multiple terraced pyramid, well faced with cut stone, has overhanging cornices, single grand stairway, balustraded. In each story are blind windows, simply niches, for the pyramid has a solid, rubble interior. These are reminiscent of the blind niches of the great sanctuaries of Chaco Canyon, New Mexico, and of many Peruvian temples, notably Machupichu and Ollantaytambo. The elaborate cornice work gives the pyramid a peculiarly Oriental aspect. In fact, Papantla is the only temple in America that ever made me think of Hindu and Cambodian architecture. Its nearest relatives in Mexico are the temples at Quiengola, on the Isthmus of Tehuantepec. Excellent models of the Totonac ruins are to be seen in the National Museum of Mexico City.

The Huastecas were not noted builders. There are countless ruin-mounds of small size all over their country, even north of the Panuco Valley. It would be extremely useful if some archæologist would find the northern limit of their mounds, probably in the state of Tamaulipas. They have the language of the great Maya stock of Central America, but nothing of their splendid building culture, nor has there been found among them a trace of the hieroglyphic writings, the most noted achievement of the Maya. In short, the Huastecas would seem to be an abortive Maya group, a band left behind, perhaps, from some ancient migration, which took root there along the gulf coast, and did not have it in them to expand culturally. Again, they might be a backwash from some archaic, undeveloped Maya group farther south. The legendary history of the Haustecas and Totonacas is scanty and unsatisfactory.

A recent excellent work on the Totonacas is that of

Dr. Walter Krickeberg, of the Ethnographic Museum of Berlin, translated from the German into Spanish by Señor Porfirio Aguirre, of the National Museum of Mexico.

3. The Zapotecs

The greatest of the non-Mexican stocks north of the Isthmus of Tehuantepec was the Zapotec, or, though the relationship is not settled, the Zapotec-Mixtec. I shall not use the hyphenated name, it being understood that by Zapotec is meant the dominant stock between Aztec Mexico and Tehuantepec, not including the low, gulf coast country. They are primarily a mountain people, singularly lacking in traditional history as compared with the Aztecs, Toltecs, and Maya, with the exception of the Mitla or Mictlan branch. There is every indication that the Zapotecs are very old occupants of their country. They consistently hold themselves to be autochthonous. Extensive occupation of caves from a far past has tended to fix this idea in their minds. In consequence of this belief, it has long been the custom of the Zapotecs to bury their dead in caves in the ancestral places of emergence from their underworld to the light of the earth and sun. They were far from being the primitives that the Tarascans, Huastecas, and Otomi were, up to the time of the Conquest. This is evident on the testimony of their archæological remains. In addition to hundreds of minor sites, two of the greatest ruins in all America are in the heart of the Zapotec land. These are Monte Albán and Mitla (in Zapotec language, *Lyobaa,* in Aztec, *Mictlan*).

Monte Albán is a lofty ridge rising a thousand feet above the surrounding valley, about five miles out from

Tarascan Temple Ruins near Tsintsuntsan, Lake Patzcuaro, Mexico (Waite)

Ruins of Monte Alban (Waite)

the city of Oaxaca. It is detached from the main range of mountains, surrounded by fertile valley land which may reasonably be supposed to have supported a considerable population in ancient times. The name of the mountain came to be attached, in recent times, to the ancient religious establishment that was built upon it. If this had an aboriginal name, it has not come down to us. It is the most extensive religious center in Mexico, south of Teotihuacan and Cholula, to both of which it bears some resemblance.

The complete excavation of Monte Albán was the dream of Mr. Maudslay, the distinguished British archæologist, to whom all students of Central America and southern Mexico owe such a vast debt for illustrative material. He believed it the most important site for study in all America, but so vast was the expense involved in his plan that he was never able to carry it out.

The builders of Monte Albán utilized an entire mountain for their purpose. Forty years ago, William H. Holmes wrote a description of the place, which cannot be surpassed. I quote at some length from his *Archæological Studies Among the Ancient Cities of Mexico,* published by the Field-Columbian Museum:

"The visit to Monte Alban was the most romantic feature of my trip to southern Mexico. Having secured a horse I crossed the river, and, passing beyond the end of the ridge . . . soon reached a village called San Pablo; from this point I turned to the right and shaped my course up the gentle slopes toward the middle of Monte Alban which rose as a great wall to the west . . . Turning to the left when near the base of the steeper slopes, I climbed the extreme southern spur of the mountain which is about five miles from the alameda in Oaxa-

ca. I passed up over alternating narrow cultivated
terraces and outcropping ledges of limestone. The
latter, interbedded with quartzites, form the body
of the mountain and dip slightly to the north, the
outcrops along the steep sides giving the mountain
a peculiar, ribbed effect. On this outer point, seen
at the extreme left in the panorama, I began to encounter small mounds, which represent ancient
buildings, besides many indications of dwelling. On
the second level, 300 or 400 feet higher and but
little below the main summit, the first well-pre-
served quadrangular ruin-group was encountered.
It . . . consists of four oblong mounds arranged
about a court, in the center of which is the usual
small conical pile of débris. The northern, southern
and western sides are represented by low, rounded
ridges of débris, the north ridge being about 8 feet
high. The eastern structure is a pyramid, nearly
25 feet high and with steep sides. The main level
of the summit is about 40 feet square, and is occupied by a heap of débris representing a superstructure—a house or temple—set back toward the
east side. . . . This ruin is on a wide cultivated
terrace, supported by a succession of inferior terraces encircling the promontory on three sides.
Small mound-like remnants of buildings are seen
on all hands. Passing over the cornfield to the
northwest I reached, at a distance of 500 feet, a
second group of mounds that includes one typical
quadrangle. The court of the quadrangle is some
80 or 90 feet square, and has the usual low mound
in the center. The south member is 20 feet high by
45 feet long and 40 feet wide, and has the ruin of
a superstructure—a mere heap of stones—on its
summit. The other sides are from 5 to 10 feet high
and are rounded ridges representing ruined houses.
At the southeast corner of the quadrangle, rises
a mound showing considerable loose stone all
over its sides. It is a few feet higher than the

south member of the quadrangle, which it approximates closely in horizontal dimensions. At the
north base is a deep depression separating the
east ridge of the quadrangle from a lower ridge
at that end. Rising from this at the north there is
a terrace about 80 feet square supporting the much
reduced remains of a building. The mountain
ridge, here quite narrow, falls off rapidly in terraces on both sides. Following the ridge to the
north some 300 feet, still over a narrowing field,
another quadrangle of usual plan and proportions
was observed. The buildings are represented by
ridges of stone and earth, which are at no point
over 10 feet high.

"One hundred feet farther on I ascended the face
of a terrace, upwards of 40 feet high, which crosses
the ridge at right angles, the left margin following
the oblique trend of the mountainside, and the
right descending to a marginal terrace which continues north for a long distance on the east side.
Crossing this terrace and some low mounds I
ascended a second terrace 10 feet high and came in
view of the southern member of the great central
group of remains. The latter is a pyramid more
than 400 feet square and 40 or 45 feet high, supporting two pyramids on its summit. The slopes
of this great mass are precipitous all around and
covered with trees and the débris of fallen walls.
I climbed the south face by a steep pathway, leading my horse up with much difficulty. From the
main level I ascended the central pyramid, which
is the crowning feature of this part of the crest,
and obtained a magnificent panorama of the
mountain and the surrounding valleys and ranges.
Turning to the north the view along the crest was
bewildering in the extreme.

"In years of travel and mountain work I had
met with many great surprises—such as that experienced on emerging suddenly from the forest-

covered plateaus of Arizona into a full view of the
Grand Cañon of the Colorado, or of obtaining un-
expected glimpses of startling Alpine panoramas
—but nothing had ever impressed me so deeply as
this. The crest of Alban, one-fourth of a mile wide
and extending nearly a mile to the north lay spread
out at my feet. The surface was not covered with
scattered and obscure piles of ruins as I had expected, but the whole mountain had been remodeled
by the hand of man until not a trace of natural
contour remained. There was a vast system of level
courts inclosed by successive terraces and bordered
by pyramids upon pyramids. Even the sides of the
mountain descended in a succession of terraces, and
the whole crest, separated by the hazy atmosphere
from the dimly seen valleys more than a thousand
feet below, and isolated completely from the blue
range beyond, seemed suspended in mid air. All
was pervaded by a spirit of mystery, solitude and
utter desolation not relieved by a sound of life or
a single touch of local color. It seemed indeed a
phantom city and separated as it is by half a dozen
centuries from the modern city—barely traceable
as a fleck of white in the deep valley beyond the
saddle of the Lesser Alban—furnishes a tempting
field for speculation.

"I have endeavored to convey some notion of this
remarkable scene. . . . In the foreground is the
great terrace referred to above, crowned by its two
pyramids, one placed at the southeast corner and
the other, the main mound, situated a little to the
left of the center.

"Behind this group is the central feature of the
ancient city, a vast court or plaza, a level, sunken
field 600 feet wide and 1,000 feet long, inclosed by
terraces and pyramids and having a line of four
pyramids ranged along its center. The great lines
of mounds at the right and left border the abrupt
margins of the mountain, and beyond is the most

astonishing feature of all—a broad terrace 600 or more feet square, within which is a sunken court surrounded by numerous pyramids that rise in a culminating group at the distant right. Beyond this at the left are other groups of mounds, and still other groups occupy the spurs and subordinate crests into which the north end of the mountain is broken. At the left and farther away are two independent, rounded, mountain crests crowned by groups of mounds. At the right is the extreme west end of the Lesser Alban, and beyond and far below are caught glimpses of the valley with its villages and farms; and rising beyond this are the lofty ranges of the continental divide, so obscured by the haze of the dry season that their serrate profiles can hardly be made out.

. . . . . .

"The group of structures occupying the foreground in the panorama forms the southern member of the great, composite quadrangle of Monte Alban. The substructure is a low truncated, pyramid upwards of 400 feet square at the base, with regular though now slightly broken slopes rising at a steep angle to a height of 40 feet or more. The summit is quite level and approximates 300 feet square.

"The pyramid occupying the southeast corner is 80 feet square at the base and perhaps 60 feet square on the summit. The height is about 25 feet, and the outer slopes are nearly continuous with the slopes of the substructure. The presence of piles of débris covering the crest and sides makes it apparent that the building was faced with stone—not dressed, however, as this quartzite is too hard to be cut readily with stone tools.

. . . . . .

"The chain of pyramids extending from north to south along the middle of the great square constitutes one of the most interesting features of

121

these remains. . . . In viewing these works one is tempted to indulge in speculations as to the conditions that must have prevailed during the period of occupation. How striking must have been the effects when these pyramids were all crowned with imposing temples, when the great, level plaza about them, 600 to 1,000 feet in extent, was brilliant with barbaric displays, and the inclosing ranges of terraces and pyramids were occupied by gathered throngs. Civilization has rarely conceived anything in the way of amphitheatric display more extensive and imposing than this."

Mr. Maudslay and Mr. Holmes did not exaggerate the importance of Monte Albán in the archæological history of Mexico. Early in the year 1932, Señor Alfonso Caso, chief of the Department of Archæology in the National Museum of Mexico, announced a thrilling discovery. Pursuing at Monte Albán his favorite study of Zapotec hieroglyphics, in the hope of establishing the relationships between Zapotec and Mixtec stocks, and between them and the Maya and Mexican, he opened a number of tombs, all of which contained some cultural material, and of which Number 7 proved to be among the richest in archæological treasure ever found in America. Let us have Señor Caso's own story of the finding of the tomb and its excavation, as related by him in *Natural History,* for September-October, 1932:

"The mound of Tomb 7 at Monte Alban lies immediately next to the western edge of the road which goes from Oaxaca to the place where the ruins are situated. This mound is very little elevated in relation to the general level of the soil, but it is located at the foot of a small hillock which is some four meters high and represents undoubtedly the substructure of a temple. On the other side of the road and in front of the tomb and the temple are the tombs numbered 3, 8, and 9. Next to Tomb 7 is another little mound which shows a depression and doubtless contains another tomb which I could not explore in this season's work, but which I intend to uncover in the next.

"We began the exploration of the mound over Tomb 7 by cleaning off the upper part, encountering what seemed to be the remains of the walls of some small rooms located on top of the mound, the floors of which were covered by a thick coating of the stucco used in Monte Alban to surface walls, their sloping bases, stairways, and pavements.

. . . . . .

"In opening up a vertical pit to find the tomb, we had to break through a second stucco floor, before we encountered the stones forming the vault. We removed two of these vault stones and were then able to descend into the tomb and to measure its interior length, with a view to finding the door. To do this, however, it was necessary to open another vertical pit before we reached a little antechamber, roofless and full of dirt, in which appeared, intentionally broken, three great Zapotec urns with their pedestals. . . . The central one of these very common urns represents an old god, probably the god of fire, whom the Mexicans call Huehueteotl, and who in their mythology was the lord of the central region of the universe. The urns at either side are representations of the Zapotec god called Cocijo, who, as I have demonstrated elsewhere, is equivalent to the raingod, called Tlaloc by the Mexicans. . . .

"After carefully removing the urns and fragments, we were able to find the entrance to the tomb. It was closed by means of large stone slabs, and when we removed these we discovered that the door was almost completely blocked by a great heap of earth. Between the top of this earth and the lintel of the door there remained only a small opening, which we had to enlarge in order to pene- trate to the interior.

"None of the stones which sealed the entrance had inscriptions, but on the other hand, forming part of the vault of the antechamber and resting directly on the lintel, we found a stone . . . which has about the same dimensions as the doorway, so that it is extremely probable that at first it oc- cupied this position.

"The inscription on this stone is indubitably Zapotec and I was able to read on it the year 'serpent' and the day 'flower,' as well as the num- ber 8, formed by a bar and three dots; but I could not say whether the sign ought to be attributed to the glyph 'serpent' or to the glyph 'flower,' al- though the first seems to me more probable. Be- neath the second of these signs there is a glyph which I do not know how to interpret, but it could be the number 4, united to the day sign.

". . . there was a layer of earth inside which varied greatly in thickness. In the second room, next to the end of the tomb, it had a depth of merely 30 cm., while at the entrance it almost hid the door, and we found in the projecting portions of the walls and the lintels, small heaps of dirt which indicated that the layer of earth originally reached that height and later owing to settling, subsided a little until it left, as I have said, a small opening between its upper level and the lintel of the tomb.

"Furthermore, after cleaning away the earth which covered the tomb and taking out the objects from the principal burial, there appeared under- neath, small clay vessels, a fragment of a Zapotec urn like those found in the antechamber, and a piece of a metate. The little pots are like those which I found in Mound B during the excavations there, and are of the type which has always been considered Zapotec.

"Therefore it seems to me unquestionable that Tomb 7 in Monte Alban was used twice. The first burial was made directly on the floor of the tomb and was accompanied by the vases, metates, etc., which I have just described, and by the Zapotec urns. The door was sealed, probably with the stone which is now in the vault of the first room and which has the inscription of the year 8 'serpent' and the day 4 (?) 'flower.' Thus both the urns and the inscription show the first burial to have been Zapotec. Furthermore, the very architecture of the tomb is Zapotec.

.   .   .   .   .   .

"We can say that all the objects found in Tomb 7 show great similarity with Mixtec objects and codices and no stylistic similarity to the style hitherto called Zapotec, that is, that of the urns and stelæ. We are forced, then, to accept one of the two following hypotheses:

"Either the objects of Tomb 7 are Mixtec, as contrasted with other objects found in Monte Alban and even those placed with the first burial in the tomb, which are Zapotec, or else what we call Zapotec is merely an older style which was replaced later by a new one which we call Mixtec. . . ."

Señor Caso reports no less than five hundred articles catalogued from this tomb, and this includes, under one number, necklaces of gold, pearl, turquoise and jade, composed of hundreds of beads each. One of the most remarkable specimens was an urn of rock crystal, a mineral of great hardness and yet worked very successfully by Zapotec and Mixtec artists. Among the objects of gold found was a great breast piece in a form called by Señor Caso the "jaguar knight." It represents a human head with jaguar's head helmet, carrying imitation feathers of golden thread. Another object of gold of especial note is a small mask believed to represent the head of the god, Xipe-Totec. Numerous armlets and earrings of gold were found, also many necklaces of cylindrical and spherical beads. A golden crown or diadem with a plume of gold was one of the most striking specimens recovered. Jet and amber beads and plaques are among the finds, together with innumerable specimens of shell ornaments. Carved bones carrying hieroglyphic characters are considered by Señor Caso to be among the most important of all specimens found, from a scientific standpoint.

The great stairway uncovered by the expedition was found to be about one hundred and thirty feet wide, forty-two feet high, and contained thirty-three steps. It is believed by the excavator to be the widest stairway yet found in ancient American ruins. He notes, in connection with the various structures, a phenomenon that is quite common in Mexico, that is the superposition of one structure upon another. The great stairway of the north platform exhibits three periods of construction.

At the base of the great stairway was found pottery which is pronounced of very recent origin, probably not more than fifty years old, indicating that offerings are still made at these ancient sites by the native Indians of Oaxaca. I noted exactly this same thing at the ruins of Monte Albán and Mitla, while studying there a number of years ago. These were clearly echoes or survivals of ancient ceremonies.

Señor Caso pronounces the finds of Tomb 7 to be of both Zapotec and Mixtec origin. He contends that the tomb is primarily Zapotec, re-used by Mixtec people who were responsible for the major part of the valuable specimens found in the tomb. He ascribes no very ancient date to the treasure, believing it to belong to the period immediately preceding the Spanish *entrada*. The skeletons found in the tomb as yet afford no convincing data.

It is sincerely to be hoped that the Mexican Government will enable Señor Caso to continue this most profitable piece of research at Monte Albán. It is certainly deserving of the most liberal public and private support.

Considering the wholesale, systematic looting of tombs carried on by the Spanish conquerors under official orders, it seems remarkable that any treasure of such great value should have escaped them. It is a matter of great good fortune that this one tomb with its contents remained intact, to be found and excavated by scientific methods and by competent scientists of Mexico, the country that has afforded such vast opportunities in the past to the archæologists of America and Europe.

The late Mrs. Zelia Nuttall, for whose work all Americanists have long had profound respect, on viewing the Monte Albán jewels expressed great surprise and interest on finding, on a gold pendant of exquisite workmanship, the hieroglyphic name of the historic Quahtémoc (Cuauhtémoc). The name was likewise on gold rings, and on a pendant, the eagle appears in ascending form. As a result of her observations, Mrs. Nuttall announced a theory of such absorbing interest that it is here reproduced:

"On October 12, 1524, Hernán Cortés left Mexico City upon his unfortunate expedition to Hon-

127

duras which was to last for twenty months, taking
with him as hostages (so he wrote to the Emperor
Charles) 'all the lords whom I believed to be responsible for the insecurity and revolt of these
parts,' and among them Cuauhtemotzin whom he
considered 'a bellicose man.'

"These principal lords whom Cortés took along
with him were six in number, besides Mexicaltzin,
brother of the 'king' of Michoacán, who was the
one who denounced them as traitors and conspirators to Cortés when they were in the province of
Alcalán, at the beginning of Lent, 1525. Cortés,
after an investigation, ordered the hanging of
Cuauhtemotzin and Tetlepanquetzal, the ex-king
of Tacuba, releasing the others. . . . The road
followed by the expedition was from Mexico City
through Oaxaca, where the provinces of Zapoteca-
pan and Mictecapan had been cruelly subjugated
in 1521 by Spaniards under Captain Francisco de
Orozco and who probably at that time plundered
the temples of Mitla and Monte Albán.

"The expedition headed by Cortés consisted of a
hundred and fifty Spaniards, mounted, and about
3,000 Indians most of whom were servants of the
chief Indian lords. As it appears that many Indians
joined the allied army on the road, it is not haz-
ardous to suppose that among them were Mixtec
and Zapotec lords.

"It is well known that after the death of Moctezuma (Montezuma) his remains were delivered to
his own people that they might do him funeral hon-
or and give him worthy burial. The same must
have happened in the case of those executed in
Izancanac, namely, Quauhtémoc and Tetlepanquetzal, and it is impossible to think that the other
Mexican lords (among whom the writer Torquemada mentions a brother of Quahtémoc) and all
the lamenting servants would have interred and
left in a strange land the sacred remains of one

who, according to historians, was always treated
with the same honors and homage as those which
were given to Moctezuma. Their greatest desire
must have been to effect the burial of the remains
in a secure and secret place which might not be
discovered by the Spaniards nor in their proximity
but at the same time a place sacred and worthy of
the high rank of the Mexican lord. When the
mourning Mexicans set forth upon what Bernal
Diaz del Castillo called 'the road from Mexico',
passing by way of Tehuantepec and Oaxaca, they
could not have found a place more appropriate
for the deposit of their precious burden than the
ancient sacred city of the Zapotecs, which was
abandoned and had been pillaged by the Spaniards, who would not return there a second time
in search of treasure, but which would indeed be a
magnificent and worthy sepulcher for the last
king of the Aztecs.

"Among other data, positive and negative, which
seem to confirm the theory is the fact that no offensive or defensive arms were found in the burials,
which would fit the case of men who were cap-
tives and disarmed. Nor were any idols found in
exploring the tomb, which is in accord with the
fact that they were accompanying Spaniards and
apparently had been converted to the Christian
religion.

"Among the artifacts never before seen in Mexico until now are noted some strings of colored
beads, fine and precious, made of shell. In his
Fifth Letter to the Emperor, Hernán Cortés relates how the Indians of the province of Acalán
traded for certain colored shell beads which they
esteem highly for their personal adornment; and
farther on he says that on the road to Taica the
lord of that region sent him as a gift 'a little gold
and certain beads of colored shell.' Since, among
objects of this kind found in Monte Albán in

tomb number 7, there are beads, some in the form
of an eagle's head and a pendant, it may be conjectured that they were offered in homage to
Quauhtémoc by the natives of the province of
Acalán where he died.

"The ring in the form of a *copilli* or diadem,
already mentioned, from which depends an eagle
in the attitude of soaring may very well have served
as evidence against Quauhtémoc, and as proof that
he entertained the ambition to recover his power
over the country. The fact that two of the remains
in 'tomb 7' are noteworthy for the richness of their
jewels seems to confirm the assertion of Cortés,
who declared that he had never written a lie to his
emperor and that he had ordered the execution of
only the two principal conspirators."

Mrs. Nuttall was insistent in calling attention to
the hieroglyph of Cuauhtémoc which started her upon
the investigation of this hypothesis, and predicted
that if the scientists of Mexico analyze the matter
with calmness and deliberation, it may well serve to
identify the two skeletons which were encountered in
Tomb Number 7 of Monte Albán, and that Mexico
will gain what will be worth a thousand times more
than all the treasures—nothing less than the location
of the mortal remains of the greatest of her heroes,
Cuauhtémoc.

Mitla, the ancient Lyobaa, thirty miles east of Oaxaca, is richer in tradition than Monte Albán, in fact
than almost any other site in Mexico. There can be no
doubt that it was one of the most sacred of all Zapotec
religious establishments, the "resting place," the "place
of sepulcher," in short, the traditional burial place of
their priests and chiefs for ages. A sanctuary of unusual holiness, the ancient Zapotecs lavished upon it all

the esthetic embellishment of which they were capable, and they came near surpassing all other efforts of the kind in ancient America. It lies in open country, at the eastern end of the lovely Valley of Oaxaca, a few miles out from the foothills, broken spurs from the Continental Divide, from which the material for its construction was obtained. The trachyte of which the temples were built was quarried a few miles away from the ruins, as shown by Mr. Holmes. It was admirably suited to the carrying out of a truly remarkable artistic conception. The series of quadrangles (a perfect Southwestern pueblo plan), with their halls, corridors, and broad entrances, called for monolithic lintels and cylindrical columns, such as were handled in few ancient American temples. Some of the lintels were twenty feet in length, fifteen tons in weight. The quarrying and carving of the huge trachyte blocks was quite within the abilities of Zapotec workmen, though equipped only with stone chisels, picks, and axes. Monte Albán had only almost unworkable quartzite and granitic rock for its facings. The splendid, undecorated monoliths of the "Hall of Columns," at Mitla, are unique in the architecture of Middle America. Mr. Holmes produced an excellent reproduction of one of these galleries, illustrating especially the roofing. Without questioning the accuracy of his work, or the fact that they supported a roof, as mentioned by Father Burgoa, who speaks as an eyewitness (1674), I venture to make the suggestion that it is not necessary to presuppose, as a function of these columns, that they were supports for anything. The ancient Zapotecs of this region, as well as their modern descendants, have had a singular idea about the column. In exploring this part of Mexico, I have seen many examples of columns of this kind used as gate posts or supports for well wheels, in which a column capable of carrying many tons actually supports a weight that could be carried by two by four pine timbers. The Mitla temples were one story only, with some subterranean crypts. Structurally, they introduced no new problems for Stone Age builders, except in the quarrying, transportation, and raising into place the huge lintels and columns. This called for some engineering skill.

The thing that makes Mitla unique among American buildings is the amazing system of façade construction and decoration in a relief-mosaic. While the hearting of the thick wall is of rubble, the usual thing in Middle American construction, the outer casing is produced by setting into the surface, in mortar, long, equal-sided wedges of the trachyte, so carefully cut and fitted together as to leave almost no space for mortar in the surface seams. The size of the wedge-shaped blocks varies; some that I examined being ten or twelve inches long, by one and a half to two inches square on the head, which takes its place in the facing of the wall. The number of these stone wedges or pegs that had to be cut and shaped to set into the walls, would, for all the quadrangles, run into the millions—almost rivaling in number of worked stones for wall construction the great community houses such as Chetro Ketl, in Chaco Canyon, New Mexico. From the state of preservation of the Mitla temples, one must concede this to be fully as substantial as any dressed stone surface devised by the ancient Americans. But the remarkable thing about it all was the way these builders utilized this method of surface construction to produce an unparalleled artistic effect. Horizontal sunken panels in the walls are developed in geometric patterns, almost Moorish in conception, and a use of mosaic totally different from any Old World work, but quite as effective, except as to color, these designs being in white, the background red. The pattern is brought out by being on a raised plane considerably higher than the plane of the background.

This mosaic style of architectural adornment, suggesting textile motives in design, was virtually monopolized by Mitla, even in the cruciform tombs and subterranean passageways, rarely if ever to be seen. The style of decoration was meticulously carried out, suggesting the ancient Pueblo corrugated pottery, constructed in excellent geometric patterns, though applied to cooking pots that were normally buried in the ashes. Very sparingly, the Mitla mosaic has been used in two or three other Zapotec sites.

Another unique contribution of Mitla to the cultural history of Mexico and Central America is that of the paintings which adorned the walls of some of the closed courtyards, for the saving of which, in sketches, we are indebted to a distinguished German-Americanist and his talented wife. Doctor Seler's extensive and profound studies of Mitla are especially commended to those who desire to pursue the subject further. So important it seems to me are the wall paintings of Mitla, true frescoes in part, since painted on stucco, that I wish to quote here Doctor Seler's conclusions concerning them:

"Defective and incomplete as they now are, these paintings of Mitla, taken as a whole, present an important document. They are, up to the present day, the only known picture writings of mythologic content, whose origin has been indisputably established, that date from ancient heathen times. Since these paintings show in the style of the fig-

ures and the subjects of the representations an unmistakable relationship to the Borgian codex, it
follows that this large, beautifully and brilliantly
executed manuscript cannot have originated far
from the place where the designers of the frescoes
of Mitla received their inspiration, their knowledge, and their skill in art. . . . I believe that
these picture writings are tangible evidences pointing to the idea we ought to form of the Toltecs,
whose name has been so often mentioned and so
much abused, for they were neither mere mythical
forms dwelling in a fantastic region beyond the
clouds nor the inhabitants of a single small city,
least of all an exotic civilized race that spread over
the whole American continent, coming from the
primal Asiatic home of man, lying somewhere near
the biblical paradise. As Father Sahagun's authority emphatically declares, the Toltecs, or their descendants, spoke Nahuatl; yet they were not the
Nahua tribes of the highlands, those who later obtained predominant political power, but the Nahua
tribes who lived in the coast region as neighbors of
the Mixtec-Zapotec and Maya tribes, and who,
in and by means of this contact, in active peaceful
intercourse with the other tribes, developed the
calendar and the philosophy which afterward became, to a certain extent, the common property of
all the civilized peoples of ancient Mexico."

Everyone should be permitted to read the first known
description of Mitla. It was written by Father Francisco de Burgoa of Oaxaca, who saw the place in 1674.
It reads as follows:

"They built in this square this beautiful house
or Pantheon, with stories and subterraneans, the
latter in the concavity which was found under the
earth, equalling in style the halls which enclose it,
having a spacious court; and to build the four equal

halls they worked with what force and industry they could secure from a barbarous people.

"It is not known from what quarry they could cut such great pillars of stone, that with difficulty two men could embrace them with their arms extended. These, although without capital or pedestal, straight and smooth, are more than five yards long composed each of a single stone, and served to sustain the roof. The roof was of flat stones two yards or more long, and one broad, and half a yard thick, laid upon the pillars successively. The flat stones are so much alike and so well adjusted one to the other, that without mortar or cement they appear in their construction like tables brought together. The four halls are very spacious, covered in the same way with this kind of roof. The walls excelled in execution the work of the most skilled artificers of the world, so that neither the Egyptians nor the Greeks have written of this kind of architecture, because they began at the lowest foundations and followed upwards, spreading out into the form of a crown, which projects from the roof in breadth and appears likely to fall.

"The centre of the walls is of a cement so strong that we do not know with what liquid it was made. The surface is of such a singular construction that it shows something like a yard of stones. The sculptured blocks serve to hold innumerable little white stones that fill it, beginning with the sixth part of an ell and the half of an ell wide and the quarter part of an ell thick, so smooth and similar that it seems as if they were made in a mould. Of these there was so great a variety, and they were so connected one with the other, that various showy pictures an ell wide each, the length of the hall, were constructed with a variety of decoration on each as high as the capital. And it was so neat that it exceeded the description, and what has caused astonishment to great architects was the adjustment of these little stones without mortar or any instruments. They worked them with hard flints and sand and produced a building of so much strength that, being very old and beyond the memory of the living, it has lasted to our times. I saw it much at my ease thirty years ago (1674). The rooms above were of the same style and size with those below, and although portions were somewhat ruined because some of the stones had been carried away, they were very worthy of consideration. The door frames were very capacious, composed of a single stone of the thickness of the wall at each side. The lintel or architrave was a single stone which held the two below.

"There were four halls above and four below. They were divided in this way: That in front served as a chapel and sanctuary for the idols, which were placed on a large stone that served as an altar at the great feasts or at the funeral of some king and principal chief. The Superior gave notice to the lesser priests or inferior officers that they should arrange the vestments and decorate the chapel, and prepare the incense. They went down with a great escort without any of the people seeing them, nor was it ever permitted them to turn their faces toward the procession, being persuaded that they would fall dead in the act of disobedience. Upon entering the chapel the priest put on a large white cotton robe, and another one embroidered with figures of beasts and birds in the manner of a surplice or chasuble. Upon his head he had something after the style of a mitre, and upon the feet another invention woven with threads of different colors, and thus clothed he came with great pomp and circumstance to the altar. Making great obeisance to the idols he renewed the incense, and began to talk very much between his teeth with these figures, the depositories of infernal spirits. In this kind of communication he continued with these deformed and horrid objects, that held all overcome with terror and amazement, until he recovered from his diabolical trance, and told the spectators all the fictions and orders which the spirit had persuaded him of, or which he had invented.

"When he was obliged to make human sacrifices, the ceremonies were doubled and the assistants bent the victim across a great stone, and opening the breast with some knives of flint they tore it apart with horrible contortions of the body, and laying bare the heart they tore it out with the soul for the Demon. They carried the heart to the Chief Priest that he might offer it to the idols, putting it to their mouths with other ceremonies. The body they threw into the sepulchre of the blessed as they called it. If after the sacrifice any one wished to detain those who officiated, or to demand some favor, he was informed by the inferior priests that he could not go to his house until his gods were appeased, commanding him to practise penance . . . etc.

". . . One hall was the burial place of these priests, and another hall was for the kings of Theozapotlan. . . .

"The last hall had another door at the rear into an obscure and fearful opening that was closed with a great stone to shut the entire entrance, and into it they threw the bodies of those that they had sacrificed . . . and there have been men and curious priests of good faith, who in order to undeceive the ignorant entered below and went down some steps . . . where they found a species of alleys like streets . . . they ordered that infernal place to be perfectly closed up with masonry, and the upper halls were separated from the lower ones, the fragments existing up to now. . . .

"One high hall was the Palace of the Chief Priest in which he gave audience and slept . . . and such

was the authority of this minister of the Devil
that no one dared to pass through the square and
to avoid it they had the other three halls with gates
at the rear through which the officers entered both
above and below. They had outside passages and
alleys for entering and going out from an audience. . . .

"The second hall was that of the priests and
their assistants. The third that of the King when
he came and the fourth that of the other leaders
and captains. . . .

"All the halls were well covered with mats and
very clean. . . ."

The excavations by the Mexican Government and by
Professor Marshall Saville have brought Mitla very
well to light, though a great deal more could be done
there to advantage. It is the last site of first magnitude as one approaches the Isthmus of Tehuantepec,
with the exception of Quiengola, on the Isthmus, which
will not be discussed here except to call attention again
to its resemblance to the Totonac temple of Papantla.
That it is Zapotec is generally conceded.

I know of no other Zapotec ruins of importance east
of Quiengola, or where the continent reaches its nar-
rowest above Panama, unless it should turn out that
Tonala is Zapotec.

The Tonala group is in the state of Chiapas. The
ruins are situated upon the crest and southern slope of
a secondary range of mountains lying between the sea
and the main range of the Continental Divide, about
equally distant. Peaks of the main range in sight from
here reach an altitude of from ten thousand to twelve
thousand feet. The secondary range on which the ruins
are situated reach in places an altitude of two thousand feet. Between the foot of this range and the

A Ruined Temple at Mitla (Waite)

Subterranean Chamber, Mitla, Mexico

Ruins of Tonala, Isthmus of Tehuantepec, Mexico

ocean is a level coast plain of from ten to twenty miles in width.

The ruins may be reached in four hours' walk from the town of Tonala. In general type they are the same as those of Monte Albán in Oaxaca. In extent, possibly in importance, they rival that famous group. In magnificence of situation they are incomparable. The stupendous panorama of ocean on the one side and lofty mountains on the other is beyond description.

Here, as at Monte Albán, the natural hills have been shaped, terraced, walled, on a scale that would be considered almost incredible if undertaken without modern appliances for grading and handling heavy stonework. The whole is crowned with a succession of pyramids built of massive granite. Fragments of a wide *calzada* paved with irregular blocks of granite are still to be found leading from the plain up to the temples.

All stonework is of refractory granite; the terrace walls, inclined planes, etc., being laid in irregular blocks, while the principal façades are of hewn stones, samples of which measure ten and one-half feet by four feet by nine inches; nine and one-half feet by five and one-half feet by one foot. The large pyramid measures about three hundred and fifty feet square. The grand stairway, or rather incline, by which it is mounted is about eighty feet wide. The buildings are unusually low, due probably to the great weight of the stones used in their construction. Due also to the refractory character of the stone, there is little in the way of sculptured embellishment. However, the builders were not without a certain degree of skill in low relief carving.

My stay at Tonala, with a single Indian guide, was

too brief to enable me to do any accurate mapping, but it would be safe to say that there are many miles of these terraces and sculptured hills with an area of pavement and mural facing that puts the site in the big class. The country is wild, uninhabited, after ascending from the coast plain. At the head of a small canyon at the top of the divide, I came face to face with a jaguar. Both parties were equally discreet in retiring from the scene. My photographs from this and from a subsequent expedition were not entirely successful, but one view is presented anyway. Tonala is a rich site for study. I do not as yet hazard an opinion as to where it is to be grouped ethnically.

The Zapotec country presents endless attractions for exploration and study. Much that has been written about it is purely speculative. Some archæologists find strong Toltec influence; some are equally certain of Maya relationship. Both are probably right. It is a transition area, and the Zapotecs a transition people. They lie between the Aztec-Toltec and the Maya-Quiché lands, with indefinite boundaries. They have many things in common with both neighbors. They had the calendar; they had the hieroglyphic writing; they had common linguistic traits; they had the architecture, arts, and industries of both sides. In all these respects there were local variations that stamp them as a well differentiated people with a specialized culture of their own. Whatever population movements occurred, up and down the narrowing continent, and there were many, had to pass over their land, except, possibly, on a small gulf coast strip. So there was ample opportunity for their fertilization by other cultures, and for them to communicate their culture traits to others. If Central Americanists will tell us which was the hen and which the egg, Maya or Toltec, the position of the Zapotecs will be clearer. However, the Zapotecs may be as autochthonous as they think they are. They may have been generous contributors to the cultures on both sides of them, and possibly may deserve more than has been ascribed to them in the way of culture genesis. The indications of great antiquity are as distinct among them as in any of the Middle American peoples. If it ever becomes possible to arrange stocks definitely in chronological relationship, through study of linguistics and culture stratification, it is not rash to predict for the Zapotecs a high place as a mother culture. At present, the whole business is extremely chaotic. The late Dr. Nicolas Leon's *Lyobaa* is still a classic work on Mitla.

PART FOUR

DÉBRIS OF AN ANCIENT WORLD: CENTRAL AMERICA

"But yesterday its people passed
    Into their silence and their night,
Leaving their broken walls to glow
    Encrimsoned by the shafted light."

—HARTLEY BURR ALEXANDER

PART FOUR

DÉBRIS OF AN ANCIENT WORLD: CENTRAL AMERICA

I. Maya-Quiché Land

1. The Western Frontier

From the Isthmus of Tehuantepec the trend of the continent is eastward. The Continental Divide hugs the Pacific shore, leaving only a narrow coast plain, along which population movements doubtless passed to the south from very early times, and trade flowed back and forth, borne by Aztec and Guatemalan carriers. Watching the lines of Indians in the highlands of Guatemala today, shuffling along their mountain paths, across deep *barrancas,* and over high ranges, loaded with produce and work, even furniture, to be finally displayed for exchange in markets a hundred or more miles away, sometimes as far as Salvador is from Chiapas, it is easy to visualize the ancient trading expeditions. Romantic historians have glorified these ancient burden-bearers into "merchants" on commercial expeditions, comparable to those of the Orient. What they are today, they were in the pre-Conquest age. Time stands still in that country.

The north side of the Continental Divide, the gulf coast plain, is of more ample breadth. It is broken hill country, almost all the way from Vera Cruz, south and east, but well adapted to all the tropical products. Fol-

lowing the trend of the coast line to the east, one reaches
the drainage basin of a great river, the Usamacinta,
which has its rise in the highlands of Guatemala, and
flows to the north, bearing slightly westward, into the
Gulf of Mexico. When this basin is reached, we are
in a new ethnic province, definitely in the country of
the Maya. The Usamacinta drainage may be regarded
as its western frontier. West and north, following the
trend of the gulf coast, are ruins of minor importance,
some disclosing evidences of the characteristic Maya
culture, and, far to the north, in the state of Vera Cruz,
as heretofore pointed out, is the small ethnological
island of the Huasteca; Maya in language, but in virtually nothing else. The lack of Maya hieroglyphic
writing to the west is convincing testimony that the
true Maya lies east and south from the Usamacinta
frontier. There is a Maya record, the earliest known,
on a small effigy, the "Tuxtla statuette," named from
the assumed place of its origin, San Andreas de Tuxtla,
in the southern part of the state of Vera Cruz, Mexico. Archæologists have attached too much importance
to this small object, as evidence of Maya occupation of
this region, or evidence by which to date Maya migration in one direction or the other. The finding of a little
fetish of nephrite, which could be carried in one's coat
pocket, or in an ancient priest's medicine bundle, must
not be used for too positive generalizations. It may
have been picked up hundreds of miles from the place
of its origin.

In the Maya, true to ancient American type in essential racial characteristics, we see a variant that sets
them apart as a people of singular ability in many
ways, yet lacking in the qualities that make for survival. The spread of their history covers at least a

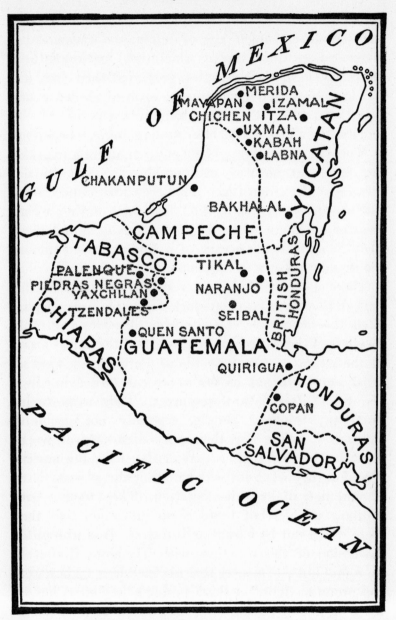

Map of the Maya-Quiché World (after Morley)

millennium and a half. They flourished at two periods—an older, Golden Age, of indefinite duration, surely several centuries, during which they developed their pantheon, built their temples, perfected their arts, social structure, and government; evolved almost a national character. They then went into a period of obscurity, their Dark Age, later undergoing a renaissance in Yucatan, which brought them up again to a flourishing state—in no way comparable, however, to the apogee of the olden time. This they maintained for a few centuries, then went into their final decline, which was far advanced when the white invader found them (1517), and, in the course of a few years, completed the dissolution of a great people.

The cause of that slump, from the height of the old period, has never been satisfactorily explained. It parallels the experience of the ancient Pueblos and cliff-dwellers of the American Southwest, of the Toltecs, and of the strong pre-Inca people of Peru. They were of good somatic breed, as far as we can tell, living in a country of fair natural resources. They were an industrious, thinking people, certainly not declining through inaction, for their vast architectural works went far beyond their actual needs. Like the ancient Pueblos, they went out with startling abruptness, showing no sign of long degeneration. They were a nonmilitary people, but there is no indication that they were wiped out by barbarian invaders. In a protracted discussion of this question, with Theodore Roosevelt, he found but one answer that satisfied him, "They were too proud to fight." I think perhaps they were, but we know of no one having taken advantage of their pacific disposition. Perhaps we will have to admit that a people who exalt the esthetic and spiritual values of life cannot survive on this planet as at present inhabited. But I must also maintain, on the testimony of history, that neither is consecration to physical force a sure guarantee of racial or national longevity. Present indications are that material culture is pretty efficient in self-destruction. Anyway, the Old Maya eclipse remains a profound mystery, as does the ancient Pueblo.

In describing Maya-land and its antiquities, I shall proceed in geographical order, about as I have personally explored it, without regard to chronology. It is not a spacious country—only some five hundred miles in extent north to south. With some archæologists it is customary to divide Maya history into "Old Empire" and "New Empire"; the latter embracing the northern Yucatecan sites; the former, all the rest— west, middle and south—on the assumption that this is a correct chronological grouping; even though, as generally admitted, the implication as to type of government is all wrong. I long since rejected the term "empire" as being totally inapplicable to any government that ever existed in aboriginal America. Thomas Gann, in his history of the Maya, in collaboration with Eric Thompson, criticizes the term from another point of view. He says, "The history of the Maya was formerly divided up into that of the Old and the New Empires, the former occupying the southern part of the Maya area up to about the beginning of the seventh century A. D., the latter, the peninsula of Yucatan, from that period on to the Spanish Conquest. Later research, however, has shown that this classification is inaccurate and misleading, as both Yucatan and the south were occupied simultaneously from very early times." Mr. Gann, however, retains the term "as a matter of convenience." Since it is inaccurate and misleading in both vital respects, I do not feel justified in using it, however convenient it might be.

If, then, we take the Usamacinta Basin as the home of the western Maya, we may choose for detailed discussion from the major sites, Palenque, Piedras Negras, and Menche or Yaxchilan; the one first named being the most extensive and most representative of western Maya culture. Although the extreme western outpost, it took the lead among all Old Maya sites, in many respects. The Palenqueños were decidedly nonconformists. In its architecture and art the place classes quite by itself, and its inscriptions are utterly erratic. That it belongs to the Old Maya period cannot be doubted, but when it comes to dating, it goes outside the range of the Old Maya group. Dates are found at Palenque that run into mythological figures, but there is no reason for considering it older than most of the Old Maya sites. Some place it among the most recent. It was, at any rate, entirely prehistoric. It was not mentioned by the early chroniclers.

Palenque is of vast extent if we include the small house foundation walls that are to be seen for many miles around, in all directions, but these may be omitted except for technical study not contemplated in this work. Excavation on a large plan has not yet been undertaken. My concession lapsed with the onset of revolutionary conditions in Mexico. Still, the sacred precinct has been well cleared and in its larger aspects we know the place quite well. It is unique in the embellishment of its buildings in stucco, also in the three-storied, square tower. In low relief ornament, it has no peer among its contemporaries. Wall panels of the highest artistic quality abound, to many of which color was doubtless added. Some of its altar

pieces, notably that in the Temple of the Cross, its
three long-separated panels now reassembled in the
National Museum in Mexico City, and the one in the
Temple of the Sun, are beyond compare in aboriginal
art of this character. The panels that face the entrance
to the Temple of the Sun are masterpieces of low relief. One, a ghostly figure with tiger-skin robe, blowing smoke or flame from a straight tube pipe (the
"cloud blower" of the Pueblos), is startlingly reminiscent of the *koshare*—impersonators of ancestral spirits in the ceremonies of the Rio Grande villages. The
other, a priest of the normal Palenque type, is an exquisite piece of stone carving, and must have been
equally brilliant in color. In elaborate headdress and
other elements of costume, the Palenque figures are
superb. The Temple of Inscriptions, with its lengthy
hieroglyphic record of over six hundred characters,
bears the stupendous date of nearly 1,247,653 years.

Like all Maya buildings, no matter how imposing or
for what purpose, the Palenque temples are devoid of
the true arch. Neither did they use the flat roofs of the
Pueblos, who, with roof beams and columns, covered
council chambers that would accommodate up to a thousand Indians. The Maya built no halls for assemblage
of the people. All their gatherings must have been in
the open. The walls of their buildings were of great
thickness, of rubble with dressed facings; their halls
without windows, narrow, of any desired length, but
permitting very little room space. Without a true arch
for roofing, the span was necessarily small. From the
top of the side walls the faces were drawn inward by
slightly overlapping courses until they came almost together, forming high vaults. The principle of the keystone was never discovered. Had it been, the true arch

would have developed, and the story of Maya architecture vastly extended. Instead of the keystone, a flat slab capped the apex, completing a roof of doubtful stability. The great thickness of the walls compensated to some extent, so that not only the normally heavy roof was borne, but in addition a high, massive "roof-comb" was carried for architectural effect. The roof-comb was a favorite element in the western Maya towns. It was used also in Yucatan. The buildings were only one story, though having the appearance of two, because of the façades being divided by a decorative cornice into two horizontal zones, the upper one usually loaded with ornament, the lower nearly always plain. The doorways are always in the lower zone, extending up to the medial cornice.

The buildings at Palenque, as in nearly all Maya towns, were set on solid, pyramidal bases, thus elevating the structure above the plazas. The elevation was increased by placing them on natural hills. The Maya built no high buildings, the three-storied tower being their limit. A single story was the rule. Structurally, their architecture was far behind that of the Peruvians, who handled blocks of almost incredible weight, and keyed them in so securely that they resist even modern vandalism. Maya masonry was almost devoid of effective keying. But they achieved esthetic effects that would have been pronounced marvelous in any country.

Again it may be pointed out that, coercive as tradition was among all the highly cultured peoples of ancient America, almost every Maya community developed its own specialty in art. The pre-eminence of Palenque in stucco was mentioned before. Menche, or Yaxchilan, on the Usamacinta, specialized in beautiful lintel carving; Tikal, in the central area, in wood sculpture. Quirigua's specialty was colossal, sculptured, monolithic monuments, in both stela and animal form. Chichen Itza developed the magnificent "serpent column." Uxmal could boast perfection in what may be called the stone lattice work of its façades, a raised mosaic in geometric patterns, reminiscent of Mitla, but technically entirely different in construction. That, with foundations in such set tradition, the Maya could produce in almost every separate community a distinguished and characteristic art form is high testimony to the eminence of their artists.

I am aware that much that has just been said here seems to belong to the later section of this work, which treats of the esthetic achievements of the Middle American peoples. It illustrates a fact that is becoming clear as we go along with this study, that the integration of culture exhibited by the American Indian race is something that has been approached by no other people, even in their primitive stages of development. Maya art is Maya religion, and Maya architecture and Maya life. It is impossible to disintegrate these factors in their culture so as to analyze them separately, but the attempt first to describe the ruined towns as they appear to the explorer today, and as they have been known to traditionist and historian, will have obvious advantages in the end.

2. *The Yucatecans*

In considering the western Maya there is the satisfaction of dealing with an unmixed culture. As far as known, it is pure Old Maya. Going on to the east, into the peninsula of Yucatan, we find ourselves in a maze of confused tradition, contradictory chronologies, mixed cultures, complicated interpretations by historians and archæologists. Stating the situation summarily, it may be said that we have Old Maya, Late Maya, Toltec, and Aztec, admittedly present. It is not within the scope of this work to attempt to straighten out this tangle of evidences. We may safely assume an Old Maya period of some centuries in the early part of the Christian era; then several centuries of obscurity; a renaissance that lasted to the Conquest; a Toltec immigration, somewhere along the line, and finally an Aztec invasion—all together making quite a jumble of Yucatecan archæology.

The country was not the most inviting in Central America. There are no springs and streams, consequently no fertile river valleys. There is subsurface water, accessible by way of large, natural wells, *cenotes,* where the limestone or coral crust breaks down to the underground flow. Some of these are roughly circular, attaining a diameter up to one hundred and fifty feet. From the ground surface down to the water may be from fifty to sixty feet, and the depth of water in the *cenote* equally great. It was only in the neighborhood of these *cenotes* that permanent settlements could be made. There was no system of water distribution from them. Not a very large population could be supplied by carrying water in clay vessels from these storing places. So I think we must regard the ancient population of Yucatan as quite rigidly limited in number, doubtless far below most of the estimates. One hundred and fifty thousand men killed in their civil wars, as estimated by Bishop Diego de Landa, would, I imagine, have depopulated the peninsula. Their "cities" were simply centers of religious life. The people lived in the bush round about, as now, naturally sticking close to the *cenotes*. Chichen Itza, Uxmal, Mayapan, Labna, Izamal, Kabah, Coba, Tuluum, were their principal settlements. Some of these were occupied at the time of the Conquest, others in ruins. Of these the first named is best known, partly because of the early chroniclers, but mainly on account of the excavation that has been carried on there for several years by the Carnegie Institution of Washington, under the direction of Dr. Sylvanus G. Morley, with important restorations by the Mexican Government. John L. Stephens, William H. Holmes, Alfred Maudslay, Edward Thompson, all made valuable contributions to our knowledge of the northern Yucatecan ruins, but it fell to Doctor Morley to plan and carry out on an adequate scale the uncovering of Chichen Itza. His first work there, under the direction of the School of American Archæology, was a survey of the Chichen site with a view to determining the practice of the Late Maya in the orientation of their buildings. Out of this grew his plan for a work of excavation commensurate with the importance of this ruin.

This was one of the largest and most important of ancient Yucatecan settlements. Its ruined buildings cover an area of at least a mile square, and minor structures are to be found in every direction for a considerable distance. The ruins are in the northeastern part of the peninsula of Yucatan, about a hundred miles from Mérida, the capital. The place belongs to a later time than Palenque, Tuluum, Copan, and Quirigua. It was contemporaneous with Uxmal and Mayapan. The ancient settlement takes its name from a tribe, the Itzas, supposed to have founded it, and from two natural reservoirs, *cenotes,* around which the place was built. While its history is obscure, students have reached

the conclusion that it had its origin as a settlement of
Maya people, as above stated, in the early centuries
of the Christian era, and that after its first period of
development, followed by a hiatus of unknown duration and an epoch of resettlement, it underwent a
change of occupancy, passing under the domination
of the conquering Aztecs from the Mexican plateau.
Numerous evidences of Aztec culture are to be seen
at Chichen Itza. In fact it is, by some authorities, held
to have been Aztec rather than Maya. My own conclusion is that we have here something of Maya, both
Old and Late, strongly overlaid by the virile cultures
from the north and west, probably both Toltec and
Aztec.

Important buildings at Chichen are: the Pyramid
of Sacrifice *(El Castillo),* the Place of a Thousand
Columns, the Temple of the Warriors, the Ceremonial
Ball Court, the Temple of the Tigers, Casa Colorado,
the Temple of the High Priest's Grave, the Iglesia, and
the *Caracol. El Castillo,* or as I prefer to call it, the
Pyramid of Sacrifice, occupies the center of the picture
in the Chichen plan. It is a pyramid, in the main well
preserved, minor restorations having been made at several points, without introducing any feature not reasonably well verified. Its approximate measurements are
one hundred and ninety by two hundred and thirty-one
feet at the base, eighty feet in height, and about sixty
feet square at the summit. In design and execution, this
structure is of a high order. It has four great stairways, each about thirty feet in width, and flanked by
balustrades, those on the north side terminating at the
base in two great plumed serpent heads, each about ten
feet in length, each carved from a single block of stone.
The pyramid is built of coarse rubble, cemented with

Restoration of Chichen Itza, from Painting by Vierra, San Diego Museum

Restoration of Uxmal, from Painting by Vierra, San Diego Museum

—*Courtesy of the Carnegie Institution*

The Caracol, Chichen Itza, Yucatan, in Process of Excavation

blocks of hewn limestone, neatly dressed and tastefully paneled. The temple which surmounts the pyramid is about forty-four by forty-eight feet at the base, and twenty-four feet in height. It is well preserved, save that a portion of the façade went down as the result of the decay of the wooden lintels which spanned the doorway. The walls and roof are four feet or more in thickness, and the stones of the facing so well cut and fitted as to require little mortar. As usual in Yucatan buildings, the exterior walls of the lower story are plain and separated by heavy molding from the upper story, which is ornamented with panels and surmounted by a cornice. In this case the cornice was, according to Maudslay, crowned by a coping of open fretwork of exceptional beauty. The lower story is pierced by four doorways, that on the north being twenty-one feet wide, eight and one-half feet high, divided by two massive stone columns. These supported the wooden lintels and are carved to represent the ever-present feathered serpent deity. Passing through the outer chamber or vestibule between these columns, and through a second doorway, a large chamber is entered, which is spanned by pointed arches, the separating walls being replaced by square, sculptured columns. This chamber was a sanctuary, serving some vital purpose in the religious rites of the people.

From the base of the north stairway, a paved road extends to the Cenote of Sacrifice, around which clusters much Maya tradition. Of especial note is the story that has come down through the ancient chronicles, known as the Sacrifice of the Maidens at the Sacred Well. This is alleged to have been a propitiatory ceremony to the rain gods in time of drought. The maidens, prepared in the temple for the sacrifice, proceeded along the paved causeway to an altar upon the brink of the *cenote*. From here, at daybreak, occurred the plunge into the water of the holy well, from seventy to one hundred feet below. If one survived this plunge, she might be rescued at midday, after which she would be regarded as a person especially favored by their gods. The story of this sacrifice is quaintly told in a letter written by the original *conquistadores* of Yucatan, in response to a circular sent out by the Council of the Indies in 1579, asking for information about the discovery and conquest of the country and the native inhabitants. That the Sacred Cenote was a place for the deposit of votive offerings was confirmed by the dredging that took place there some years ago, during which ornaments and vessels of gold of considerable value were recovered.

The most beautiful of all Chichen buildings is the Temple of the Tigers. It overlooks the Ball Court, an Aztec feature of ceremonial precincts, which warrants some discussion as indicative of the integration of recreational and ritualistic life among Middle American peoples. The court, in size between a modern football field and a tennis court, was confined between massive side walls of stone, with pavilions at the ends for the seating of dignitaries. A massive stone ring was set in one of the side walls, near the top, and through the hole in this fixture the ball used in the game was cast. This ball, according to the chronicle, was "made of the gum of a tree that grows in hot countries, which having holes made in it distills great white drops which soon harden and being worked and molded together turn as black at pitch." Here we recognize one of the earliest uses of a well-known product of the tropics, our so-called India rubber. The ball was struck with any part of the body. Sometimes it was necessary that it should rebound from the hip, upon which was fastened a piece of stiff leather. When the ball was cast through the great ring upon the wall, the game was won, and the winner entitled to the mantles and other objects of wearing apparel of which the spectators could be deprived. The successful player often acquired loads of mantles and, sometimes, much gold and feather work. This characteristic Aztec game or ceremony was widespread. I found the stone rings in the Casas Grandes district, Chihuahua, and in the cliff ruins of Pajarito Plateau, New Mexico. "Courts" are reported to have been found in north-central and eastern Arizona.

A unique building at Chichen is the *Caracol*, or Round Tower. It rests upon a massive platform, taking its name from the spiral or shell-like passageway that extends upward through the center of the building. The lower terrace is one hundred and fifty by two hundred and twenty feet square and twenty feet high. The second terrace is sixty by eighty feet square and twelve feet high. The upper level is occupied by a ruined turret, twenty-nine feet in diameter. The building, now completely excavated and described in detail, conforms only in a general way with my rough notes made when the *Caracol* was a mass of ruins. It has been called an astronomical observatory by the excavator, a designation that I am not prepared to accept. It implies a level of scientific attainment that may be unwarranted.

As Doctor Morley is the outstanding authority on Chichen Itza, readers are advised to secure his numerous papers and reports for detailed information. Among the most important achievements of the project under his direction are the excavation of the *Caracol*, above referred to; the excavation of the Temple of the

Warriors (read Mr. Earl Morris' report on this); together with the clearing and repair of numerous other buildings, and the rescue of the entire establishment from its jungle environment. With liberal assistance from the government of Mexico, it has been made one of the great show places of ancient America.

It would seem that in the Old Maya period the places of note were on the east side of the peninsula. Coba and Tuluum were probably earlier than Old Chichen. Tuluum was on the coast of the channel of Yucatan. Its ruins are visible from the ships that keep inside the Island of Cozumel, passing up and down the coast. It has been a rather difficult place to explore because of the unpopularity of the white race with the Indians of that region, a branch of the Maya that has not been "too proud to fight." They have long had the idea that, to reverse an ancient epigram, the only good white man is a dead white man. They were there, if a single dated stela is sufficient evidence to prove it, in Old Maya times, 304 A.D., if we adopt one way of counting. They were there a thousand years later; there when the Spaniards arrived and reported it "as fine as Seville," though this is one of their extreme flights of fancy. It is unusual in being a walled precinct, but its ruins are not impressive as compared with the greatest of Maya sites. My account is from a short expedition that I sent there in 1913, which, under the impression that those Indians still held their traditional view about white men, remained only a few hours. The place has since been visited several times, a good report being that of Dr. S. K. Lothrop.

Mr. Morley's report on the expedition to Tuluum, above referred to, is here reproduced in part for the information of aspiring young archæologists as to the kind of training they are sometimes put through in preparation for this dry and dusty science:

"The east coast of Yucatan is occupied by small groups of the Sublevado Indians who have maintained their independence by guerrilla warfare for the last sixty-five years. These independent Mayas regard every intrusion into their midst with suspicion and act accordingly. In a thick, impenetrable bush, with every trail and corner of which they are perfectly familiar, they have held the Mexican soldiery at bay time and time again, exacting a heavy toll in human life every time they have been attacked. In this general hatred for outsiders, Americans have not been excluded. . . .

"On April 5, the expedition [School of American Archæology, 1913] landed at San Miguel on the west coast of Cozumel island. This island is indeed one of the gems of the Caribbean sea. It is about twenty-four miles long and twelve miles wide. Graceful groves of coconut, banana, and other tropical trees overhang the strand. The water is blue, presenting a wonderful and ever-changing play of color, running from palest Nile green through all the medium shades of green and blue to the rich, deep blue of the sapphire. This water is so clear that stones at the bottom, seventy-five to one hundred feet down, appear to be just beyond reach of one's hand. And, of a moonlight night, the water is so crystal clear that the shadow of a boat, far below on the bottom, makes the boat itself appear to be floating in air.

"This tropical paradise, for such in truth it is, has a rich history. Here it was, in 1519, that Hernan Cortez landed on his voyage to Mexico, where later he was to achieve such enduring fame, and clearing one of the Mayan temples of its idols installed there the image of the Virgin instead. . . .

"A sailboat was rented and, in addition to the

crew of three, a guard of five Mexicans was taken along as a protection against the Indians. The collection of arms carried by these bravos was worthy of installation in an archæological museum, the most modern gun being an antiquated shotgun, loading at the muzzle. We could but hope that the Sublevados would have no better armament.

"After an exceedingly rough passage of nine hours, the boat was off the ruins of Tuluum, tossing in the midst of a high surf. The captain declared it would be impossible to pass through the reef, which parallels the shore at this part of the coast, in such high seas, and that it would be necessary to go ashore in the small dugout canoe with which the boat was equipped.

"The passage to the shore was fraught with the gravest dangers and it is still a matter of amazement that the little craft did not capsize, drowning all on board. Then it was, a high wave broke over the canoe just as it grounded on the beach, and the first thing the writer realized was that he was floundering in water waistdeep, amidst a tangle of legs, arms, photographic material, guns, and lunch.

"This episode effectually disposed of the muzzle-loading shotguns of the guard, not one of which could be discharged after this saltwater bath. Much more serious, however, was the damage done to the photographic equipment. The wide angle shutter was put out of commission entirely, and all the plates were ruined. Fortunately, five had been left behind on the boat, and one of the guards was sent back for them.

"It must have been a sorry spectacle that the expedition presented at that moment. Drenched to the skin, weakened from nine hours of continuous seasickness, the writer welcomed *terra firma,* with all the possibilities of Indian attack, in preference to the terrible buffetings of the sea in a cockle shell of a boat.

"The second trip of the canoe brought the remainder of the guard and the last five dry plates. After a brief rest on the beach, the party started for the ruins up a steep bluff and through a dense tangle of scrub palm, the guard leading the way. Presently, after climbing the high defensive wall of the site, the writer stood within the ruined city of Tuluum.

"The ruins of Tuluum are surrounded by a wall twelve or fifteen feet in height and of equal thickness. This wall incloses a rectangular area 1,500 feet long by 650 feet wide. The wall begins at the high bluff overhanging the beach, runs west for 650 feet and then makes a right angle turn to the north. At the corner this wall is surmounted by a watchtower or lookout. The wall continues north for 1,500 feet, at which it makes a right angle turn to the east and thence continues for 650 feet back to the edge of the bluff. The bluff took the place of a wall on the sea side.

"The north and south walls are entered by two narrow doorways each. The west or land wall has but one doorway. This walled inclosure contains about twenty-one acres, and is filled with vestiges of ancient structures, some in a fairly good state of preservation and others entirely demolished. . . .

"Toward evening the party returned to the beach and made preparations for boarding the boat. The sinking sun painted the principal temple a golden yellow, and the green sea, pounding on the rocky shore below its base, every now and then threw a cloud of spray swirling in the air. In silence, as we found it, we left the ancient city until some other more fortunate time.

"During the stay on shore, the sea had risen and it was with grave doubts that the writer entrusted himself to the dugout canoe again. Twice this unseaworthy shell was capsized before getting beyond the breakers, and it was only with the most energetic baling that it reached the sailing boat at all. The sun was just setting as the last of the guard climbed over the heaving gunwale and the anchor was weighed.

"A gale was blowing dead ahead. Time after time the captain tried to tack out to open sea, but as often was buffeted back by the mountainous waves. In one of these encounters, the little boat caught in a hollow between two lofty crests, was battered down it seemed to the very bottom by an avalanche of water. To the writer in the hold, too ill to raise his head, it seemed as though a young Niagara had broken over him. Under this continuous assault, the boat sprung a leak and it was all the wheezy little pump could do to hold its own. The bilge water rushing from end to end, as the boat one moment was stern up and the next stern down, sounded as though the whole Gulf of Mexico had been shipped and was racing back and forth.

"By seamanship worthy of the highest praise, by teamwork little to be expected in such a ragged, misfit crew, the boat was gradually coaxed out to open sea where, although the swell was heavier, the perilous whitecaps were fewer. A night of pitching and tossing followed, and it was the middle of the morning before San Miguel was sighted.

"The expedition did not linger long at Cozumel island. That same night, the 8th of April, the gunboat on its return trip touched at San Miguel and neither Mr. Nusbaum nor the writer were reluctant to leave. Another 'norte,' however, had to be encountered before the gunboat made Progreso, on the 11th, and the Cozumel expedition was over. Although there were no cannibalistic features anticipated or encountered, there was sufficient risk by land and more than enough danger by sea to make this trip linger long in the writer's mind as a perilous undertaking, and one not to be lightly repeated in the future."

As results of this brief expedition to Tuluum, Mr. Morley verified the former accounts by Stephens and Howe as follows: First, that Tuluum was a walled city and, with the possible exception of Mayapan, the only one of its kind in the Maya area; second, that Tuluum is the only city in the Maya area which shows a flat type of roof, there being here several structures of that kind; third, that Tuluum has some exceptionally fine mural decorations; fourth, that Tuluum has very little sculptural decoration, the greater part of the façade embellishment being in stucco.

While there are two noticeable periods of occupation of this ruin, there is no proof that the ancient Maya ever abandoned the place entirely. The late occupants held on for quite a while after the Spaniards came; so perhaps Tuluum had as long a history of continuous occupation as any place in America.

Uxmal is the most beautiful of Maya ruins. It was settled, according to tradition, near 1000 A.D., by a clan or band known as the Xius. It has no old period, as Chichen and Tuluum have, but some see Toltec and Aztec influence in its buildings. It was badly located in a level, undrained country, which, once infested with such fevers as yellow and malaria, would remain so. Its unsanitary history has prevailed down into modern times, few children ever surviving in its pestilential atmosphere. In the time of my explorations there it was inhabited by the hottest and most vindictive breed of hornets that I have ever pitched camp among.

Amid its buildings were the magnificent group surrounding the main quadrangle, the *monjas;* the incomparable Palace of the Governor (badly named also), three hundred and fifty feet long, its façade a mosaic of over twenty thousand pieces of stone; the Great Pyramid, and the House of the Pigeons, with its roof-comb fifteen feet high, extending the entire length of the building, two hundred feet. The façades abound in mosaic masks, roof-comb ornament, open tracery suggesting lattice work in stone—a wealth of geometric decoration, rivaling Mitla in design, and surpassing it in the variety of its patterns. The buildings could have had slight, if any, residential function, and no civic purposes. No place of assembly was provided, though the open plazas would have served admirably for outdoor congregation. The proportion of solid masonry to room space in the buildings was forty to one. The great edifices with their small, dark interiors were places of mystery to the populace, cells for the priests for secret ritual, affording the seclusion that was necessary for maintaining the pall of superstition over the people.

A description of Uxmal, written in 1586 by an associate of Father Ponce, Franciscan delegate in Yucatan, may to this day be utilized as your Baedeker in exploring Uxmal. Every place described by him is identifiable. Everyone should be permitted to read it:

"On the north of the ranchos where the father delegate was lodged, as has been seen, which is about twenty leagues from Merida, to the south of that city, stands a *ku* or *mul,* very tall and made by hand. It is very difficult to ascend this by its 150 stone steps, which are very steep and which, from their being very old, are very dilapidated. On the top of this *mul* a large building . . . has been built, consisting of two vaulted rooms, made of stone and lime, the stones being carved with great care on the outside. In old times they took the Indians who were to be sacrificed to these rooms, and there they killed them and offered them to the idols. The father delegate went up this *mul* as soon as he arrived there, and this surprised the others greatly, since many others did not dare to go up and could not have done so if they had tried. Close to this *mul* and behind it on the west, there are lower down many other buildings built in the same way with stone and lime and with arches. The stones are carved with wonderful delicacy, some of them having fallen and others badly injured and ruined, while others can still be seen, and there is much in them worth examining. Among these there are four very large and handsome buildings . . . set in a square form, and in the middle is a square plaza, in which grew a thicket of large and small trees, and even on top of the building there were very large and dense trees growing. The building which faces the south, has on the outside four rooms, and on the inside eight others, all arched with cut stone, and as carefully joined and put together as if very skillful workers of the present had built them. These arches, and all the other old arches which have been found in this province, are not rounded over in the form of a cupola nor like those which are made in Spain, but are tapered as the funnels of chimneys are made when built in the middle of a room, before the flue begins, since both sides draw together little by little and the space between becomes more narrow, till on the top one wall is separated from the other by about two feet and there they place a layer, which extends inwards four or five inches on each side, and over this they place flags or thin stones in a level position, and with these the arch is closed, so that there is no key to the arch, but with the great weight of stone and mortar, which is placed on top and which strengthens the sides, the arch is closed and remains fixed and strong. The ends of this arched building are continuous and straight from top to bottom. At the door of each of the rooms of this

building on the inside, there are four rings of
stone, two on one side and two on the other,—
two of them being high up and two lower down
and all coming out of the same wall. The Indians
say that from these rings those who lived in these
buildings hung curtains and portieres, and it was
to be noticed that no one of these rooms, nor of
all the others, which we found there, had any
window, small or large. The rooms were therefore rather dark, especially when they were made
double, one behind the other, so that even in this,
this idolatrous race gave evidence of the darkness
and obscurity of the error in which it was en-
shrouded. The high lintels of all these doors were
made of the wood of the chico zapote, which is very
strong and slow to decay, as could well be seen,
since most of them were whole and sound, although they had been in position from time im-
memorial, according to the statements of the old
Indians. The door jambs were of stone carved
with great delicacy. On the façades of the building, both on those which face the plaza or courtyard, as well as on those which face outward,
there are many figures of serpents, idols and
shields, many screens of latticework, and many
other carvings which are very beautiful and fine,
especially if one looks at them from a distance
like a painting of Flanders, and they are all carved
from the same kind of stone. In the middle of this
building a great arch is made, so that it takes in all
the depth of the building, and therefore it is the
entrance to the courtyard or the abovementioned
plaza. It would appear that this entrance had
been plastered and that on the plaster paintings
had been made in blue, red and yellow color, since
even now some of them remain and can be seen.
Nearly all the rest of the stones had been plastered
but not painted.

"The building which stands at the west, behind

the previously mentioned mound of sacrifices, was
in the best condition and uninjured. It had four
doors which opened on to the courtyard or plaza
with as many rooms, arched in the same way as the
others, and beyond each room was another, so
that there were eight in all. Between these four
doors, two on one side and two on the other, there
was still another door which opened on the patio,
and within this was a very large hall, long and
broad, with two small rooms on the sides; and
beyond this hall there was another—a little smaller,
with two other small rooms—one on each side, so
that inside of this one door there were six rooms,
four small and two large, making, with the other
eight, fourteen rooms which this building contained. On the inside façades and ends of this
building, there were carved many serpents in stone,
and heads of savages and other figures in the manner of shields, and at the four corners (since each
building stood by itself and not joined or connected with the other) there were many other carvings cut in the round like a half curve, with tips,
which looked like serpent heads, and which stood
at half a vara from the rest of the carvings.

"The building on the north is the tallest, and
has more carvings and figures of idols, serpents
and shields and other very beautiful things about
it, but it is very much injured and the most of it
has fallen. It has ten doors which open on the
plaza and another which opens on the eastern end,
and inside each one there are two rooms, and so
among them all there are twenty-two rooms in that
building made of stone and lime, and arched like
the others, but the most of them, especially those
inside, have fallen. Before the ten doors above
mentioned there has been made a terrace, *paseo,*
or walking-place, somewhat broad and open on all
sides, to which one ascends from the plaza by steps
which are now half in ruins. All this terrace has

below it other arched rooms with doors opening on the same plaza, and these are covered and stopped up with stones and earth and with large trees which have grown there.

"The building on the west is very elegant and beautiful on the outside façade, which looks on the plaza, since serpents made of stone extend over the whole of it so as to enclose it from end to end, making many turns and knots, and they finally end with the head of one of them, on one end of the building, joined with the tail of the other, and the same thing happens on the other end of the building. There are also many figures of men and idols, other figures of monkeys, and of skulls and different kinds of shields—all carved in stone. There are also over the doors of the rooms some statues of stone with maces or sticks in their hands, as if they were mace-bearers, and there are bodies of naked Indians with their *masteles* (which are the old-fashioned loin-cloths of all New Spain, like breeches), by which it is shown that these buildings were built by Indians. In this building are seven doors, of which six open on the patio and the seventh on the end which faces the north, and inside of each door are two rooms, so that there are fourteen rooms in all, arched like the others.

"Besides these four buildings there is on the south of them distant from them about an arquebus shot, another very large building built on a *mul* or hill made by hand, with abundance of buttresses on the corners, made of massive carved stones. The ascent of this *mul* is made with difficulty, since the staircase by which the ascent is made is now almost destroyed. The building, which is raised on this *mul*, is of extraordinary sumptuousness and grandeur, and, like the others, very fine and beautiful. It has on its front, which faces the east, many figures and bodies of men and of shields and of

170

forms like the eagles which are found on the arms of the Mexicans, as well as of certain characters and letters which the Maya Indians used in old times—all carved with so great dexterity as surely to excite admiration. The other façade, which faces the west, showed the same carving, although more than half the carved part had fallen. The ends stood firm and whole with their four corners much carved in the round, like those of the other building below. There are in this building fifteen doors, of which eleven face the east, two the west and one each face the north and south, and within these doors there are twenty-four rooms arched like the others. Two of these rooms are in the northern end, and two others in the southern end, while two are in the west front, and all the rest in the eastern front—all made with special accuracy and skill.

"The Indians do not know surely who built these buildings nor when they were built, though some of them did their best in trying to explain the matter, but in doing so showed foolish fancies and dreams, and nothing fitted into the facts or was satisfactory. The truth is that to-day the place is called Uxmal, and an intelligent old Indian declared to the father delegate that, according to what the ancients had said, it was known that it was more than nine hundred years since the buildings were built. Very beautiful and strong they must have been in their time, and it is well known from this that many people worked to build them, as it is clear that the buildings were occupied, and that all about them was a great population, since this is now evident from the ruins and remains of many other buildings, which are seen from afar; but the father delegate did not go to these ruins, since the thicket was very close and dense, and there was no opportunity to open and clear out a path so as to reach them. And now they all serve only as dwellings and nests for bats and swallows and other birds, whose droppings fill the rooms with an odor more disgusting than delightful. There is no well there, and the farmers of the vicinity carry their drinking water from some little pools of rain-water which there are in that region. It may be easily suspected that these buildings were depopu-lated for want of water, although others say that this is not so, but that the inhabitants departed for another country, leaving the wells which were there choked up."

Recent studies of Uxmal have been made by Dr. Franz Blum of Tulane University. His reports will bring the investigation of Uxmal down to date.

In the Late Maya period there seems to have been a time of unification for about two hundred years, when three strong clans or tribes, the Cocomes of Maya-pan, the Itzas of Chichen, and the Xius of Uxmal, came together in a confederacy that has been called the League of Mayapan. Its period was the ten and eleven hundreds, and to this age is ascribed, by some, the greatest building activity of Yucatan. The League worked only indifferently, it seems, but it must have had its advantages, for after it broke up, near 1200 A.D., Yucatecan culture declined rapidly. Like the Mexi-cans in the time of Cortéz, the Yucatecans appear to have hated one another so bitterly as to make the way of their conquerors easy. They were by this time a poor lot of degenerate Maya, Toltec, and Aztec, with little sense of racial unity.

There can be little of mystery left in accounting for the disappearance of the formerly adequate temple builders of Yucatan. Diego de Landa, Bishop of Yucatan soon after the Conquest, is our best eyewitness. He burned all the sacred books that he could get his hands on, making a fairly complete job of it (we have only three left), and did other things not exactly necessary to the saving of pagan souls, but at the same time he preserved for us a mass of facts, derived first hand, that have opened the way to about all we know of the history, tradition, and religion of those people. He has to be studied critically. Reading conservatively the accounts of one hundred and fifty thousand men killed in battle; the horrible epidemics, smallpox for one, newly acquired from the Spaniards, that swept the land; the swarms of locusts that devastated the country; the severe drought of one period; and the terrible hurricane that wrecked everything, we have quite enough to account for the abandonment of the country. Some, of course, remained, and from these have descended the modern Yucatecans. For the large proportion that fled the country, there would be only one reasonable thing to do, that is to drift back into the highlands of Guatemala and Mexico. They would at least get away from malaria and yellow fever there; would be among their kindred—virtually all the languages up there are Mayan—and, moreover, they would be in a land of much more certain subsistence where they could practice, happily, the arts and industries that the Indians of that region have always loved, and, above all, get away from the abhorred white man.   ,

The Late Maya knew white men from 1511 A.D., the landing of the shipwrecked Spaniards on the mainland, and knew nothing but evil at their hands. The twilight of this remarkable people is one of the saddest chapters in human history.

3. The Central Towns

There is no definite boundary between the Maya areas. A large group of ruins lies in the central section, the northern part of Guatemala, or Peten District. They belong to the Old Maya period, though tradition connects Yucatecan Maya with some of these settlements. As we have rigidly limited the scope of this work, it will be necessary to pass briefly over these middle area towns: Uaxactun, with its earliest dated monument in all Maya-land; Tikal, with its steep-sided pyramids, numerous roof-combs, and superb wood carvings, both lintels and altar pieces; Naranjo with its many stelæ; the ruins about the Lake of Flores with its wealth of tradition. These formerly remote places are now reached by air service.

Uaxactun has come into note in recent years because of its excavation by the Carnegie Institution, and because of the finding there of the earliest dated Maya monument. Because of this, archæologists have pronounced Uaxactun the oldest of Maya settlements. This cannot be admitted upon such slender evidence, nor can it be conceded that the great Tikal site, only fifteen miles away, one of the largest and most important in the Maya world, was colonized from Uaxactun. Trailing groups of ancient wanderers from one location to another is uncertain business. Archæologists need to adopt some rules of evidence, comparable to the requirements in courts of law.

Tikal is a vast group of ruins occupying approximately a mile square in the interior of Guatemala, in the District of Peten. It is situated on three hills that have been leveled on top and terraced on the sides for the purpose of building thereon a great religious establishment. There are five temples situated upon steep-sided pyramids, with flights of narrow steps for stairs, and high roof-combs for architectural embellishment. All are on solid platforms. One is two hundred thirty feet high. The walls of the temples are of great thickness in proportion to room space. There are numerous dated stelæ. There is but little authentic history of the place. Mention is made of its having been explored in 1848, and various reports were published during the latter part of the past century. Its best known explorers were Mr. Alfred Maudslay and Mr. Teobert Maler. The ruins have been well studied and published by Peabody Museum, Harvard University.

An important specialty of Tikal was the remarkable wood carving found in its temples. From nowhere else in Central America, and from but few places in the world, do we have such beautiful examples of ancient wood sculpture. Of especial note is the altar piece of zapote wood now in the museum at Basel in Switzerland. It is a master work of the highest order, unsurpassed in my estimation by any piece of wood sculpture in the Old World. The design is exceptionally elaborate even for Maya art. The subject is a richly costumed personage holding a standard or baton in his right hand, his face framed in the open mouth of a grotesque monster. He is inclosed beneath the arched body of a feathered serpent of extraordinary design, the head appearing at the left. Perched on the serpent arch above is the figure of a mythical bird monster. The whole probably represents the major deity of the Central American pantheon, the plumed serpent; Kukulcan of the Maya, Quetzalcoatl of the Aztec and Toltec. The central design is surrounded by hieroglyphic inscriptions, among which are exquisitely carved portrait faces. It is said that a companion piece to this remarkable work of ancient American art was lost in the jungle in the process of transportation from Tikal to the seaboard.

4. *The Southern Maya*

For typical southern Maya sites, Copan and Quirigua, both in the Motagua drainage, are chosen for description.

Copan is the southernmost of important Maya towns. It is a high-water mark in Maya culture, among the earliest of the great establishments, and one of the richest in sculptures, pyramids, temples, and inscriptions. Its plan may be understood by studying the accompanying photograph of Maudslay's model.

The ruin of Copan is situated near the frontier between Honduras and Guatemala. It is in the Valley of the Copan River, a tributary of the Motagua, upon the banks of which, some thirty miles away in an air line, are the ruins of Quirigua, from which it is separated by a high mountain range. Unlike the majority of the Central American sites, Copan was built in the hills at an elevation of approximately two thousand feet above sea level. The district is not heavily forested, as is the main Valley of the Motagua, though from early accounts it would appear that the place was once surrounded by heavy jungle.

Of Copan there is little that is satisfactory in recorded history. We have a description of the ruins in a letter of Diego Garcia de Palacio, written in 1576 to the King of Spain. He speaks of "ruins and vestiges of a great population and superb edifices of such skill and splendor that it appears they could never have been

Model of Copan (after Maudslay)

Restoration of Copan, from Painting by Vierra, San Diego Museum

Restoration of Quirigua, from Painting by Vierra, San Diego Museum

built by the natives of the province." His description
of the ruins will still pass as reasonably accurate. As
to his information concerning them, he states, "I endeavored with all possible care to ascertain from the
Indians through the traditions derived from the ancients
what people lived there or what they knew or had
heard from their ancestors concerning them, but they
had no books relating to their antiquities nor do I
believe that in all this district there is more than one
which I possess. They say that in ancient times there
came from Yucatan a great lord who built these edifices,
but at the end of some years he returned to his native
country, leaving them entirely deserted."

Little of value was recorded concerning Copan until
the year 1839, when Mr. John L. Stephens explored
Guatemala and, with the aid of the artist, Catherwood,
prepared a most interesting and valuable account of
many of the ruins of Guatemala and Yucatan, which
to this day ranks as a classic. For important investiga-
tions of Copan we are indebted to the English explorer,
Mr. Maudslay, also to Peabody Museum, Harvard
University, during the years 1891-95, the results of
which may be read in their valuable reports. Doctor
Morley commenced his work at Copan under the
auspices of the School of American Archæology, during our expedition of 1910, and has continued inter-
mittently ever since. His chief contribution to date is
his monumental "Inscriptions at Copan," published by
the Carnegie Institution, in 1920. Copan has as yet
only partly told its story, though the Carnegie Institution is of late making substantial additions to our
knowledge of it.

Copan is not easily reached. There is an air service
that is reputed to be thoroughly bad. You can ride

across the mountains on horse or mule back from Quirigua in the Motagua Valley, but it is over high mountains with little or no trail, and what there is likely
to be belly deep in mud. Some distance can be ne-
gotiated by automobile from the railroad, but the un-
certainties are great. A saddle horse and the old reliable pack mule from Gualan or Zacapa is the surest
transportation. Supplies are meager and unsatisfactory at Copan village. Sleeping accommodations are
primitive, to say the least, when not non-existent. If
a bedroll is carried, a floor to spread it on under roof
is usually available.

The Copan River at every flood season for many
years ate into the temple area, destroying great masses
of the building and carrying away who knows what
priceless archæological records. The process, disastrous
as it was, has been friendly to the archæologist in a way
by laying bare a vertical section of over one hundred
feet in depth. Copan has suffered not only from these
catastrophes of nature, but desperately from human
vandalism. During the years when little or no scientific
work was going on in Central America, monuments
were broken up for building stone, even corrals and
pig sties being enriched with fragments of sculptured
stelæ. It is hoped that all that is past now.

Copan was favorably situated for agriculture as
well as for architecture and sculpture. The latter art
was in high favor because of the abundant and easily
carved stone, giving rise to a rich, ornate style not
equaled elsewhere in Maya-land. A unique feature,
almost completely lost, was the famous hieroglyphic
stairway, approximately thirty-six feet wide, ascending
one of the principal temples of the place, the vertical
face of every rise, about ninety steps, being covered

with hieroglyphic writing. Excavation saved ten complete and five incomplete steps in place. The inscriptions consisted of upward of twenty-five hundred glyphs, the next longest known being in the Temple of Inscriptions at Palenque, containing six hundred and seventeen glyph blocks. Extending from bottom to top at regular intervals, in the center of the stairway, was a row of seated figures of heroic size, each made of several pieces of stone. Only one remained in place, it being six of the stairway steps high. At the middle of the base stood a sculptured altar.

The glyph blocks and statues of the hieroglyphic stairway lie in the plaza in front of the temple, a hopeless jumble. Although Doctor Morley has succeeded in partly unscrambling it, this most remarkable of all monumental hieroglyphic inscriptions of the Maya must be put down as almost a total loss. A timely and on the whole charitable comment on the excavation of the hieroglyphic stairway appears in the "Guide to the Maudslay Collection of Maya Sculptures from Central America," published by the British Museum. The comment is quoted here in no spirit of unkind criticism, but as a suggestion concerning archæological field work that is worth heeding:

"The hieroglyphic stairway at Copan, discovered since Maudslay's expeditions, originally provided an even longer series of glyphs [than those of the Temple of Inscriptions], but a land-slide had occurred here. Unfortunately this fact was only recognized late in the process of excavation. Had the excavation been conducted from its inception with a knowledge of the true conditions, a restoration of the inscription, by the exercise of the greatest care, should have been possible. Unluckily the component blocks were removed without the meticulous record which the circumstances demanded, and there is little chance, in the light of our present imperfect knowledge, of reconstructing this wonderful inscription, which is estimated to be composed of some 2,500 glyphs. The unhappy fate of this monumental record demonstrates the narrowness of the line which divides excavation from destruction, and emphasizes the responsibilities of the excavator. One of the salient features of Maudslay's extensive pioneer researches is constituted by the fact that they, in no single case, resulted in the destruction of evidence."

The art of Copan, displayed mainly in the sculptured stelæ, comes in for description in a later chapter. It will be in place, in this description of Maya ruins, to tell briefly, without technical details, of the work of uncovering a ruin in the tropical jungle. Old World excavation consists largely in clearing away oceans of drifted desert sand, or removing, layer by layer, the accumulated débris of city built upon ruined city from Bronze Age to modern times. To the archæologist trained in Old World or even American Southwest excavation, the tropical jungle is a new experience. While the trowel, pick, and spade constitute the standard equipment of the dirt archæologist, almost everywhere jungle archæology calls first of all for the *machete* and the ax. Mush under foot and moisture overhead take the place of desert dust and scorching winds, but the broiling sun of the desert is equally torrid in the tropics.

The description of Quirigua, the remaining southern Maya site to be described, may be made the occasion for presenting a picture of jungle excavation, not only because it was the best of all jungle sites, but because it was the scene of our own work for five consecutive seasons. Anyone wishing to pursue the subject further may read our Quirigua Papers, published by the School of American Research, and the definitive "Handbook of Quirigua" (Carnegie Institution of Washington), by Doctor Morley, who was my assistant there. We will here describe only in part the methods and results of the work.

The ruins of Quirigua are situated on the flood plain of the Motagua River, within less than half a mile from its banks. The Motagua is here a majestic stream carrying a large volume of water during the entire year to the Bay of Honduras, which it reaches between fifty and sixty miles below Quirigua. The trend of the valley in this section is toward the east, and its flood basin, several miles in width, is one of the richest valleys on the globe. The soil, of inexhaustible fertility, consists of the deep alluvial deposit of the flood plain enriched by the vegetable mold of ages. In all directions, except to the east, the horizon presents an irregular boundary of mountain contours. To the south rises the range which separates Guatemala from Honduras. On the north and west are the spurs of a range which extends out from the main cordillera. The country is heavily watered, the rainy season lasting from eight to nine months annually and the so-called dry season from three to four months, this being more or less broken by light rainfall.

Quirigua is in as fine an example of tropical jungle as can be found. The vegetation is indescribably dense; almost every tree, bush, and flower known to the tropics is to be found there. The forest seen from adjacent hills presents the appearance of a solid mass of green, the top of which rises about one hundred and fifty feet above the ground, some trees reaching a still greater height. There were trees more than twenty feet in circumference, giants of the jungle, growing in close proximity to the monuments, and because of their enormous weight and short lives, constituting a constant menace. It was evident that the removal of such trees from the temples upon which some of them grew and from other places close to the monuments would be among the most difficult tasks that had ever confronted an archæologist in any land.

Quirigua forest is also a zoölogical garden, exhibiting in its natural habitat the fauna of the torrid zone. The largest animal to be found there is the tapir. Deer abound, also monkeys, sloths, anteaters, armadillos, and many other singular species. Birds are numerous, and of wonderful plumage. There are parrots, parroquets, macaws, toucans, herons, and many smaller species. Reptiles exist in great abundance, and insect life is seen in vast profusion. Then there are the ancient ruins; and in the jungle are a few houses and families of native bush people living in primitive fashion.

During the first year came the underbrushing of the site. For this work we had at our disposal a force of native laborers varying in number from twenty to fifty. These men, while not physically strong, are remarkably efficient with the *machete*. With this implement a native or two will quickly cut a way through what seems an impenetrable tangle of underbrush.

On returning to Quirigua the second year, the magnitude of the task of uncovering a ruin in the heart of the tropics became obvious. In the plazas of the ruined city which had been left perfectly clear nine months before, a tangle of vegetation was now found reaching a height of twenty-three feet, thus representing the almost incredible growth of one inch per day.

The real work of subduing the tropical jungle and removing it permanently from the proximity of the ruins was now commenced. As foreseen the previous year, another important problem presented itself in the matter of sanitation. The native conditions of the tropics are comparatively easy to cope with individually, but the bringing together of large numbers of laborers whose habits, even under thorough supervision, can be but imperfectly controlled, greatly increases the difficulty. During the first expedition to Quirigua, but one member of our party suffered from the prevailing fevers of the region, and he for only a few days. During the second expedition, attacks of fever were experienced by everyone except the Director. The fever was not of a malignant type, but the difficulty of work in the hot regions was greatly augmented by it.

The first work consisted in clearing the forest from the entire temple area of the town. This work was of great difficulty. About three hundred and fifty large trees and countless smaller ones had to be removed. The area cleared was about twenty acres in extent. It comprised that portion of the ground occupied by buildings and monuments, leaving around the margin the natural growth where the native fauna and flora were left undisturbed.

In removing the trees it requires much calculation to overcome the chances of damage. A large tree standing upon a temple may extend its roots out and clasp almost the entire structure. It must be so felled that it will not crush walls, stairways, or stone shafts in its descent, nor tear up masonry by disturbance of its roots.

It is often necessary to anchor the trees with cables,

and by means of ropes and pulleys throw them to a certain place. In such cases the tree is first climbed by a native, who carries up with him to the branches, perhaps more than one hundred feet from the ground, a small rope, by means of which he draws up the cable, an inch and a quarter thick, that is designed to control the movement of the tree. In many cases the only possibility of climbing the trees is by means of the vines which cling to the trunks. After anchoring the cable in the top of the tree the climber descends, and the pulleys are brought into play as the choppers fell the tree. In some instances two cables are used, and even then, unless handled with correct judgment, the weight of the tree will snap them. From twenty to fifty natives man the ropes and pulleys while the Caribs cut down the tree. That we were able to remove every one of these giants of the jungle without injury to a single monument is something for which we do not claim the entire credit. Those Carib ax-men are wonders. There may be five chopping on a single tree at once, so big that no two choppers are in sight of one another. When the old foreman sends the word around, "She's talkin'," they scurry away and he does the fancy calculating and final chopping that sends the monster where he wants to place it. I never knew him to make a mistake in judgment.

After the trees are felled the *machete* men cut up the branches, and the ax-men divide the trunks into logs that can be handled. These are rolled away from the ruins. The brush is piled and, when dried, after clearing fire paths around the monuments and buildings, the great mass is burned.

Toward the close of the season excavations were commenced in the area which we have called the Temple

Court. This is surrounded by massive terraces of cut
sandstone, and surmounted by a number of buildings
completely covered by débris. The preliminary excavations laid bare portions of the façades of these buildings.
They disclosed numerous sculptures, which apparently
had been used for mural embellishment, and a hieroglyphic cornice which starts at the northeast corner
of the building. A number of small human heads, beautifully sculptured in the gray and red sandstone of the
region, were uncovered in this area.

As in the majority of the Maya settlements, the
residential part of Quirigua probably consisted of huts
built of bamboo and thatched with palm. These houses
were of perishable character. They were especially
adapted to a tropical climate. No other type of house
can be quite so comfortable in this region as the bamboo with thatched covering. In sunshine or in rain
it affords the most grateful shelter that can be had.
The religious aspect of the civilization found expression
in the building of massive temples, "palaces," and
pyramids, and the setting up of monuments. But for
the destruction occasioned by the falling of trees and
by the rending power of the roots which have penetrated
the crevices of stairways and temple walls these buildings would have stood intact for untold ages. As it is,
stairways have been torn asunder, temple walls have
been broken apart, and a vast amount of destruction
has been wrought by growing vegetation. Because of
the isolation of the ruins and their obscurity in the
jungle, vandalism, which more than all other causes put
together has leveled to earth the monuments of antiquity, has done little damage to the ruins of Quirigua.

It is, then, the religious architecture and sculpture
of the place that have survived. In all probability what

is shown upon the accompanying plan of Quirigua constituted the sacred precinct. This consists of a number
of quadrangles, either wholly or in part surrounded
by terraces, some of which were surmounted by structures of sandstone, variously termed palaces, temples,
and pyramids. These ruins, when first seen in the
dense jungle, presented the appearance of rounded
mounds of earth. In only a few places were there
evidences of stairways of cut stone, and nowhere were
the façades of buildings visible. The entire assemblage
is comprised in the following quadrangles: First the
Great Plaza, almost a quarter of a mile in length, inclosed on three sides by terraces and open on the west,
thus presenting the appearance of an unfinished quadrangle. Grouped within the Great Plaza are eleven
of the sculptured monuments which have given Quirigua a place among the most famous of ancient American ruins.

Adjoining the Great Plaza on the south is a smaller
quadrangle which we named the Ceremonial Plaza.
This was, perhaps, the place where the principal religious ceremonies were held. It is surrounded on three
sides by massive stairways of red sandstone, rising to
a height of from twenty to fifty feet. Upon these steps
a large congregation of people could be assembled for
the purpose of viewing processions, religious rites, sacrifices, or games. Were it not for its rectangular form,
it would present the appearance of an amphitheater
rivaling in capacity those of the ancient Romans.

To the east of the Ceremonial Plaza is a small quadrangle completely surrounded with massive terraces.
Almost nothing could be determined concerning this
inclosure until after the clearing was effected. It then
became evident that this quadrangle was one of the

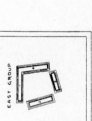

Monument No. 1, Quirigua, Guatemala

Monument No. 2, Quirigua, Guatemala

most important features of the sacred precinct. Not less than five temples stand upon the terraces which surround this inclosure, named by us the Temple Court.

Still farther to the east lies a small quadrangle, consisting of four low terraces which have not been cleared and which appear to be constructed almost entirely of cobblestone. Whether any cut stone has been used in them remains to be determined.

To the south of the Ceremonial Plaza a few hundred feet lies another quadrangle which has been named the South Court. It consists of an arrangement of low terraces built of rubble. Upon the north side of the court is a small pyramid of rubble and earth, with one side faced with cut stone. A stairway is visible upon the north side of the pyramid.

It is thus clear that the sacred precinct at Quirigua, embracing, as we have seen, about twenty acres, consists of five courts somewhat irregularly arranged and quite devoid of symmetry in their orientation. But these are by no means all the ruins. From the western boundary to the foothills is a distance of one and one-half miles. Here the land rises in successive benches from the flood plain up to the high mountain peaks. The first bench above the flood plain is from fifty to sixty feet high, and upon this we find ruins exceeding in extent those of Quirigua proper. They begin just east of the Quirigua River and extend in a series of low terraces forming quadrangles for a distance of several miles along the foothills. Nowhere do the terraces attain to the massive size found at Quirigua proper and nowhere is there such a display of cut stone in their construction, yet excavation will doubtless lay bare in these minor ruins a number of interesting structures.

The monuments at Quirigua were not buried in earth but in tropical jungle of incredible density. They were covered with moss, water soaked, and in many cases badly mutilated by the falling of trees against them in past centuries. To remove this menace of the jungle, free them from destructive vegetation, and expose them to the sunlight where they could be studied was the job to which we set ourselves. We did this; then, by means of glue molds, made replicas of eight of them for the Museum of Archæology, at San Diego, California. That is another interesting story, which cannot be told here.

Our preliminary study of the monuments may be briefly put down. We consider them in two classes, the "greater" and "lesser." To the former class belong the sculptured shafts which, in size, surpass everything else of their kind upon the American continent, and the huge zoömorphic figures which bear the same kind of hieroglyphic inscriptions and show the same sculptural features as the shafts. No evidence can be found that the zoömorphs had any different function from the shafts. They have been considered altars, but there is no evidence justifying such classification. Accordingly, we designate them the zoömorphic group.

i. THE GREATER MONUMENTS

The Greater Monuments will be considered first. These are arranged about the Great Plaza and in the Ceremonial Plaza. The material is sandstone. There are thirteen of them, and they fall into four groups. It is interesting to note that this structural sequence checks with the chronology of the monuments. They are dated at intervals of five years from No. 1 to No. 13.

Group I: The High Pedestal Group

In this group the figure stands upon a sculptured pedestal three to four feet above the ground level; the pedestal, however, is a part of the monolithic shaft.

Monument No. 1 is a large prostrate shaft (now erected), the most archaic in style of all the monuments of Quirigua. The shaft was imperfectly prepared for the carving. The human figure of heroic size on one face of the monument is archaic in treatment and comparatively expressionless. The hands rest upon a bundle which extends across the chest from shoulder to shoulder. The sides of the monument are covered with decorative elements, and upon the back, covering almost the entire surface, is an inscription in which the glyph blocks are arranged diagonally. This monument is south of the center of the Great Plaza. The face is beardless and evidently female, as are all the statues in the southern part of the sacred precinct.

Monument No. 2 is the next most archaic. This figure is also beardless and evidently female. The shaft is between sixteen and seventeen feet in length, and, like No. 1, had been thrown down, but is now set up. The figure grasps in the right hand a wand or scepter. This is held across the body in a position which corresponds closely to the position in which the *tiponi* is held by the snake chief in the snake dance of the Hopi Indians. In the left hand is held a small ceremonial shield. On the back of the monument and on each side are well preserved inscriptions.

Monument No. 3 is next to the largest of all and better prepared than No. 1 or No. 2 to receive the sculptures. This is the first of the double figured monuments; that is, with figures of heroic size on two sides. The human figure displayed on the south side is that of a man, with face singularly lacking in strength as compared with the fine strong faces of the next two monuments in the group. The hands rest upon the bundle across the chest which, for reasons explained later, I call the "medicine bundle." The north face is somewhat damaged. The right hand clasps the manikin scepter, while the left is covered with the tasseled shield. The upper third of the monument is devoted to the feathered headdress. On the two narrow sides are inscriptions in an excellent style of carving.

Monument No. 4. Some advance is noticeable in the style of sculpture when we pass to the next of the great shafts, especially in the carving of the face. The high pedestal is noticeably well carved. The shaft has been more carefully prepared for the sculpture. Like the other figures on the monuments at the north end of the plaza, both figures are bearded and represent men. The figure on the south side has been badly defaced, evidently by the falling of a tree, which has shaved off the principal features of the face. The right hand grasps the scepter, upon which is to be seen the manikin figure, the plumes at the top of the wand, and the feathered serpent's head at the lower end. The figure on the north side is in a fine state of preservation and beautifully carved. The scepter is held in the left hand, the right supports the tasseled shield. On the narrower sides are hieroglyphic inscriptions.

Monument No. 5. This is an enormous shaft, the largest at Quirigua and in fact the largest in the whole Maya-land. It is twenty-six feet high above the ground, with an unknown projection below the surface. It is approximately five feet broad and three and a quarter

Monument No. 3   Monument No. 4

Quirigua, Guatemala

Monument No. 5—North Side   Monument No. 5—South Side

Quirigua, Guatemala

feet thick. It leans (or did when we were excavating Quirigua) thirteen feet from the perpendicular, and because of its great weight this inclination raises an interesting question. By the laws of physics the shaft should have fallen, if partly overthrown by an earthquake shock, or when it settled into this position. It was reported by Catherwood, in 1840, to be leaning twelve and one-half feet from the perpendicular. This indicates some settling during the past century, but I am disposed to question the accuracy of the earlier observation and to consider the monument virtually immovable. It could hardly settle at all, either suddenly or gradually without falling. As it marks the limit of size of the great shafts, it is possible that the people found themselves unable to handle stones of such weight and were driven to adopt a different type, in which size would not be so essential. I am inclined to suggest as a possible explanation of the leaning position, that the shaft was never erect; in short, that the builders finding themselves unable to raise it to perpendicular, left it on an incline, cribbed with stone, until it settled into place and remained there. It was noticeable that the upper, exposed side was badly weatherworn, while on the under, protected side the carving was sharp and unworn. Had the monument stood upright for some centuries the two sides would have weathered equally, as with the other near-by shafts.

There is involved in the discussion of this monument a consideration of the methods used for the transportation of stones of such weight by people possessing no beasts of burden and no mechanical contrivances other than the most elementary, such as levers, pulleys, cables, and inclined planes. Stones of such size could be hauled from the quarries several miles away by means of ropes pulled by hundreds of men, with the aid of rollers and inclines. When it came to the problem of erecting the great shafts, we can see that this might have been effected by the simple method of prying and cribbing, and that on being brought to the angle seen in this particular example the limit of power that could be applied may have been reached. In that case, the leaning position records the failure of the most ambitious attempt of the Quirigua people in handling stones of great weight. Years after our work there, the shaft fell. It lay prostrate for some years. In 1934, the Carnegie Institution raised and reset all the fallen monuments at Quirigua. To my regret, the "leaning shaft" was set upright, a position that, as above stated, I think it never occupied. In the process, the monument got out of control, snapped the cables, fell, and was broken in two. It was well repaired and successfully erected. The incident is mentioned here simply to show that trained engineers with modern appliances are not so reliable as were the Old Maya with their primitive tackle.

The human figures sculptured upon the two broad faces of this shaft are the most imposing to be seen at Quirigua. They are of heroic size, both male. Both present the appearance of great strength. They are noticeably different in type. We note particularly the heavy lips of the figure on the south side, and the prominent nose of the northern. Each figure bears the manikin wand in the right hand and a tasseled shield on the left. The two narrow sides of the monument are covered from top to bottom with hieroglyphic inscriptions.

Group II: The Low Pedestal Group

Monuments Nos. 6 and 7. The attainment of such great size in the monuments of the first group, and the probable failure in the erection of the last example, would lead to the devising of a type of shaft easier to handle. Two monuments constitute what I have called the Low Pedestal Group. These are respectively thirteen and fourteen feet high. Both face the south, and are sculptured on the southern face with bearded human figures. The north side, or back, of each shaft is covered with a grotesque figure in low relief. Each figure occupies a peculiar position with one knee flexed, and, instead of being presented full face, is in profile. We surmise that in each case this figure is intended to represent the Death God. The treatment of the two monuments differs noticeably from all others of Quirigua. They are unique in the carving of the inscriptions upon the narrow sides and in the dress and treatment of the human figures on the south faces, as well as in the designs upon the north sides.

Group III: The Zoömorphic Group

Monument No. 8. The first of this group is at the north end of the Great Plaza. It is carved to represent a huge dragonlike monster. From the mouth issues a human head with bearded face and crowned in the same manner as the heads previously noticed upon the sculptured shafts. The hands rest upon the chest. On the arms and legs of the monster, which extend back along the sides and around the rear of the figure, are inscriptions in what is known as the full-figure style.

Monument No. 9. Another monument of the zoömorphic group occupies the north end of the plaza. The identification of this animal has been a matter of varying conjecture. It has been called the giant frog or toad, the great tiger, and the armadillo. It is doubtful if any attempt should be made at identification. In all probability the significance of the monument did not rest upon its resemblance to any particular animal, but rather upon a conception of a mighty power embodied in an animal form of totemic significance, purely mythical in character. Human heads, bearded and crowned, look out of the mouth and from under the the sides.

Monument No. 10. No other monument at Quirigua has suffered so much as this one. The stone has been badly broken away in places and many characters in the inscriptions erased. It is difficult to determine the design, and any suggestions as to its meaning would be purely conjectural.

Monument No. 11. The last of this group is called the Great Turtle. There is very little upon which to base the name. This is undoubtedly the crowning achievement of native American sculpture, so far as now known. In the beauty of its design, the richness of its execution, and the breadth of its conception, it is not approached by any other specimen. The seated figure placed upon the side facing the Ceremonial Plaza is that of a young woman bearing the manikin wand and ceremonial shield and also the crown and elaborate headdress which characterize all the monuments of Quirigua. The entire surface of the block is carved. The principal inscription occupies the end which faces the stairway. The people who executed this work probably reached in it the limit of their powers; accordingly

Monument No. 6   Monument No. 7

Quirigua, Guatemala

Monument No 8, Quirigua, Guatemala

Monument No 9, Quirigua, Guatemala

we now witness a change to a different form of sculpture. (This monument is the subject of critical analysis in a following chapter of this work.)

Group IV: The Group Without Pedestal

Monument No. 12. This is a fallen monument (now erect) bearing a female figure upon one side. It is the first representative of our fourth group, those without pedestal; the figures stand at the level of the ground. The carving is exceptionally deep and the relief affords a pleasing example of the more refined art of the Quirigua sculptors.

Monument No. 13. This is the last example of the greater monuments. It is only eleven and one-half feet high. It has a female figure in relief on each of the two broad sides, with glyph columns on the narrow sides. In dress and ornament the figures conform closely to those of Groups I and III. The faces are full and beautifully rounded; the figures very short. The one facing west, fancifully called "the Queen," bears a manikin wand and tasseled shield. This is the latest monument set up at Quirigua, and while lacking in the cruder strength of earlier shafts and in the richness and beauty of the Great Turtle, yet displays a fineness of work not to be seen in any of the earlier groups.

ii. THE LESSER MONUMENTS

The Lesser Monuments consist of three specimens found near together in the Ceremonial Plaza. The first is double and without inscription. Upon one end is a grotesque female face; upon the other a face and head half animal, half human. The monument was broken in two; it was restored by us and placed upon a cemented base.

Another of the lesser monuments is a disk, called the Great Seal, three and one-third feet in diameter and carved upon one side. A seated figure is surrounded by glyphs in an archaic style. (This monument has been taken to Guatemala City and set in a public park where it looks very homesick.)

The last of the lesser monuments has been called the Alligator's Head. It seems to resemble more nearly the head of a tiger. The inscription extends over the back of the head, which has never been attached to a body.

The excavations have brought to light numerous minor sculptures. These consist of some very archaic disks and several human heads carved from the sandstone of the region. An example of the ceramic ware from Quirigua is shown in a later chapter.

The work of clearing off the tropical jungle occupied nearly two seasons, after which the time was devoted to excavation, exploration, the making of replicas of the monuments, and the study of special problems. An important result was the establishment of the historical stratification at Quirigua. So far as we know, no work in Central America theretofore had revealed any substratum for the Maya culture. In the excavation of one of the smaller temples it was found to have been built almost entirely of a different material from that of the larger ones. Here was very little of the conspicuous red sandstone. The material was a grayish, volcanic rock, containing many black particles. This stone was interspersed with a fine, compact white marble, the best of all building stone yet discovered in the Maya region. A search for the origin of the gray volcanic stone has not been successful. It is the same as that which was used in a small, low temple previously uncovered, and also the same as that of the great monument known as the Dragon, and of the two lesser monuments, the Great Seal and the Tiger Head. These too have inscriptions in a very archaic style which students of Central American chronology have not been able to place in any assured sequence. The building material of this temple, its foundation level, and method of construction, conform to that of a small building on the south side of the quadrangle. These two single-story structures underlie the greater temples of the higher levels which were built of red sandstone. They are more archaic in construction, much smaller, devoid of inscriptions, and lacking in ornamentation. They may be placed in time with the lesser monuments.

We have now the remains of the two distinct culture strata of Quirigua. The upper one at its foundation level, is about one meter below the present surface of the Motagua Valley which has been silting up gradually during the past ages at an approximately uniform rate. The study of several miles of railroad cuts and of the ditches through the plantations of the United Fruit Company, leads to the conclusion that the overflow of the river, which occurs annually, results in a slight building up of the general level. If we are correct in our study of the chronology of the monuments, this gives a "yardstick" to apply to the stratification that has been going on in recent centuries. The conclusion is that from a yard to a meter of silt was deposited in from fifteen hundred to eighteen hundred years. This amount was not only accumulated around the foundations of the larger temples, but also around the bases of the great monuments. Additional confirmation of this is found in the study of hundreds of

197

small sites scattered over the valley, in which only the tops of the mounds appear above the surface. Excavation shows that these were situated upon the flood plain as it existed when Quirigua was flourishing. These sites doubtless represent the homes of the people who were tributary to Quirigua. They are so numerous in the valley and upon the adjacent hills as to indicate a pretty large population within a radius of five miles, taking the great plaza as the center. They contain no important temples, and in only two of them have monuments been found.

Returning now to the two smaller temples that have been laid bare, we find their foundations far below those of the larger ones in which their superstructures are partly embedded. We connect with the buildings the lesser monuments which were built of the gray, volcanic stone. The bases of the lower temples lie from three and one-half to four feet below the most recent culture level. Accordingly, we have established two strata of culture in the operations above described.

Sinking shafts at four different places in various quarters of the plazas, the following facts are disclosed:

First, at the depth of one meter below the surface is a culture stratum containing potsherds, charcoal, and red sandstone building blocks belonging to the later Quirigua. We then pass through approximately a yard of silt containing little or no cultural material.

Second, at a depth of not quite seven feet below the surface, another culture stratum is reached, containing potsherds, charcoal, and building material of gray volcanic stone belonging to the period of the older or second level of temples and the lesser monuments.

Third, going through another stratum of silt to a depth of ten to twelve feet below the present level,

Monument No. 10, Quirigua, Guatemala

Recently Discovered Altar, Quirigua, Guatemala

The Great Seal, Quirigua, Guatemala

The Tiger Head, Quirigua, Guatemala

we come to a third culture stratum which lies at least six feet below the present normal level of the Motagua River. It contains an abundance of potsherds, charcoal, and flaked stone, and has yielded no evidence of building material or inscriptions. A study of the sherds shows something much more archaic than anything found in the upper levels. We, therefore, reach the conclusion that we have found a substratum of the great Maya culture. It is doubtless the undifferentiated "archaic" of the Valley of Mexico and farther north.

Revisiting Quirigua several years after the excavations above described, I am moved to attempt a revaluation of the work in the light of subsequent conditions.

The first decision to be made at Quirigua years ago was on the removal of the dense jungle in which the ruins were buried. No accurate survey could be made, no effective excavation done, no protection of the monuments accomplished, without it. Practically all the damage to the great monuments during more than a millennium of abandonment was occasioned by the impact of the enormous falling trees of the jungle.

The decision was in favor of a complete clearing of the site. It was a formidable task, a new operation in archæological work, and was achieved without a casualty. Not a monument was scratched in the removal of the gigantic growth from the temple precinct, nor in the process of making the replicas of the principal ones. Apprehension was expressed in some quarters at the time that with the clearing a protection was being removed from the monuments; that, out in the open, exposed to the tropical sun and rains, the surfaces would disintegrate and the carvings be obliterated. Wild projects were conceived for protective treatment, painting, oiling, shellacking, etc. It is a satisfaction to note that all such fears were groundless. Comparison with the replicas in the San Diego Museum, which we made from glue molds, thus preserving every hair line and retaining the perfect surface texture of the stone, shows no perceptible deterioration in the years that have passed. On the contrary, freed from the constant soaking of the humid jungle, the surfaces have hardened and become more resistant to disintegration. With the menace of the falling trees removed, not the slightest mishap occurred to the ruins in all this time. Left alone, they are good for another millennium—and more.

Herein is illustrated the importance of perfect reproduction of monuments. Disaster to originals is not thereafter irreparable. Questions like the one raised above are rendered undebatable. The replicas of Quirigua monuments in the museum in San Diego, California, constitute a perfect record. Those in South Kensington, of which there are some duplicates in American museums, do not. They were made by an inferior process in which surface texture of the stone is lost. We reproduced eight of the monuments with glue molds. The remaining eight should be done by the same process.

The Carnegie Institution of Washington has just finished a commendable job of erecting the three monuments that have been prostrate since before Quirigua was first described, and the great monolith known as "the leaning stela" which fell of its own weight some years after we worked there. In the process of the work, two fine additional monuments, which for the present may be called "altars," were uncovered.

One feels a deep sense of gratitude to the officials of the United Fruit Company. The broad policy of the late president, Minor C. Keith, and superintendent,

Victor M. Cutter, in liberally supporting the original work, has been perpetuated by the subsequent management. They have preserved what we accomplished with great fidelity. The clearing made has not been allowed to become overgrown, as it would in a short time without attention. The margin of magnificent jungle that we left surrounding the cleared plazas has been kept intact. The site is made reasonably accessible and travelers are always assisted in visiting the ruins.

In reviewing briefly this early work at Quirigua, certain items stand out rather clearly:

1. The rescue of the monuments from the jungle and their preservation from further damage.

2. The perfect duplication of the monuments and their preservation in the form of casts in the San Diego Museum.

3. The numerous studies, reports and published articles on the ruins, all of which are assembled for republication in a single volume on Quirigua.

4. The identification of an archaic or first culture stratum underlying Quirigua, to which corresponding strata have since been discovered in the valleys of Guatemala City and Mexico City, in Chaco Canyon, New Mexico, and in various lesser sites of Middle and Northern America.

5. The stimulus given to Middle American research, leading to renewed activity in many directions.

6. Not the least, probably the greatest, of all those early Quirigua activities is liable to be overlooked. The young men who were attached to the expeditions from year to year, in the early stages of their careers, have since done distinguished work and attained to eminence. They are today leaders in American research. Quirigua served as an effective training school for archæologists.

5. *The Highland Ruins of Guatemala*

There is a convincing unity running through the pattern of all the sedentary cultures of ancient America. In the American Southwest, the débris of ancient life consists of what was left behind by the cliff- and mesa-dwellers, with a residuum of population that outlived the great exodus and continues to the present day, now called the Pueblo Indians. In the Mexican highlands, Yucatan, and the lowlands of Guatemala, Toltec, Aztec, Zapotec, Maya, and lesser breeds ran their allotted courses, left the wreckage of their culture, described in these pages, and after generations of disintegration survive in the peoples of modern Mexico. So, in the highlands of Guatemala, there was early development of virile clans, Quiché, Maya, Cakchiquel, Zutuhil, builders of substantial towns, of which only ruins now exist, victims of a merciless conquest, the survivors of which we see in the gentle, inarticulate communities of modern Guatemala, constituting a large part of the three million population of that Central American republic. Underlying the débris of all these culture areas is the archaic stratum, bringing scanty, elusive evidences of the first people to disperse over the American continent, a basic population, mostly undifferentiated in culture, but furnishing the groundwork for what America was to bring forth.

No other part of the American continent could have been more inviting to settlement by ancient migrating clans than the highlands of Guatemala. No other could so firmly hold its population, once established in its valleys and mountains which, from the scenic standpoint, justify the name, "the American Switzerland,"— a tropical Switzerland, however, for in climate, flora, and fauna, it is anything but Alpine.

The region to be described here is mainly the great cordillera. There is the narrow Pacific coast plain (*tierra caliente*), twenty to forty miles wide, extending back to the mountain base; then the subtropical, rapidly rising, western slope and tableland (*tierra templada*), up to six thousand feet altitude. Above this to ten thousand feet are the high plateaus and mountain slopes and valleys (*tierra fria*), broken by deep *barrancas,* wooded to the mountaintops with sylvan growth that gave to the land its Aztec name, Guatemalan (place of great forests). The distance between palm and pine can be covered in a few hours, even on horseback, the ideal way to see any country. In the lower zone is the dense tropical vegetation, precious woods, palms, bananas; in the middle zone, corn, sugar cane, coffee, rice, and many subtropical fruits; in the high valleys and plateaus and on the mountain slopes, corn, wheat, potatoes, and many of the vegetables, with fruits of the temperate zone.

A land more adequately endowed by nature would be hard to find, and it should be especially noted that these natural resources of the highlands were available to man in the primitive stages of culture. Vast resources of the lowland tropics have been made available only through the expensive equipment and operations of modern civilization.

The conditions for subsistence in the highlands were, and are today, singularly dependable. Failure of food crops over a large area was practically unknown, failure of water supply from the splendid mountain rivers and lakes, inconceivable. The natural catastrophes, floods, earthquakes, volcanic eruptions, were all confined to narrow limits—inflicting only local inconvenience, which could be met by supplies from not distant localities.

These facts, together with the remarkable healthfulness of the country, account for many things in the archæological history of Central America. In the American Southwest, sudden failure of water, always imminent, could depopulate the country in a week. In the lowlands of the Caribbean and Mexican gulf coasts, embracing practically all of Yucatan and the Guatemala Peten region, with the jungle Valleys of the Usamacinta and Motagua, forces adverse to man were prevalent and widespread. Hurricanes, floods (in Yucatan, also droughts), epidemics, swarms of tropical insects, conflicting breeds of people (Maya, Toltec, Aztec), all these made for instability, even extermination.

The ancient peoples of Guatemala were ideally situated. While they had their internal troubles and some local disasters, their habitat was comparatively an earthly paradise. Mountain fastnesses protected them from invasion. If subsistence was never superabundant, it was dependable. The reputed exuberance of the low countries not far away might entice the more restless, and might lead to a rapid efflorescence of culture there during favored periods. It might also result in a return drift to the old homeland by a defeated people, when the years of disaster came to the lowlands.

This is probably exactly what happened in Maya-Quiché land. Early population movements to the south, from New Mexico to Peru, appear always to have followed the high country, found there their greatest security, and there undergone their most stable culture evolution. In the Guatemalan highlands one sees today, ancient American culture in its least modified state. Industries proceed as in the ages past. Subsistence is simple, dependable, satisfying, as of yore. Arts are practiced in the ancient ways and with all the ancient skill and pride in perfection of what the hand creates. The fabrics of ancient Peru are not more exquisite in design, color, and execution than those of the Guatemala Indians of today, while those of the modern Peruvian and Mexican Indians have fallen far behind.

Religious ceremonies go on, veneration of the ancient deities, pilgrimages to the old shrines, pagan reverently blended with Christian. All this may be seen today, bringing conviction that something of the old contentment still exists here, at least a partial immunity from the unrest that modern civilization, in the name of progress, breeds.

The conclusion has been forced upon me, in thirty years of personal observation in Middle America, that the primeval seat of Maya culture was in the highlands of Guatemala; that it naturally flowed out under the urge of great expectations to the prolific lowland regions; that it experienced there, in a favored epoch, the exuberant growth that has often come to a transplanted culture; that with the continual disasters, met with in the newer habitat, there came the sense of defeat, the degeneration that results from a long struggle against relentless misfortune, and then the inevitable drift back into the upland regions, where life might be normally harder, but free from the losing fight against appalling disasters, such as we know afflicted the later Maya peoples of Yucatan. My advice to prospective field workers in Central America, for years past, has been to go into the most remote districts and communities of the Guatemalan highlands for remains of the oldest Maya culture, for survivals of the old rituals, for clues that may lead to the unraveling of the ancient symbolism, even of the foremost Maya mystery, the hieroglyphic writing. In other

words, go to mountainous Guatemala for the origin of
Maya culture and for survivals brought back from its
centuries of spectacular efflorescence and period of
abrupt decline in the Caribbean and Yucatecan low
countries. High Guatemala is pre-eminently Maya-
Quiché land. The regions that figure more prominently
in Maya archæological history are its abandoned out-
posts. The headwaters of the great rivers, Usamacinta
and Motagua, in the valleys of which we find the principal western Maya and southern Maya ruins, and from
which the central and Yucatecan group may have derived, proceed from the heart of the old Maya-Quiché
country, natural channels for the flow of migrating
clans to new destinations; equally natural roads by
which to retreat to their ancestral homes and kindred.

Without introducing the technicalities of linguistic
study, not permissable in this work, it may be said that
the principal tribes of high Guatemala,now, as in times
past, known as Maya, Quiché, Cakchiquel, Zutuhil, are
of one original breed which may be called the Maya-
Quiché. Among these there are no greater variations
of culture than among the Pueblos of New Mexico.
Quiché and Cakchiquel are most in evidence in the
history of the Conquest. The archæological remains of
these two groups are found in the ruins of their so-
called capitals, Utatlan and Iximche.

Utatlan has been vividly described by numerous
writers. While its wealth and splendor are vastly
exaggerated, as usual in these early chronicles, recent
exploration (1934) discloses the fact that in the main
the early accounts as to situation and plan are reliable.
That it was a site of great antiquity cannot be doubted.
It was built upon a high platform, not far from the
present town of Santa Cruz Quiché. It was surrounded
by deep *barrancas* and had only two points of entrance,

one by way of stone steps up a nearly vertical cliff, and the other by a narrow causeway which could be easily removed, across the gorge. A four-storied watch-tower and a pyramidal fortress, one hundred and twenty feet high, guarded the entrances.

Some have considered Utatlan in the class with Mexico's Tenochtitlan and Peru's Cuzco. There was the usual central structure, called by the Spaniards, of course, the "Palace," built of dimensioned stone in mosaic style. The historian, Torquemada, states that it had a frontage of three hundred and seventy-six paces, over one thousand one hundred feet, with a depth of seven hundred and twenty-eight paces, possibly two thousand two hundred feet. The pictures of magnificent quarters for kings, queens, and concubines, with baths and gardens and lakes, may be rejected. But there was certainly one great central mass of buildings for ceremonial and defensive use. My own conclusion is that Utatlan was an exceptionally strong, almost impregnable fortress. This is borne out by a study of the existing mounds that constitute the ruins of the once great Quiché "capital." It is one of the most inviting prospects for excavation in all Middle America.

Iximche, the Cakchiquel "capital," was built upon a similar plateau, near the present town of Tecpan. It also occupied a high, level plain, surrounded by *barrancas* of five to six hundred feet deep, giving to the place a wellnigh impregnable situation. It is alleged that it could be entered only by way of a narrow causeway, which was closed by two stone gates. The plateau was two miles by three miles in extent. Its central feature was a building some three hundred feet square, of dressed stone, in front of which was a plaza surrounded by "palaces." The place was laid out with the points of the compass and, from the descriptions that

have come down, must have been guarded by breast-
works and towers. Iximche, like Utatlan, was no doubt
a strong fortress, built for ceremonial use as well.
Almost nothing now remains visible of this once great
Cakchiquel establishment. The story of the overthrow
of these two strongholds, by Pedro Alvarado and his
indomitable little army, belongs to a later chapter.
Eyewitness information comes down to us from the
letters of Alvarado to his chief, Cortéz.

A priceless literary monument of the Maya-Quiché
people is the *Popul Vuh,* the Sacred Book, the mythological account of the origin and migrations of the
ancient people. The original manuscript, written doubtless by a native Quiché priest who had learned to use
the Spanish script after the Conquest, was found by the
priest, Father Francisco Ximenez, in the Indian village of Chichicastenango. He copied and translated it
into Spanish but never published his translation. His
manuscript was found in 1855, in the library of the
University of San Marcos in Guatemala City, by
Scherzer. The Spanish text was published in Vienna
in 1856. Brasseur de Bourbourg made a translation
into French which was published in Paris in 1861. This
remarkable document will come in for some further discussion in the later chapter of this work dealing with
the intellectual and spiritual life of Middle America.

Another important native work was the *Annals of
the Cakchiquels,* the manuscript of which was obtained
by Brasseur de Bourbourg at the Franciscan Xahila.
It is a migration legend of the period preceding the
Conquest by two or three centuries, and is a valuable
source of information on the two great Central American peoples, Quiché and Cakchiquel. It was translated
and published by Brinton in Philadelphia in 1885.

II. The Archaic Stratum

In all the great centers of sedentary culture of pre-Spanish America, the Pueblo Southwest, Mexico, Central America, and Peru, we have two clear periods of archæological history to deal with, an ancient and a recent, the latter ending with the European conquest. It began at an indefinite time which marks the decline of the ancient, which was invariably the higher, finer culture, and the rise of a stronger, cruder, more materialistic people. Equally certain is it that in each of the larger culture areas there are remains of an older, more primitive, undifferentiated population. This lowest stratum of remains in the Valley of Mexico connotes an old, old occupation which antedates the Toltec by some centuries, and which, in all probability, eventually merged into the latter. It is seen to best advantage near Coyoacan, where a geologically recent flow of lava produced what is known as the *pedregal*. It varies in depth from ten to thirty feet, and presents the usual aspect of not the heaviest of basaltic flows, but a somewhat porous stratum full of vast crevices which make it difficult and dangerous crossing for man and beast. In places it is of the nature of coarse breccia; again, there may be seen areas as solid as the basaltic river that overwhelmed Herculaneum. The age of these volcanic deposits has been a subject of wide diversity of opinion among geologists.

Professor Byron Cummings, of the University of Arizona, excavated near Tlalpam, southwest of the city of Mexico, a conical mound of large size, known as Cuicuilco. My own impression was, on studying Professor Cummings' excavations, that Cuicuilco be-

longed to the archaic stratum. As Professor Cummings
is the authority on this site, I quote here, with his permission, part of what he has to say about it in his
report published by the University of Arizona.

"The oldest of the shrines of primitive America
so far uncovered is Cuicuilco, a great truncated
cone situated near Tlalpam, in the Federal District
of Mexico, about 12 miles south of Mexico City.
From the rim of the mountains that form the southern boundary of the Valley of Mexico, and separate
it from the Valley of Cuernavaca in the state of
Morelos, rises Ajusco which pushes its peaks
12,664 feet into the blue of heaven. From its older
craters terrific eruptions shot out rock and pumice
and ashes that from time to time covered the surrounding hills and plain with shroud upon shroud
of yellow, gray and black. A little to the north
of Ajusco rose the hills of Zacayuca and Zacatepec.
To the north and east of Zacatepec, on the slope
that bore away from these hills to the northeast,
rose a massive temple—the great shrine of the
people who then inhabited the plains and the hills
of this region.

"Like primitive homes and shrines throughout
the world, it was circular and reared in the form
of a truncated cone. It measured some 369 feet
in diameter, and its top platform was 60 feet above
the base. The outer wall slopes inward from the
base at an average angle of 45 degrees, and is
formed by placing large and rather long chunks of
lava at right angles to the surface and bedding
their inner ends in smaller chunks of lava. No
chipped or hewn stone and no mortar of any kind
are found in these walls. They are of crude cyclopean masonry and give no indication of having been
worked except possibly some of them may have
been broken by stone mauls; but so far no stone
mauls or hammers of any size have been found on

the level of the base of the structure. Behind this surface wall were thrown irregular chunks of lava such as the builders evidently were able to gather from the plain and slopes round about. At the top, this stone work was leveled into a parapet 26 feet wide that formed the outer rim of the platform. On the inner side of this parapet the stone work dropped $2\frac{1}{2}$ feet in a perpendicular wall and then continued inward toward the center about 50 feet more. The remaining central space was filled with clay and sand that had been covered with pebbles and fragments of lava to a depth of 8 to 12 inches. The crevices in the surface of the stone were filled with smaller stones and pebbles and all covered over with dark clay that had been trodden and packed down to form a hard, smooth pavement 6 to 8 inches thick. In the center of this pavement rose a platform of hard packed clay, $12\frac{1}{2}$ inches high, with sloping sides and rounded corners, that probably served as an altar for offerings. It stands 35° north of true east. The altar and surrounding pavement were painted red.

"From the eastern side extended two massive walls similar to and at right angles to the surface wall of the temple. These walls stretched out onto the plain, 2° north of east, and were backed with a filling of rock some 28 feet thick behind the northern wall and 16 feet behind the southern, while the center of 42 feet was filled in with clay, thus forming an inclined approach 86 feet wide that reached from the level of the base up to the bottom of a low incline that led on up to the encircling terrace and thence to the central platform. This low incline was 33 feet wide and made of large boulders placed so that they made it easy to step from one to the other in the ascent to the platform above. This is the only approach to a staircase found in the structure, and plainly demonstrates that the builders of Cuicuilco had not yet learned to construct steps with anything that gave a regular horizontal tread and a vertical lift. The eastern approach was evidently the original means of mounting to the first platform, as it ended at the bottom of the boulder incline which led only to the top of the earliest platform, while the western approach was an ascending roadway that ended on a level with the latest platform that had been in use. This western grand calzada, 45 feet wide, extended down the western slope slightly south of direct west and out onto the plain some 150 feet from the base of the temple.

"Generation succeeded generation. This old temple cone lifted its hoary head toward the eternal blue and tried to raise the children of its builders nearer heaven and nearer the true understanding of Nature's phenomena. The Fire God often interfered in those days to disturb the equilibrium of the Valley of Mexico; and Cuicuilco seems to have received its share of shocks and baptismal fire. Cracks were made in and many huge boulders dislodged from the edge of the terrace and the outer wall. Later some powerful chief undertook to repair the damage done and appease the wrath of the gods—by enlarging the temple. Another wall was built 10 feet thick at the base and 6 feet thick at the top outside of the former structure. The old wall was repaired and carried higher, the outer stone parapet was raised, and the central portion filled to a depth of $4\frac{1}{2}$ feet. Over this was laid a new pavement of clay and in the center, directly over the old altar, was raised another of hard packed clay painted red. No one knows how many generations of ancient men danced and sang upon this platform, and laid their offerings of fruits and flowers upon this bright red altar. No one, perhaps, will ever be able to tell why these in turn were covered with $3\frac{1}{2}$ feet of yellow clay, the parapet raised still higher, and the whole temple enlarged again by a second encasing wall that increased its diameter on an average a little more than 12 feet, making the total diameter of the enlarged structure 387 feet. Thus there are really three great truncated cones, of which the outer and larger two are like great flaring circular boxes that telescope down over the inner and original structure, preserving and protecting it from further destruction. . . .

"Time passed on. Men tilled the plains below and terraced the hillsides that the ever increasing population might grow and be happy. Women gathered the rushes from the swamps and plaited mats that served for beds and for burden baskets. They sought out the fine soft clays and moulded plates, bowls, cups and ollas in which to cook and serve their food. The abundant remains of human artifacts uncovered at the level of the base of the great temple, as well as the material and form of the edifice itself, are ample evidence of a large, vigorous and aggressive population.

"Periods of flood must have alternated with volcanic eruptions. Torrential rains swept the volcanic dust and pumice down from the hills and flooded the valleys. The waters rose and swept around Cuicuilco, filling its walls with fine sediment to a depth of six feet. On the north side of both the eastern and western approaches the causeways have been widened by the addition on the western side of three walls, respectively 12, 14 and 6 feet in thickness, and on the eastern side by two walls each $6\frac{1}{2}$ feet thick. It would seem that the great force of inundations and floods had swept in from the northern side and necessitated the reenforcing of these projecting northern walls to prevent the undermining of their bases and the sweeping away of the great approaches. Each of these walls was faced with boulders in a manner similar to that of walls of the edifice and filled behind with a mass of lava without any earth packing. Thus one realizes why this structure has withstood the inroads of time for so many centuries. It is a veritable mass of rock so placed that the force of gravity holds each boulder in place and the great structure has maintained its identity against the forces of destruction.

"When the waters subsided, and the people again occupied this part of the valley and wished to offer their prayers from the top of Cuicuilco, they found the lofty platform covered with a mass of volcanic ash and pumice. Around the eroded slopes of this low hill they built a low cyclopean wall of lava chunks and river boulders and filled in the space behind by levelling off the top of the mound of volcanic soil that had accumulated. The space between this encircling wall and the outer edge of the old platform was thus turned into a terrace and a raised dirt platform occupied all of the central portion. Trenches cut across the top of the mound at right angles to each other disclosed the clay pavement of the parapet and the central area and a strangely fashioned rock altar in the center.

"Upon a clay pavement rests a pavement made of large chunks of lava and water-worn boulders bedded in clayey soil. This pavement is circular in form and averages 68 feet in diameter. This was built around and upon two clay altars that stood end to end and extended east and west. They were made of hard-packed clay 10 inches high. Above these clay altars was built an altar of river boulders and clay 22 feet long and 9 feet wide. This consists of two parts, an eastern portion 3½ feet high, and a western portion 1 foot high. These surround and overlie the two clay altars.

"How many generations of men chanted their prayers about these altars one can only conjecture. But time evidently continued to produce great changes and the altars of Cuicuilco seem to have been abandoned and forgotten. Five feet of yellow clay and sand covered the old rock pavement and altar before the temple seems to have been used again. A floor of hard-packed earth marks the dancing place of this last and highest level; but no altar, either of rock or clay, marks the spot that had served for so many centuries as the sacred center of this holy temple. But instead, toward the northwestern rim of this last lofty platform, rose a cone of rock and earth some 12 feet in height and 50 feet in diameter from whose crest must have risen a wooden structure that either formed or covered an altar. All that was left to tell the story were the large post holes in which timbers had been set to support some platform, roof or canopy.

"Over this clay pavement and rock cone was spread a stratum averaging 12 inches thick of pumice, volcanic pebbles, and sand. Above this lies from 3 to 5 inches of black sand and ashes, which undoubtedly represents the surface level when Xitli sent out its showers of dust and ashes preceding the eruptions that produced the lava flows of the Pedregal. Since then decaying vegetation and windblown sand have produced a stratum that varies from 2 to 2½ feet in thickness. This forms the surface soil in which are growing great pepper trees and hoary cacti that must have looked down benignly upon passing humanity for a century or more.

"Thus the surface covering and this central filling tell us a story that cannot be misunderstood. These six pavements, with their six corresponding shrines, all lying at different levels below the carbonized stratum that indicates the time of the eruption of Xitli and the coming of the Pedregal, speak in a language that is clear and convincing. The lowest pavement lies more than 18 feet below the surface. Eighteen feet of gradual fill on top and

12 to 20 feet of debris overlying the base, all accumulated probably before the Christian era, and the composite condition of the structure itself bespeaks a lapse of time that pushes its builders back into the dim beginnings of things in the Valley of Mexico.

"These people of Cuicuilco were undoubtedly leaders in the archaic age in Mexico. They built this great temple, the only one of the period yet uncovered, but other mounds in that vicinity probably conceal structures reared by their hands. They developed the ceramic art and produced forms of artistic merit and attempted to mold the human form in clay. The presence of broken pottery and clay figurines close to the base level of the temple places the people in the neolithic stage of culture; but the absence of well-shaped and polished stone implements is puzzling. Rude, unworked hammer stones and polishers selected from water-worn pebbles and rudely chipped obsidian knives and scrapers formed their chief implements. Their skill in pottery contradicts their seeming lack of skill in working stone. Perhaps, however, we have not yet found the best of their stone implements and the ruins of their homes. These people seem to have attained skill in working in clay before they had developed good methods of successfully chipping and polishing stone into useful utensils.

"The ruins of the Valley of Mexico show three extensive periods of culture: (1), the oldest, called archaic, (2), the most highly developed that is best classed as Toltec, and (3), the later that held sway at the time of the Spanish conquest, known as Aztec. The archaic or the earliest period covers the time preceding the last great lava flow—the Pedregal—and is believed to antedate the Christian era. At Cuicuilco the excavations beneath the lava, and yet overlying the base of the temple, reveal artifacts of the archaic age, while the surface covering of the top and upper slopes contained articles of Toltec and Aztec workmanship.

"Cuicuilco tells its own story quite clearly. Its crude cyclopean masonry without mortar of any kind, its massive conical form, and its great elevated causeways for approach instead of staircases, all demonstrate that the structure was the work of primitive men, and that its builders hardly knew the rudiments of architecture. Its base lies buried beneath from 15 to 20 feet of accumulated debris, which in turn was covered with three lava flows that have crowded around its slopes and piled up upon each other in rapid succession to the depth of 10 to 20 feet. The old temple had been so completely covered with rock and soil, volcanic ash and pumice in successive strata that the noses of the lava streams as they pushed around the mound and crawled up its slopes were no where able to touch the walls of the ancient structure. Centuries must have elapsed and several eruptions of old Ajusco must have buried its platforms and slopes under successive mantles of ash and pumice before Xitli poured forth its baptisms of fire. Two and a half to 3 feet of surface soil have accumulated above this scorched and blackened stratum that marks the footprints of Xitli's consuming blasts. Careful measurements were taken in several places of this accumulation since the eruption of Xitli, and of the accumulation directly beneath between the pavement surrounding the temple and the blackened stratum just underlying the lava, and the story was always the same. If it has taken 2,000 years for the deposit to form since the eruption of Xitli, then by the same yardstick it took some 6,500 years for the debris beneath the lava to have accumulated, and so Cuicuilco fell into ruins some 8,500 years ago. The late Mrs. Nuttall, a noted Aztec scholar, found that the word Cuicuilco signified a place for singing and dancing. Everything about the structure bears out that interpretation. Here men and women met to pay tribute to the great spirits who, they thought, controlled their lives and their destinies. Here they danced and sang in honor of their gods and for the benefit of their fellow men seemingly through many centuries of time. Cuicuilco stands out as a monument to the religious zeal and to the organized power and perseverance of the earliest inhabitants of the Valley of Mexico. It is a great temple that records devotion to their gods and subservience to the will of great leaders. It shows the beginning of that architecture that developed into the pyramids and altars of Teotihuacan. It certainly gives evidence of being the oldest temple yet uncovered on the American continent. Everything about it so far revealed bears out its great antiquity, and it should serve as a strong incentive to the further investigation of the archaic culture of Mexico."

Doctor Gamio's excavations at Copilco near San Angel, southwest of Mexico City, consisted of tunneling under a hard cap of lava. His work preserves both the skeletal and cultural remains as found *in situ*. Graves, pottery, many other artifacts discovered, show the Archaic people of this valley to have been of considerably higher culture than the cave man of Europe, to have been in fact advanced Neolithic, if we care to transplant that term—which I do not. They practiced agriculture, made pottery, crudely worked stone for domestic and ceremonial purposes. They made tripod pots with hollow legs, and simple cooking and food bowls. They cultivated corn, thus disposing of several myths and theories about the bringing of maize to the Toltecs. They made figurines of stone and clay, the latter in a crude style of modeling, the protruding eyes and mouth reminiscent of the masks worn by the "Mud Heads" of Zuñi, in their ceremony portraying the coming of the first men from the slimy underworld. There are remains of rudimentary dwellings, architecturally as good as what we find in the lowest stratum (pre-Pueblo) in the Southwest.

Archaic man is thus fully established in the Valley of Mexico. Doctor Gamio found a like culture stratum in the high country of Guatemala, near the present capital city. I found it at Quirigua in the Motagua Valley, consisting there of stone chippings, charcoal, and a few potsherds (see report to the International Congress of Americanists, 1912). Plentiful remains of the Archaic stratum have been found in the Panuco Valley, above Vera Cruz, Mexico, and clear across the continent westward to the Pacific coast states; in British Honduras and in South America. In fact, this would seem to have been the most widely disseminated population that ever inhabited the American continent. It probably represents early population movements, in some cases centuries apart, marking the dispersion of man over the western hemisphere. In the vast extent of this distribution, with intervals of who knows how many centuries, it is to be expected that hundreds of specializations in culture will be found. It would be idle to attempt as yet any classification of these variations. I venture to suggest that in the southwestern part of the United States, where there is such a confusion of cultures, at least in the nomenclature of the archæologists, that all pre-Pueblo peoples be lumped under the term Archaic, and then let those whose interests lie in the lower levels of human history work along patiently with "Folsom Man," "Basket Makers," "Pit House People," "Slab House People," etc., until a logical framework is constructed for the classification of the first Americans. My own opinion is that the study of climatic fluctuations will eventually afford some such assistance to the archæologist, as the "tree ring calendar" has done. I see no reason why the nomenclature of the Mexican archæologists should not be fully accepted, and this lowest, ancient population from one end of the continent to the other called the Archaic. We would then have this simple diagrammatic scheme for the archæologic history of the sedentary cultures of America:

AMERICAN SOUTHWEST	MEXICO	CENTRAL AMERICA	PERU
Recent Late Pueblo	*Recent* Late Mexican—Aztec—	*Recent* Late Central American—Maya-Quiché ("New Empire")	*Recent* Late Peruvian—Inca
Ancient Old Pueblo and Cliff-dwelling	*Ancient* Old Mexican—Toltec	*Ancient* Old Central American—Maya-Quiché ("Old Empire")	*Ancient* Old Peruvian—(Quechua, Colla, Chauvin, Megalithic)
Archaic Pre-Pueblo (undifferentiated)	*Archaic* Pre-Mexican (undifferentiated)	*Archaic* Pre-Maya-Quiché (undiffentiated)	*Archaic* Pre-Peruvian (undifferentiated)

I venture to say that the spread in time between "Folsom Man" of northeastern New Mexico, and "Basket Maker Man" of southern Utah, or between the latter and the Rio Grande Pueblo, is no greater than that between "Sub-Pedregal Man" of the Valley of Mexico, and Montezuma; nor than the Archaic man of lowest Quirigua stratum and the sculpture of the great stelæ. It must be understood too that these terms represent culture sequences, with little relation to chronology. The living Hopi of Arizona are a hold-over of the ancient Pueblo and cliff-dwellers, while modern Zuñi was recent Pueblo when first seen by Coronado. So "Archaic Man" of Mexico and Guatemala probably exists today among living bush people of those countries. In the Otomi of Mexico, pre-Toltecan blood may predominate. Old Maya and Late Maya represent stages in archæological history, but overlapped and interpenetrated. In short, to some extent they existed contemporaneously. The great community builders of Chaco Canyon, New Mexico, the cliff-dwellers of Mesa Verde, Colorado, may have been in part absorbed in modern Pueblo or Mexican tribes. Culture cannot be fitted into any exact chronological picture. That is why I do not attach so much importance to studies in chronology as many archæologists do.

So it seems to me that the Archaic people constituted the general, undifferentiated mother-breed from which the American sedentary cultures derived. They were wanderers, but not in a strictly nomadic sense. They settled and to some extent developed, but they pushed on. They were the forelopers of America. It is logical to believe that, as they dispersed, bands would find and settle favored localities; that is to say, places favorable to specialization in certain modes of life, in types of building, in arts and crafts, in religion. No tribe or community could become great at pottery making unless settled in a region of good clay and paints. None could become good basket makers and weavers of fabrics unless grasses, barks, and fiber material were at hand. Metal work in ancient America, confined mainly to gold and copper, necessitiated a convenient source of supply. Lapidary art flourished where jade, turquoise, serpentine, etc., could be found or obtained by trade. The Archaics proper contented themselves with houses of the "jacal" type, or something equally primitive—their offshoots or descendants in favored regions becoming builders of magnificent structures of stone. They shifted rather readily. Their descendants in places adhered to the soil and developed the idea of permanent land tenure. Water gods in the tropics would be totally different from the beneficent rain deities of the arid Southwest. So the great middle stratum of all the areas of sedentary culture that we have described above represents the exuberance, the stimulated life of people out from primitive, the Archaic, under environments that release cultural potentiality, that induce the culture germ to sprout and grow and flourish.

PART FIVE

INTELLECTUAL, ESTHETIC, AND SPIRITUAL ATTAINMENTS

"Where tireless striving stretches its
arms toward perfection"—TAGORE.

PART FIVE

INTELLECTUAL, ESTHETIC, AND
SPIRITUAL ATTAINMENTS

I. Attempts at Knowledge

Like all humanity the ancient Americans made incessant efforts to know their world and to learn how best to live in it. The resulting attainments of hand and mind constitute their culture. Attempting to separate these into component factors, that is, the esthetic (artistic), industrial (mechanical), institutional (social), linguistic (literary), and religious (spiritual), throws interesting light upon the psychology of the Indian and affords a basis for comparative study of the achievements of races. This analysis of culture may be roughly charted as shown in the accompanying diagram. The predominating trend of the Indian mind has been toward the exercise of an esthetic sense by the creation of objects of beauty; the working out of an orderly mode of life, modeled upon what he observed in nature; and the creation of a pantheon of deific powers whereby he arrived at a satisfactory explanation of the forces in the universe about him and of his place therein. He lived in a world of color, of social order patterned after the phenomena of nature that he witnessed—male and female, day and night, cold and heat, light and darkness, summer and winter— a dualism observed and accepted as requiring no investigation. By analogy he reasoned out a spirit world, peopled with beneficent and malevolent beings, to account for what he observed and had to find explanation for. His industrial life remained elementary, non-mechanical. Expression was through color and line, through symbol, ceremony and ritual, rather than by spoken or written language. His type of religion necessitated a priesthood which, in time, became absolute, authoritative. Out of this trend of racial mind—empirical, non-scientific, fatalistic—could evolve a civilization characterized perhaps by high morality, ideal social relations, noted achievements in the imaginative phases of culture, but limited in intellectual accomplishment to the elementary stages—for the most part, static, non-progressive.

Comparing in the diagram the level reached by the native American in each factor of culture, with the corresponding factor in the other races, evaluated in like manner, it is seen that the greatest resemblance is found in the Mongolian; the most striking difference in the industrial or material culture of the European. The analysis will not be discussed further here, but it is suggested that some time might profitably be devoted to the diagram as a graphic illustration in comparative culture history.

In the study of the aboriginal American race, no other fact stands out so prominently as that every phase of culture, before adulteration by the European, took its color from the religious life. The various esthetic activities of the people—temple building and embellishment, sculpture, painting—were the daily manifestations of the religious spirit. So also was the rich mythology, folklore, ritual, drama, that would have afforded a wealth of material for a national literature had the culture of the people proceeded, without interruption, to the level of civilization.

Comparative Culture Chart

EUROPEAN

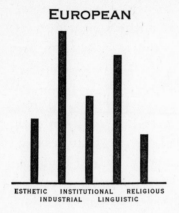

ESTHETIC INSTITUTIONAL RELIGIOUS
INDUSTRIAL LINGUISTIC

AMERICAN
(INDIAN)

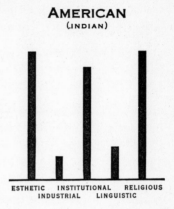

ESTHETIC INSTITUTIONAL RELIGIOUS
INDUSTRIAL LINGUISTIC

AFRICAN
(NEGRO)

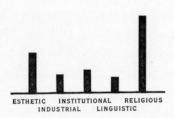

ESTHETIC INSTITUTIONAL RELIGIOUS
INDUSTRIAL LINGUISTIC

ASIATIC
(MONGOLIAN)

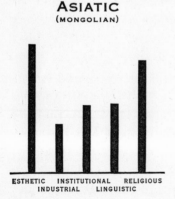

ESTHETIC INSTITUTIONAL RELIGIOUS
INDUSTRIAL LINGUISTIC

ASIATIC
(SEMITIC)

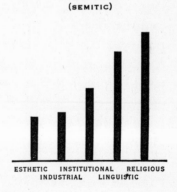

ESTHETIC INSTITUTIONAL RELIGIOUS
INDUSTRIAL LINGUISTIC

The social order too, and the political if they had any, was dominated by the religious hierarchy. No other race developed such a closely integrated culture. In attempting to study any one cultural element—art, religion, society, mythology, drama, language—one finds oneself studying all the others. Even industry was under the shamanistic regime.

The above observations, if valid, will account in a measure for the paucity and character of the purely intellectual attainments. Such knowledge as was obtained by the trial and error method was soon under sacerdotal control. This is illustrated in the most elementary of their industries, that of agriculture, which was, from planting to harvesting, controlled by seasonal ceremonies.

America was rich in food plants, somewhere around forty, now cultivated by us, having been on the New World bill of fare; not all by any means due to conscious development by the Indian, for nature itself went far toward preparing America for human occupation. We wonder how Old World man ever got along without the potato, sweet potato, numerous varieties of beans, calabashes, etc., cocoa, and above all the Indian corn of America. The latter constitutes one of the most stupendous of agricultural resources today, and its development into a food plant is attributed by some anthropologists to the wisdom of the Indians. This is based on the assumption that maize (Indian corn) comes from a wild plant, *teosinte,* somewhat similar to corn, capable of being crossed with it, but incapable of development without the assistance of man. From it the Indian is alleged to have bred the edible cereal that meant so much by way of sustenance to his race, and has come to mean a priceless food supply and billions in money to the white man. Some anthropologists find this theory so satisfactory that they even fix, pretty closely, the place (highlands of Mexico) where *teosinte* was "Bur-banked" into corn, and confidently outline the proce-dure whereby this was brought about. Anyway, an-thropological guesswork about corn is abundant, and out of it has grown a voluminous literature on the sub-ject. But, to the botanist will be the authentic word. Anthropology has a habit of passing authoritatively upon questions that lie outside its domain. It will be a more dependable science when it asks botany, geology, astronomy, climatology, forestry, anatomy, and various other sciences, to do the intensive research and furnish the authentic answers to many phenomena in nature that affect the life of man.

It may not be necessary to assume that corn, as found in the New World at the time of the discovery, could not have been brought to its edible state without the conscious intervention of man. At any rate, another possibility is worthy of consideration. To the late, gifted Americanist, Mrs. Zelia Nuttall, long resident in Mexico City, who had a habit of making anthropol-ogists feel uncomfortable if not actually unsettled about many of their pet theories, we are indebted for a contribution on this subject, published in the *Journal of Heredity*, May, 1930, which is of such importance that it must be, by permission of the editor, here quoted at some length. Mrs. Nuttall says:

"The Chevalier Lorenzo Boturini Benaduci, cel-ebrated for having made the greatest collection of ancient Mexican picture writings and documents ever brought together, went to Mexico in 1735 and spent the eight following years in enthusias-tically investigating its past history, this being, as he writes, 'a subject that was dying out and clamored to be extricated from its tumulus of oblivion.'

"In the preface to his book he relates how, in quest of historical data, he had exposed himself to the inclemencies of the climate and infinite discomforts and traveled long distances, often without finding shelter.

"That he was an enthusiastic lover and observer of nature is proven by his casual remarks: 'In designating the tassels of the ears of maize I shall employ the elegant metaphor "golden locks"; as agriculture has always been a fascinating delight to me.' Chevalier Boturini's contemporaries praised him as a prodigy of learning, and Doctor Borrull, professor of the University of Salamanca, wrote that he had 'sounded and discovered in Boturini a singular talent, utmost powers of penetration, indefatigable industry, cautious judgment and well-balanced critique.' He calls him 'an ornament of all sciences and a stranger to none, being indeed very much at home in natural and moral sciences, etc., and all kinds of erudition, also an expert in European languages.'

"The foregoing tribute to Chevalier Boturini's intellect and capacity for making accurate and careful observations and cautious statements lends great weight to the following which can but be of utmost interest to the botanists who have recently been dealing with the problematic ancestry of cultivated maize.

"Boturini asserts: 'I found, in New Spain, a wild maize that grows amidst the forest or woods, especially those in the hot lands, with a small ear, whose few grains are of a more delicate flavor than the cultivated kind, as though nature had located in them, as a compendium, all its essence.'

"The record, by a scholar of Boturini's standing who was also a true lover of Nature, to whom 'agriculture was a fascinating delight' and who considered his finding of wild maize and the native tradition concerning its cultivation as worthy of special mention in his historical work, deserves respectful consideration. This testimony about its habitat agrees with the native tradition that it grew in woodlands and his statement that its ears were small and had but few grains reveals that the difficulty of shelling them could not have been as great as in the case of cultivated maize.

". . . A belief in the possibility that survivors of 'wild maize' may yet be found and identified by trained botanists is encouraged by the report received by the writer from the explorer, Mr. Oliver LaFarge: 'Mr. Frans Blom was very much interested in the advance information you sent him and showed me the part of your letter about the maize . . . suggesting that I write you about something that came up on our trip which might be of interest to you.

" 'With regard to wild maize: At the finca Chanquejelvé, between Menton and Chacula in Guatemala, at an altitude of 5,000—6,000 feet, we were given what we should have taken to be elote (young ears of corn) still in the milk, save, that in early May the milpas (corn fields) had only just been planted. They were ears about two inches long, or a little longer, looking rather like oat sheaves without the whiskers, and having the unmistakable flavor of corn. They were said to grow wild in that section. In the district and around Jacaltenango, there grows wild a very tall grass which looks just like silage corn run to seed, called, I believe, sal-icim by the Indians, who say that its ears are edible, and also its tassel. This is green during the rainy season.' This account of the kind of plant food which grows wild in Guatemala and has small ears and the 'unmistakable flavor of maize,' justifies the suspicion that this may be identical with the plant Boturini described.

231

It will be for the competent botanists to determine whether this can rightly be described as 'wild maize' or not."

So, concerning the natural history of our priceless American cereal, you may take your choice between giving nature the credit for it, or creating an aboriginal Burbank to wizard an inedible, cobless grass seed into the succulent cereal that has given to humanity (American humanity at least; Europe is still a bit benighted in this respect) the *tortilla* of Mexico, the hominy, succotash and corn pone of the United States. The abundant life exemplified in corn-fed American manhood and womanhood, the saving of the English colonists from starvation, the raising of wild, western valley and plains land to five hundred dollars an acre, incidentally through juxtaposition of corn, hog, and steer, creating such an oversupply of food as to give economic indigestion and political panic to a great nation, are mighty results that have followed the evolution of that insignificant plant that came to be called Indian corn.

Now, an Indian friend, with whom I have discussed the two theories above set forth, tells me that both are wrong, and recommends that I give the Indian version of it, since the "red" man had a longer and greater interest in it than anyone else. This I have set out to do, but find that the Indians are, like the white brethren, at variance on the subject. An Aztec version is put down by Mrs. Nuttall in the article above quoted. She says:

"The oldest is the ancient Mexican legend of the origin of maize which was recorded in the Aztec language written with Spanish characters, by an anonymous writer in 1583, or 64 years after the Conquest.

"According to this, after the gods had created

men, the latter asked, 'what shall we eat, oh gods?
We are all searching for food.' Whereupon, immediately, the ant went to fetch the grains of
shelled maize from the interior of its 'hill of provisions.' One of the gods met the ant and asked
'to what place did you go to fetch these? Tell me.'
But the ant would not tell. The god worked hard
questioning the ant who finally told him that he
had brought the shelled grains of maize from a
place close by. Then the god transformed himself
into a black ant and was led to the 'hill of provisions' and entered it, and the god and the ant
overcame and made the red ant prisoner and
brought him to terms in order to increase the
amount of maize, which they then took to the home
of the gods, who immediately ate it. They then
said, 'What shall we do with the hill of provisions?'
One of the gods, trying to lift and carry it, tied
it with cords but could not raise it. Then a god-
dess began to draw lots with grains of maize and
then all the rain-gods heaped earth. . . . As soon
as the sun-god shelled the maize, beating it, the
rain-gods snatched the grains from him . . . they
also snatched all food plants or provisions."

The version of Frank Hamilton Cushing, from the
Zuñi creation myths, may be even more convincing.
In the words of the Flute Priest, Paiyatuma:

"Lo! ye children of men and the Mother,
Ye Brothers of Seed,
Elder, younger,
Behold the *seed plants of all seeds!*
The grass-seeds ye planted, in secret,
Were seen of the stars and the regions,
Are shown in the forms of these tassels!
The plumes that ye planted beside them
Were felt in the far away spaces,
Are shown in the forms of their leaf-blades!

But the seed that we see growing from them
Is the gift of my seven bright maidens,
The stars of the house of my children!
Look well, that ye cherish their persons,
Nor change ye the gift of their being,—
As fertile of flesh for all men
To the bearing of children for men,—
Lest ye lose them, to seek them in vain!
Be ye brothers ye people, and people;
Be ye happy ye Priests of the Corn!
Lo! the seed of all seed-plants is born!"

So, the corn myths, corn symbols, corn ritual, of the American Indians constitute an interesting contribution to the history and significance of corn in ancient America. As between the poetic and the scientific points of view, each reader may choose for himself.

Among the intellectual achievements of the Middle American peoples, the calendar and the hieroglyphic writings have been given high place. In the excellent *History of the Maya,* by Thomas Gann and Eric Thompson, the latter makes a statement that accurately reflects the estimate placed by most of the specialists on the Maya calendar: "The Maya calendar can rightly be described as one of the greatest, indeed one may say the greatest, achievements, in the line of pure, reasoned science, ever achieved by a people on the same cultural horizon as the Mayas. It is the concrete result of hundreds of years of patient and acute observations by scientists handicapped by the absence of any scientific instruments or the mundane rewards too frequently the aim of modern investigators."

I cannot concur in this high estimate though it is conservative as compared with that of some of the enthusiasts. Thompson further, and accurately, says: "The calendar was primarily devised to show the times when the different tasks connected with the agricultural year were due to be commenced. It was primarily a farmers' almanac." I submit that there is no need to assume that these observations were made by scientists, or that any scientific instruments would have been required. The kind of knowledge easiest to obtain is that which may be arrived at by measurement. All peoples have taken their first steps in the derivation of exact knowledge by measuring time, distance, weight, etc. This history of the formulation of the Central American calendar will be found substantially the same for all who accomplished that feat—Toltec, Aztec, Zapotec, Maya, Quiché, Cakchiquel. I cannot concede that any individual—Quetzalcoatl, Kukulcan, culture hero, god, man, or superman—invented or discovered the calendar, no more than that agriculture was ever "discovered" or "invented" by any one person. I see in it merely a culture process, extending over the ages during which the agricultural Indians of America, observers of seasonal phenomena affecting their crops, as our own forebears were, trying to derive dependable knowledge to use from year to year, gradually reduced their observations to a pictorial scheme or diagram.

The earliest stages of this process survive among the Pueblo Indians of the American Southwest. Their elaborate system of calendar observations was never reduced to diagrammatic form, though a few of their elementary symbols relate to such. Their observations, tending always toward a divinatory character, were embodied in their seasonal ceremonies. Drama dances accompanied the turning on of the water in the irrigation ditches in the spring, the preparation for planting of the seed, germination and growth ceremonies, rain invocation, maturation and protective rituals, harvesting and thanksgiving celebrations, occupying the entire agricultural season, from early spring to late fall. These were followed by a shorter cycle of hunting or winter ceremonies, all constituting an ever recurring round of events to get and keep the food quest on an assured basis. Here again is seen the integration of cultural factors, the industrial and religious, with the latter dominant, illustrating further the Indian type of mind—empirical, imaginative, esthetic, spiritual, non-scientific. I have known Indians to become artists, philosophers, priests, poets, statesmen, but never one who readily took to the natural sciences such as botany, zoölogy, geology, physics, chemistry.

The ancient Pueblos attained to fully as high a culture as the Toltecs, Aztecs, or Maya. The difference was in modes of expression. They had just as much of a calendar as the Middle Americans had, but they never diagrammed it. They dramatized and acted it. The Toltecs, Aztecs, and Zapotecs got it formulated in a simple way. The Maya carried it further, as they did picture writing. The Pueblos depended mainly upon symbols; the Aztecs and their forebears upon pictures, sometimes in rebus arrangement, and elementary symbolism; the Maya upon pictures and highly conventionalized symbols, but never attaining to our phonetics—a conventionalized symbol standing for a sound. The native American race brought forth no alphabet.

All the calendar-making people of Mexico and Central America recognized a "sacred year" of two hundred and sixty days, divided into thirteen months of twenty days each. We have no evidence that they used any smaller unit of time than the day. This "sacred year" of two hundred and sixty days was the foundation of

the calendar. Its derivation is a matter of wide dis-
agreement among Americanists. Father Sahagun, foremost sixteenth-century authority on the Aztecs, says
flatly: "Those who say that the Indians were natural
philosophers are sadly mistaken, for this count of two
hundred and sixty days did not occur to them by any
means of a natural law, but is an invention of the
Devil." Doctor Spinden, eminent twentieth-century authority on American chronology, says: "This does not
correspond to any natural period and is an invention
pure and simple." As to individual responsibility, he
is not so specific as Father Sahagun.

Madam Nuttall calls attention to the simple fact of
nature that at every point between the Tropics of
Cancer and Capricorn there are two days in the year
when the sun is exactly overhead, and at that moment
no object casts a shadow. She brings much documentary proof to show that this, to the ancients, was the moment when the beneficent sun-god descended to earth,
bringing his supreme blessing upon the crops essential
to the welfare of the people. This phenomenon and
the general belief concerning it is believed to explain
the many stelæ and similar objects found in the sacred
precincts of Mexico and Central America. The "descent of the sun-god," the "seat of the sun-god," are
archaic expressions pertaining to these phenomena.
Mrs. Nuttall points out that at latitude fourteen degrees
forty-two minutes north, there is a zone (which, by
the way, crosses the Old Maya area) in which the sun,
in the month of August, passes the zenith on its way
south, and in the month of April, exactly two hundred
and sixty days later, on its way north, again passes the
zenith; that at this latter date the rainy season begins,
filling out the solar year with a period of one hundred

and five days of vast consequence to the production of the crops. She considers this incontestable proof that upon the dense populations of these fertile regions a period of two hundred and sixty days was imposed by nature, and that it was through observation of this phenomenon that the two-hundred-and-sixty-day calendar, or *tonalamatl,* was derived. It seems reasonable. If valid, it will not only afford a basis for the formulation of the Central American calendar, but will give a starting point for the interpretation of the whole chronological system of the Aztecs and Maya. It will likewise involve a reinterpretation of much of the symbolism of that country. It certainly renders unnecessary the creation of any mathematical or astronomical genius to devise the calendar system. It becomes a simple cultural process, brought to maturity through the observations of many generations, finally reduced to diagrammatic form.

The solar year of three hundred and sixty-five days has been a matter of simple, elementary observation common to agricultural people throughout the world. It naturally co-ordinated with the two-hundred-and-sixty-day sacred year, with one hundred and five additional days to complete the annual round. Its twenty-day months would, in the solar year, number eighteen, and it would require no phenomenal intelligence to discover that a five-day period was necessary to fill out the year. This period to a superstitious people would be likely to have some sinister significance and was, in fact, regarded as an extremely unlucky time.

The Aztec "calendar stone" is the best example in existence of the Aztec calendrical diagram. The many interpretations of this famous specimen, found on the site of the great *teocalli* in Mexico City, and now to be seen in the National Museum of Mexico, will not be discussed here. It is said to have had a counterpart which was lost in transportation from the quarries, on the Coyoacan side of the lake, to the temple precinct of Tenochtitlan.

As the calendar and the symbolism connected therewith grew out of the agricultural life with all its shamanistic relations, so the hieroglyphic system of writing was inseparable from the calendrical system. The inscriptions are found on countless stone monuments and in picture manuscripts, a few of which survived the Conquest and have been published by numerous writers, in spite of the thoroughgoing effort to destroy them utterly. The historian, Torquemada, states that sixteen thousand of these manuscripts were recovered from five villages in the Aztec country and burned. However, the Aztec picture writing is well preserved. Their characters, partly symbolic, highly pictorial, relating to the calendar and to deities, were also extended to apply to a large number of geographical names such as are shown in the facsimile of the Boturini codex page, practically all of which are now translated and published. To Antonio Peñafiel and Cecilio Robelo, we are indebted for the most adequate studies of the Aztec picture writings.

Maya hieroglyphic writing advanced beyond the stage achieved by the Aztecs. The characters are ideographic, non-alphabetic, to some extent syllabic, and contain elementary phonetic elements. The signs used are highly conventionalized, it being impossible in many cases to determine their origin. Every glyph has its own independent meaning. Mainly nouns were written— no verbs.

A quarter of a century ago, when I was paying some

attention to the study of Maya hieroglyphic writing, and before deciding to leave it to minds more eager than mine in that line of thought, I repeatedly expressed the conviction that no Maya "Rosetta Stone" or "Rock of Behistun" existed; that no "key" would ever be found, and that when the Maya inscriptions became understood they would contribute little or nothing to our knowledge of the ancient history of America, other than in a few aspects of cultural evolution. That opinion has been sustained. As the study progresses the hopes of Maya students are waning. The expectation that something would happen, comparable to the reading of Egyptian hieroglyphics by Champollion, or the mastery of the Babylonian cuneiform writings by Rawlinson, with corresponding revelation of historic events, have not been realized.

The meaning of about one-half of the Maya characters is now known. All, including the simple, cumbersome, numerical system, relate to the calendar, to gods, and ceremonies. It is safely predictable that nothing of different character will be found when the remaining fifty per cent are deciphered. Still there is the possibility of historical inscriptions having existed. If found, they might be extremely troublesome. Practically nothing is known about non-calendrical glyphs.

The system of writing numbers is well understood. Ordinarily, bars and dots were used, a bar meaning *five,* a dot, *one.* The system was vigesimal. The number twenty had a special sign of its own, closing the period. The number eighteen, for example, is written with three vertical bars and three dots on the left. The number was written to the left of or above a sign of which it served as a coefficient. A set of face numerals was also used and these are here shown. All this is to be seen on the accompanying chart. Note the special sign of zero, the conception of which is regarded by mathematicians as extraordinary.

There is no limit to the extension of this numerical system. It could be drawn out "to the crack of doom," as Goodman observed. But I imagine large calculations, in which it is alleged to have been used, are mainly the conceptions of astronomically inclined archæologists. I doubt if the Maya dealt with large numbers or intricate calculations. The modern Maya are perfectly dumb in mathematics.

To Diego de Landa, Bishop of Yucatan, immediately after the Conquest, we are indebted for our initial knowledge of the meaning of the Maya glyphs. Without what he noted down from the testimony of native priests, we should still be nowhere in the study. Goodman, Bowditch, Morley, among Americans; Forstemann and Seler, Germans, have been devoted, lifelong, effective students of the glyphs. A writer in 1626, Lizana, states that old men still lived who could read the manuscripts. My greatest hope has been that possibly such men still exist in the mountain fastnesses of Guatemala. In New Mexico, to the present day, old men of old priesthoods conserve the lore of their ancients and the meaning of their ceremonies and symbols. If such a thing is possible in these little communities, hemmed in for nearly four centuries by an aggressive, inquisitive civilization, with no isolation except their own determined, close-mouthed conservatism, how much more likely is it to be so in the remote communities of Guatemala where white men are seldom seen and are hardly permitted to sojourn at all.

The inscriptions on stone monuments still exist in great numbers and are well preserved. Those at Quirigua, Copan, and Palenque, have had special notice in this work. The codices were native books, the hieroglyphic characters being painted in various colors on a substantial paper made from the fiber of the American agave. These books were made in folding panels. They existed in large numbers, but the pious bishop, Diego de Landa, had the idea that they were works of the Devil, and so caused huge bonfires to be made of them. This entire literature of an idolatrous people was to be "sunk without trace," and it must be admitted that a pretty thorough job was made of it. Only three books survived the holocaust. These are the Dresden codex in the public library of that city in Germany, the Perez in the National Library of Paris, and the divided manuscript in Spain called the Tro-Cortesiano, now known to be one original. The former, a page of which is here shown in facsimile, is the finest specimen of all. These three codices deal with calendrical and religious matters.

What may have been in the hundreds destroyed, *sabe Dios!* When inclined to think rather savagely of Diego de Landa, do not forget similar incidents in ancient, medieval, yes, and in modern times. Remember too that he left in this priceless *Relación de las Cosas de Yucatan,* a mine of information about the Maya of the Conquest period. And he delivered the kickoff which enabled modern students to open up the whole Maya hieroglyphic game.

This brief exposition of the calendar and hieroglyphic writing of Mexico and Central America is intended merely to set out in an elementary way the Aztec and Maya systems reduced to their simplest terms. For a first-rate, detailed treatise, read Morley's "Introduction to the Study of Maya Hieroglyphics,"

Clearing the Underbrush, Quirigua, Guatemala

Felling the Jungle, Quirigua, Guatemala

Page of Dresden Codex

published by the *Bureau of American Ethnology, Bulletin No. 57.*

The sustained efforts of the ancient Americans to understand the phenomena of time to the end that they might have a reliable agricultural program; the dramatization of this in seasonal rituals and ceremonies; the long process of developing an instrument, the calendar, to serve as a seasonal chart; the devising of pictures and their conventionalization into a system of writing that would enable them to give due recognition to their deities in the program; constitute their most conspicuous and most successful attempt at the acquisition of exact knowledge. It was elementary knowledge, to be sure. Time is a phenomenon that is susceptible of exact measurement, and because the Indian type of mind was what it was, the merging of the whole thing with the religion was inevitable. I have repeatedly called attention to the amazing integration of Indian culture, the impossibility of completely isolating the various factors for special study. The foregoing illustrates how, with this race, attempts at exact knowledge for industrial use were soon drawn into the sphere of religion, the latter dominating.

Other attempts to acquire knowledge may be mentioned here, such as the efforts to explain the creation of man and of other creatures, to trace migrations over the earth, to account for natural phenomena. These efforts, dealing largely with the supernatural, gave rise to a rich mythology and might be classed with the religious attainments of the people. However, they are equally concerned with purely mundane affairs, so may as well be classed as intellectual achievements. That question involves some consideration of the meaning of *mythology* and *folklore*. Great philosophic conclu-

sions were reached during the dawning ages of man.
These usually involved creator-deities, so belong with
the genesis of religion. These basic beliefs, of untold
antiquity, constitute the natural philosophy of the people and might be considered a basic mythological system. They do not belong with the vast body of tales of
gods and giants, culture heroes, etc., that have grown
with the life of the race and is still growing. Pueblo
mythology is increasing today, just as the literature of
civilization grows. The same is probably true in Mexico and Central America. The human mind is incur-
ably romantic. The play of imagination upon basic
themes gives rise in civilization to drama, romance, fic-
tion, in endless variety. In the cultural stages of life,
the same play of fancy upon ancient themes produces
mythology and folklore. I have known Indian myth-
makers and folklorists who would rank as creative
artists in civilized life. So I am disposed to class mythology and folklore, not with religion, but with the
intellectual elements of culture.

In Guatemala the *Popul Vuh,* previously referred
to, is a fine example of, not a "Sacred Book," as it is
usually called, but a "Book of the People"—a book of
Maya-Quiché legendry and mythic history, which would
be fine reading for young and old. Written down in
Quiché language, after the Conquest, by some native
who had learned to use the Spanish script, it deals with
creation, colored a bit by the Christian Genesis, and
then develops a great cycle of myths recounting the
performances of the "Hero Twins," Hunapu and
Xbalanque, who with their great giant-killing and various daredevil exploits parallel our cherished twin gods,
the 'Ahayutah. In fact, they must be the identical twins
translated to Central America from the Rio Grande

Valley, New Mexico. We know that our Southwestern culture heroes were born on the top of Sandia Mountain, where the father of gods, Okuwapiñ, still resides in his red cloud; that after cleaning up the giants of the Rio Grande Valley they went away to a far country. Guatemala would do as well as any, for according to Quiché mythology there were plenty of giants there. So I think the *Popul Vuh* is part of a continued story. The exploits of the hero twins did not cease with Guatemala. The entire New World claims them. We hear of them from Alaska to Patagonia.

In Yucatan, the books of Chilam Balaam represent another intellectual effort of the Maya. Like the *Popul Vuh,* these books were written after the Conquest, in native language, by native scribes who had learned the Spanish. Several of them have been found and translated. They relate a very fragmentary legendary history of the Maya, go somewhat into family history, are as the title indicates the work of soothsayers. They are important, as every scrap of Maya literature is, but add little to dependable Maya history, and do not go far toward relieving the confusion that beclouds the Maya world.

Had the invention of letters been achieved, there is little doubt that a great literature would have arisen in ancient America. From the excellent compilation of songs and discourses of the ancient Mexicans, made by Professor Ruben M. Campos of the National Museum of Mexico and published by the Department of Monuments of the Mexican Government, under the title of *La Produccion Literaria de los Aztecs,* I desire to present two songs of Nezahualcóyotl as examples of the love of nature and exquisite poetic sense of this remarkable Indian poet, philosopher and chief. The intrusive Christian elements introduced in the transcription of these songs from the living voice by recorders of the post-Conquest period will be readily recognized, but the aboriginal spirit of the poems as a whole is unmistakable:

"Acolhua Song of Nezahualcóyotl

On visiting ancient Moctezuma in Mexico when he became ill. (Translated from the Nahuatl to Spanish by Mariano Jacobo Rojas)

"1. Most esteemed and august shade, look how I, Nezahualcóyotl, have come, withered like a yellowing flower. I come from Acolhuacan, where rare flowers grow abundantly.

"2. Listen to these, my songs, with which I come to entertain you, oh sovereign Moctezuma, strong and shining with my regal crest of emerald green plumage, according to the excellent Mexican custom.

"3. Yonder where the white willow stands, your forefathers, Acammapichtli and Huitzilihuit, granted you great favors. Weep, Moctezuma, and so you shall enjoy repose in the kingly abode of Teotl.

"4. Oh Moctezuma! May God have mercy upon you, showing himself compassionate toward you; because how difficult it is to come before your royal throne!

"5. Drown yourself in a flood of tears! Ay, ay, ay! Oh Moctezuma, weep, weep; for now it is not possible to contemplate again the mountains of Atloyan, where you continually looked upon your servant, Nezahualcóyotl.

"6. Give aid to this temple of Tlilapa, this dwelling place of beautiful writings, where I, Nezahualcóyotl, granted such great benefits, and improving those gifts which are freely offered there, you will recognize perfectly the displeasures which overwhelm me.

"7.   The eagle croaks and the tiger mews. Do not despise the voice of Izcoatl, so that you may gain repose in the seat of honor of Teotl.

"8.   Your voice is heard in the white willow, in the silvery cattails, and in the reed beds which grow profusely in this Mexico.

"9.   Only God, only He who is our holy father, will protect you. Take the delicious baths of the flowered lakes with willowed shores of the mountains of Atloyan, whence are loosed the mists which are scattered above us; and gather in your hands the precious flowers which are found there in continuous bud, so that you will have the perfection of your history.

"10.   You will have agreeable shade, and be fanned with the wing of the rare *quetzal,* where the nobility assemble and the mist extends over us. And there, holding in your hands the beautiful flowers which are found in continuous bud, you will listen to the narrative of your deeds in sweet and harmonious songs.

"11.   Yonder bud the magnificent flowers referred to in the writings. Oh, and there, too, buds forth the warm season of the year.

"12.   All that is told about the mountains of Atloyan and Tenochtitlán was written in the *amoxtles* (codices) that our fathers, unrolling them, looked at them as soon as they directed their gaze to the sky, and returned again and again to look at them attentively.

"13.   Here is this celestial ceiling, a ceiling of lovely sapphires, the work of God, before whom all is subject, and who governs as master and lord of heaven and earth.

"14.   There you will carry in your hands branches of sweet flowers and fragrant laurel. So meanwhile in this world, direct your gaze each day toward that mountain of Atloyan, the abode where all shall go.

"15. The nobles wrote of things relative to the land of Anáhuac, and now you are writing what is relative to heaven.

"16. I, Nezahualcóyotl, and you, *Moctezumatzin,* are creatures of Him who gives life; we are creatures of God, our father who is in heaven."

"Song of Nezahualcöyotl
(Translated into Spanish by José Maria Vigil)

"1. I meditate deeply upon where I may gather some beautiful things and fragrant flowers. Of whom to ask them? Imagine that I question the brilliant *zumbador* bird, quivering emerald; imagine that I question the yellow butterfly; they will tell me that they know where the fair and fragrant flowers grow, if I wish to gather them there in the forests of laurel, where lives the *tzinitzcan,* or if I wish to take them in the green forest where dwells the *tlauquéchotl.* There will be cut brilliants of dew; there they reach their perfect development. At such a time I shall be able to see them if they have finally appeared, put them in my *cuexantli* (carrying bag), and greet the children with them, and entertain the nobles.

"2. On passing by, it sounds to me as though even the rocks were replying to the sweet songs of the flowers; the clear and murmuring waters respond; the azure fountain sings, dashes itself to pieces, and sings again; the *centzontle* answers, the *coyoltótotl* is wont to accompany them, and many musical birds scatter their trills as one melody. They exalt the earth, making their sweet voices heard.

"3. I said, I exclaimed: would that it might not cause you sorrow, my dear ones, that you have stopped to listen; would that the brilliant *zumbador* birds might come soon. Whom shall we seek,

Aztec Hieroglyphics—The Mexican Calendar Stone

10 Ahau	7 Ahau	4 Ahau	1 Ik	2 Ik	1 Kan
13 Manik	5 Lamat	2 Cib	12 Caban	5 Caban	5 Eznab
0 Pop	14 Uo	18 Zip	17 Tzec	6 Xul	4 Yaxkin
3 Yaxkin	10 Mol	5 Yax	18 Muan	3 Kayab	8 Cumhu
Cycle 9	Cycle 9	Katun 8	Katun 3	Tun 5	Tun 1
Uinal 1	Kin 4	Kin 12	Kin 8	Kin 0	Kin 8

Maya Hieroglyphics with Numerals (after Morley)
(See page 240)

oh noble poet? I ask, and I say: where are the beautiful and fragrant flowers with which you might cheer yourselves, my noble companions? Soon these flowers will tell me, singing: 'Here, oh singer, we shall show you that with which you may truly delight your noble companions.'

"4.   Then they led me to the fertile site of a valley, a flourishing site, where the dew was spread with brilliant splendor; where I saw various sweet and perfumed flowers covered with dew sprinkled around in the shape of the arc of a prism, and they told me: 'Pick the flowers that you desire, oh singer; would that you be happy, and give them to your friends, that they may rejoice in the earth.'

"5.   Then I gathered into my *cuexantli* delicate and delicious flowers, and said: if some of our pueblo were to enter here; if many of our people were here! And I thought that I could go out to announce to our friends that all of us should rejoice in the varied and fragrant flowers, and that we would select varied and delicate songs with which we would delight our friends here on the earth, and the grandees in their splendor and dignity.

"6.   And then I, the singer, gathered all the flowers to place them on the nobles, to cover them and put them in their hands; and I hastened to lift my voice in a solemn song that praises them to the nobles before the face of *Tloque in nahuaque,* in whose realm there is no slavery.

"7.   Where can I cut them? Where can I gather these fair flowers? And how can I reach that florid land, that fertile land, where there is neither servitude nor sorrow? If it is attained here on earth, it is only by means of submitting to *Tloque in nahuaque;* here on earth, sorrow fills my soul when I tell where I, the singer, saw the flowery site.

"8.   And I said: truly, there is no good place

249

here on earth; truly, happiness is in some other region; for what good is this earth? There is, indeed, another life beyond. Would that I could go there; there the birds are singing; there I could learn to know those fair flowers, those sweet flowers, the only ones which appease and mildly intoxicate."

It was in the sphere of esthetics that cultural integration became complete with the Middle Americans. In a sense, it may be said that their art and religion were identical. However, it would be a bit more exact to say that art was the visible expression of the spiritual life. The unified arts—drama, music, painting, sculpture, temple building—made of religion something tangible. It must be understood that drama as here used embraces ritual and ceremony. In the study of ancient life in Middle America, the practice of these unified arts fills the picture. In this way the worship of the deities was achieved. Accordingly, the art of Mexico and Central America will be treated at much greater length than any other cultural factor.

II. Mexican and Central American Art

A FORMER statement of mine with reference to the genesis and racial trend of native American art will serve as an introduction to what I wish to say here about the esthetic achievements of the Mexican and Central American peoples. It is reproduced substantially as it appeared in the *American Magazine of Art,* for September 1922:

Sounding the remote sources from which flow the cultural activities of peoples, one finds in ancient America conditions that invite the reflection of scientist and artist and philosopher alike. These conditions we should have clearly in mind, for they are the agencies that fashioned the native race, gave it its distinguished physical character, built its distinctive racial mind, drew from out the racial soul those peculiar spiritual characteristics which found expression in its arts and prepared its tragic destiny.

America was a continent of complete isolation, of vast solitudes, of limitless spaces, of certain well-defined physical areas, such as the great Western plains, the Southwestern desert, the Mexican tableland, Central America and the high plateau of Peru and Bolivia. It invited an expansive culture. There was not any problem of over-population. There was little excuse for conflict between tribes. There was room for all. Natural resources provided what man needed without intensive effort. There were everywhere conditions of nature which stimulate the imagination, induce reverent contemplation, bind man to his soil. These conditions were favorable to the development of religion, of esthetic life, of social structure. There was not the intensive struggle, the conflict of interests which focus the thought of people upon material things and intensify the practical activities. Moreover, the race was of a single origin, essentially Oriental in its psychology, which was fairly well established as to its type before reaching America.

This was the antithesis of Europe, where for millenniums our forebears, ethnic breeds of little degree of likemindedness, have fought for the frontiers which they deemed essential to existence. There has been incessant conflict of interest; there the struggle for subsistence, for control of the routes of trade, for access to the open seas, and for the freedom thereof, for economic advantages of every sort, for a place in the sun, for strategic positions of defense, that have, altogether, produced the seething caldron of warring nations, of ancient hatreds which have grown and intensified through the ages. While we dare to hope that Europe may be composed into peace in our time, we do not overlook the plain truth that the conditions above described have for many centuries impelled the European peoples to fight for every possible advantage. This swift advance in material civilization is the result of their early discovery and utilization of metals, mastery of forces, constructive and destructive, which have brought us to the pinnacle of material supremacy which we enjoy or, at any rate, spend our lives in maintaining.

During the same centuries, much of the Orient and all of America kept the more tranquil ways of the Stone Age. Racial mind was in the making just the same. The activities of these races, whatever they were, produced a brain development equal to any in the world and mental power unrivaled in certain ways. But these

A Palenque Design

Polychrome Urn, Quirigua, Guatemala

ways were spiritual rather than material. If we represent with a series of curves the progress of the various types of culture in the races, it is seen that with the Europeans the curve of material culture mounts to great heights, while with the Orientals and the native American race it remains at a very low level. When we consider the development of spiritual culture, the situation is nearly reversed. The European remains low; the other mounts. Europeans are people of vast material achievements. Theirs are the great mechanical inventions. Orientals, and the Indian race, gave the world great religious conceptions and high esthetic values.

Mind is made by its experiences, and experiences are partly matters of choice. It would seem that the more spiritual pursuits, such as art and religion, of those whom we call inferior races have been quite as potent in developing brain as have our material activities. We lump these races together as heathen, displace their culture with ours, which may be good for us but deadly for them. We give them a religion which is not ours to begin with, and demonstrations of efficiency which they rarely envy, while they calmly wonder why these violent people of the West never stop for the real solid enjoyment of sitting in silent meditation upon the graves of their ancestors.

The immediate result when two civilizations that rest on such radically different foundations come in conflict can never be in doubt. But the question of ultimate stability may remain open. We perhaps have not made ourselves entirely secure in our greatness; our faith in ourselves has been somewhat shaken recently. But we have wrought tragic results to the peoples whose culture rested on foundations unlike ours. Of these the best example is the American Indian race.

The art of the earliest Americans could not well be considered without the foregoing discussion of fundamental conditions of culture. The race was essentially esthetic. It developed no machinery and no literature, but out of its rich experience grew profound views of nature and of man's relationship to all created things. Art in its various forms afforded the Indian his means of expressing what he thought. One is amazed in checking up the attainments of the Indians in comparison with those of other races, at the scope, the purity, the integrity, and the universality of their arts. They may best be considered in broad culture areas.

The great western plains were peopled by tribes of fine physical and mental development which was the result of their age-long experience. The drama was the foundation art of the Indians. It was the least material of all arts. With music, from which it was inseparable, it afforded a channel of expression sufficient in itself to the needs of the people where conditions were not favorable to the arts that required material accessories. The great plains did not invite permanent construction, but out of that spacious environment came an immaterial culture, a purely spiritual structure that is almost beyond compare. Rich in imagery, in poetry, in symbolism, in religious fervor, in every emotional quality, it has all the elements of great art, even to the details of dramatic form. In the very nature of this art it cannot long survive the tribal organization. Of plastic art, the Plains Indians had little. In painting and building their achievements were rudimentary.

The American Southwest, region of unalterable deserts, exercised the same stimulating influence upon the human mind as did the great plains. Out of the vast spaces came the same profound reflections upon nature

and man's life. It opened primarily the same major
channels of expression, induced the same art forms.
Drama with song is still the basic art. As the conditions there invited fixed abode, building became an important occupation, mounting to the level of a fine art
in a few localities. But cliff-dwelling and pueblo architecture was for the most part not eminent in esthetic
character. There came, however, a vast development
in ceramic art. Like the drama, it was universal in the
region. In both, the entire people participated. It is
clearly related to the ceremonial life, for its decorative
motives are almost made known when we understand
the religious ceremonies. Their search in nature for
beautiful colors, their discoveries among minerals and
plants of the elements with which to produce paints for
their potteries and dyes for their fabrics, resembled
the intensity with which the Europeans investigated
metals and discovered and made available hidden forces
of nature. They studied fibers, barks and grasses, and
attained high skill in weaving textiles and baskets.
Their pre-eminence was in decorative art, beginning
with the ceremonial painting of the body, the extension
of the same decorative symbolism to the costumes of
the dance, and the embellishment of practically all articles of use, most notably pottery. Here they rose to
the levels of the great esthetic peoples of the Old World.
The pottery of the ancient tribes of Chihuahua, who
were the arid Southwest, challenges comparison in
color, form and mastery of line with that of the Greeks
and Orientals.

It is in the Southwest that we first notice that most
striking thing in native American culture, the integration of utility and beauty and religious thought. The
article of everyday use was invariably beautified and

almost always some phase of religion furnished the motive. Utility and beauty, as well as art and religion, were inseparable. In utilizing life forms in decorative patterns, in play of fancy with primary motives, in poetic, symbolic expression of what life and nature meant, the ancients of the Southwest rose to sublime heights. Their sculpture remained rudimentary.

In Middle America three major culture centers developed in ancient times. These were the Mexican tableland, Central America, and the plateau of Peru and Bolivia. In their civilization they were sufficiently alike to permit of one characterization. There is every reason to believe that, as with the northern Americans, the dramatic ceremonial dance was the basic art. As in the Southwest, decorative art in ceramics and preeminently the weaving of fabrics flowed in a natural evolutionary course. The ancient Peruvians made textiles that are furnishing patterns for the most discriminating manufacturers of America. The plumage of tropical birds afforded material for gorgeous robes and, among the Aztecs and related tribes, was one of their most conspicuous arts.

So far the arts of Middle America paralleled those of the Southwest, but now they add two major fine arts, architecture and sculpture. The former follows the evolutionary course of which we find the rudiments in the north. It was a product of the religious life, integrated with the social structure. While fine temple architecture was far advanced in all three of the Middle American centers, it reached its supremacy in Guatemala and Yucatan, the land of the Maya. The temples of this region rival in beauty those of any part of the ancient world, and they have endured with the most enduring.

Along with his other accomplishments, the Indian of Middle America developed sculpture, and so generally was this art practiced that from Aztec Mexico to Peru few miles are traversed without seeing the works of the ancient sculptors. It ranges from the exquisite little carvings in jade and serpentine and molded ornaments of gold up to the enormous sandstone monuments of Quirigua; while the temples at Palenque, embellished in stucco and low relief, and great ceremonial groups, such as Chichen Itza and Uxmal, are as much achievements in sculpture as in architecture. Hardly anywhere else in the world was there such a general application of sculpture to architecture as in Central America. So consistently is the cultural order held throughout Central America that where a written language has come into existence, as with the Maya, the inscriptions constitute an essential part of the decorative system.

When we consider that these monuments of architecture and sculpture were executed without machinery other than the most elementary, without metal tools, with only the mechanical equipment of the Stone Age, it starts new questionings as to what civilization really is. The arts of all the earliest Americans were products of a Stone Age, yet we would require all the facilities of our advanced civilization physically to imitate their works, and the spirit of their art we could never reproduce. Viewed from the standpoint of achievements other than material, America was a continent of distinguished culture while Europe was barbarian.

One is tempted to consider to what extent these natural conditions of America, these subtle forces of the western world, which operated in the past to produce so definite a cultural type, may still be potent to influence the new race that has invaded its ancient solitude and rudely interrupted the cultural evolution of its aborginal population.

The secondary conditions are vastly different. The human animal on which these forces have to react has nothing of the homogeneity of the first American stock, but is of diversified breed. It is for the most part European in origin, therefore of a type whose aspiration has long been to subdue and transform nature rather than to yield to its benign influence and be absorbed therein. The European seeks in nature every element that can be conscripted to serve a civilization founded on force, dedicated to supremacy of force, destined to stand or fall as the ideal of force prevails or declines in human affairs. The native American, like the Oriental, viewed Nature as the great source of all existences, found in contemplating its orderly processes the principle for the ordering of his own life, sought not in its mysterious forces something to be captured and made to serve him, but harmonies that he might share to the profound satisfaction of his soul. His was a life of the spirit; existence in a world of unreality, of mysticism, of naïve, spiritual experience. Such a mind is the product of vast spaces and solitudes, the play of thought induced by deserts, prairies, mountains, forests, skies, and elemental forces not yet analyzed, classified, controlled, and reduced to the commonplace.

No doubt isolation has been as potent in producing cultural types as in conditioning the biological variations that lead to new species. Life forms and cultural forms exhibit striking parallels in their evolution. Isolation no longer exists in the Americas in sufficient measure to induce strong, new cultural variations such as took place with the first settlers.

Nevertheless, the deeper influences of climate and soil that produced the aboriginal Americans and endowed them with a racial culture as definite as the color of the skin must still exist and, to some degree, retain their potency over the minds of men. They are profoundly felt in the elemental conditions of the American Southwest, the Mexican plateau, the highlands of Guatemala and Peru. The noted development of American art, showing as it does a strong tendency to assimilate the native American achievements in ceramics, textiles, painting, sculpture, even music and architecture, may be a happy portent of something of which those who are participating can hardly be aware; a movement that is obeying the influences that formed the mind of the earliest Americans and which, if followed in the spirit of reverence in which art has been wont to yield itself to the deep impulses of life, may teach us the lesson of the ages—that a people to be great in culture must feel to the depths of its soul the beauty and the sublimity of the forces that make it a nation, and urge it to reflect in some or all of the manifold forms of art the nobilitiy of life that is kindled by a noble environment.

In the art of the ancient Toltecs, Aztecs and Maya, sculpture may be taken as their most characteristic mode of esthetic expression. In Mexico and Central America we are able to recover such works in great numbers, but with all the profusion of material we have no problems relating to individual artists. We have the name of no single sculptor, nor is there anything to indicate that any individual ever stood out as a leader in the rich artistic life of the people. In some respects this is an advantage, for we are thus enabled to study art in its finest aspect, simply as a record of the esthetic progress of a race.

The study of Middle American art is equally a study of religion and of sociology. It can be interpreted and appreciated only through a knowledge of the social organization and spiritual character of the native American race. The Indian mind is notedly religious. Its manifestations in song, ceremony, ritual, rhythm, color, and form display always a dominant religious note. Its art products must be viewed accordingly. There is always a predominance of decorative motives, with little regard for realistic proportion. There is close adherence to fixed conventional models in attitudes, headdress, apparel and all decorative elements, for magic power is an ever present religious concept, and this is always associated with traditionary form.

In the illustrations that are shown, there may be noticed the orderly arrangement or distribution of the works of art in the sacred precincts. This may be related to a fundamental trait of the Indian mind denoted by the invariable observance of orderly sequence in the arrangement of camp, village, or town, the construction of the sanctuary, the position of men, women, and ceremonial objects in the sacred inclosure, of direction and movement in the procession, and in the use of certain articles of apparel or insignia in the performance of rites. It is an expression of the idea of all-pervading spirit, derived from the orderly procession of phenomena in Nature, day and night, light and darkness, summer and winter. There is the invariable juxtaposition of two elemental principles, male and female, represented by sky and earth, oriented as North and South.

Because of the bountifulness of Nature in the tropics, the food quest was not normally a hard one. No year

passes without exhibitions on a stupendous scale of the
forces of Nature. Floods and earthquakes are of frequent occurrence, and volcanic activity has been constantly before the eyes of the aboriginal inhabitants.
Here were constant manifestations of mighty power,
vitally affecting human destiny, which, to the Indian
mind, must be propitiated by ceremony and sacrifice.
In animal life, tigers, serpents and birds abound to
direct thought in zoötheistic channels. In a consideration of art these facts of environmental relationship
must not be lost sight of. Here, permanent establishments for religious observance would flourish, consecrated in due form with reference to ceremonial arrangement and processional movement.

If effigies were set up to represent deities of mighty
power, they were of vast size and in physical aspect often
tending toward the grotesque. If statues were carved
in honor of personages who by virtue of priestly, jurid-
ical or military authority stood before the people either
for life or fixed periods of time as the earthly repre-
sentatives of deific power, they were of imposing size
displaying authority in conventional attitude and traditionary insignia, and in apparel abounding in decorative elements derived from serpent, bird, tiger, or from
mythic conceptions and grotesque combinations of these
animals by virtue of which the wearer becomes endowed with their physical, intellectual and spiritual
attributes, and acquires something of their intermedi-
ary relationship with the gods to be propitiated in ceremony and sacrificial offering.

In Middle America religious feeling found expression in the setting up of temples and statues in great
numbers. Among the Indians of our western plains of
North America, all this existed as a purely immaterial

structure, highly elaborated and spiritualized, objectified in ceremony and song. In the remains of the ancient cliff- and mesa-dwellers of the Southwest, together with the survival of archaic ceremonies among the Pueblos, we have a condition for the study of religious expression intermediate between that of the Plains Indians and the Central Americans. The art of Quirigua and Copan will serve as illustrative of the entire subject of Middle American art in its general principles.

In the plan of Quirigua, the temple area is to the south. The open space to the north, called the Great Plaza, is partly surrounded by low terraces. Within this inclosure are all the sculptures that have been found. Male figures occupy the north end of the plaza, and female figures the south. The same arrangement is found at Copan. It is interesting to note that among the Pueblos, when men and women enter the sanctuary, the men and things pertaining to them are ranged upon the north, or right, the women and all belonging to them on the south, or left. The same arrangement of male and female in the Sacred Inclosure prevails among certain Plains tribes. With both, the south pertains to the female, the north to the male; the south to the earth, the north to the sky.

In Quirigua and Copan there is general similarity of plan. There is the same arrangement and orientation of buildings and statues. Male figures occupy the north, and female the south. At Copan, we find on the west side line of the Great Plaza a male figure; opposite on the east, a female; and between these two, a monument containing two figures—the one on the north side male, and the one on the south female.

Note how the sculptures at Copan fall into evolutionary series. The statue known as Stela H may be taken

Stela P—Archaic Stela   Stela H

Copan, Honduras

Stela B—Front   Copan, Honduras   Stela B—Back

as a type of the best group. The figure is that of a woman. There is lack of correct proportion, the body being very short in proportion to the size of head and limbs. It is executed in the high round relief of all the statues of this group. The face is well modeled and not devoid of expression. The figure stands in the conventional attitude of all the Copan statues. The manner of carrying the hands I shall refer to later. The feet are in natural position. The apparel differs from that of any other at Copan, male or female, in that it includes a skirt.

The conventional style of apparel at Copan for both male and female is shown in Stela B. The costume consists of a richly ornamented cape, a girdle, decorated with human faces, and fringed at the bottom with shells, probably representing the *conus,* and a narrow apron, or mastil, hanging from the girdle to the feet. This is simply an elaboration of the loincloth almost universally worn by the American Indians. The legs are bare and fairly well modeled in almost full round relief. There are ornaments on knees and ankles, and the feet are shod with sandals. Across the chest, supported by the upturned hands, is a bundle, which is terminated at the shoulders of the figure with highly conventionalized serpent heads, in the mouths of which grotesque faces or figures appear. In the attitude in which it is carried, it suggests the medicine bundle of certain North American tribes. I am inclined to give it a similar significance, that of the palladium of authority—the sacred insignia of the priest-chief. The headdress is the most complex article of the wearing apparel. As in that of the priest-chief in northern Indian ceremonies, the variable elements may be regarded as the emblems of clan or phratry.

An example of a more archaic group is Stela P. The proportions are here very different. The shaft is narrow and slightly wedge-shaped. The figure is tall and slender with contracted waist. The angle formed by the forearm is acute; there is little attempt at modeling. The face is expressionless, the bulging eyes giving a slightly grotesque appearance. The relief is low. Stiffness, angularity, lack of expression, characterize all the figures of this group.

A still earlier class comprises shafts devoted entirely to hieroglyphic inscriptions. There was in this group no attempt to sculpture the human figure. If there were at Copan smooth, unsculptured shafts, the evolution series would be complete.

As the stelæ at Quirigua have already been described in some detail, two or three examples will suffice to illustrate their pre-eminence in monumental sculpture. Among general characteristics to be noticed is the absence of war implements and signs of combat in the sculptures, indicating a people living at peace with their neighbors. There is an entire absence of signs of sacrifice, cruelty or bloodshed. In the delineation of the human figure there is consistent ignoring of proportion. Scant attention was paid to anatomical details. There is little in the dress, vesture, or insignia on which to base the determination of sex, but male figures are always bearded and female beardless. Another element in the delineation of sex is the elevation of the relief. In male figures the relief is low and flat, while with female figures the relief is higher and well rounded. The perfect chastity of all the sculptures is noteworthy.

While the sculptures at Quirigua may be clearly arranged in chronological sequence, all may be considered as upon the same plane of artistic achievement as

the best group at Copan. But we have, in the neighborhood of Quirigua, shafts totally unsculptured, and
are left without examples of intermediate forms. The
most archaic in style is Stela No. 1. Unlike most of
the shafts at Quirigua, it is figured on one side only.
It is the first of a series of five monoliths of nearly
double the height of the monuments at Copan, and several times their weight. The blocks were rather crudely shaped for the sculptures.

The series culminates in No. 5, the largest of all
Central American monoliths. Note the ceremonial elements of apparel which prevail throughout the monuments at Quirigua and which may be clearly seen on
the stela now under consideration. Instead of the medicine bundle supported upon the chest by the upturned
hands, as at Copan, we have a wand or scepter grasped
in the right hand and held in front of the body, while
the left hand bears a small shield. A grotesque manikin is seen upon the scepter. This probably has a significance akin to that of the serpent bundle carried by
the Copan figures—that of a symbol of authority. A
counterpart may be found in the *tiponi* or wand of the
priest-chief in Pueblo ceremonies. Here, too, we have
the elaborate headdress, bearing mythic faces and grotesque figures emblematic of clan or phratry. Upon the
knees are medallions, corresponding to the plate or
rattle of turtle shell worn upon the knee of the Pueblo
priest. Upon these are carved normal human faces.
Upon the ankle is a death-head mask, and this, too, has
a remote counterpart in the priestly apparel of the
Pueblos, there being in certain ceremonies performed
in the upper Rio Grande Valley a masking of the ankles
with the skin of some totemic animal, that of the skunk
being generally used.

In the group that I have called the zoömorphic series, Middle American art reaches its zenith in the example that I have previously referred to as the Great Turtle, by others called the Great Dragon. I wish to urge everyone to read a series of articles on "Masterpieces of Aboriginal American Art," published in *Art and Archæology*, beginning in volume one, number one, of that magazine, July, 1914. The late William H. Holmes, master mind and master hand in American archæology, therein says almost the last word on the art of ancient America. A part of what he has to say about the Great Dragon of Quirigua is, by permission of the editor, repeated here:

"The task of describing these monuments (Quirigua) has been undertaken by Maudslay, Hewett, and others, and to the publications of these explorers those who would go deeply into the subject are referred. A single example of the sculptures—a work that takes high rank in the world of art—is selected for detailed presentation in this place.

"The massive sculpture sometimes called the Great Turtle may well be regarded as the sculptural masterpiece *par excellence* of the American race. It is a somewhat ovoid mass of coarse-grained sandstone of warmish gray color weighing about twenty tons. It is upward of seven feet in height, and is eleven feet six inches in greater diameter. When the School of American Archæology began its work here, the surface was deeply coated with moss and other tropical growths which were carefully cleaned off by Dr. Hewett in 1910, repeating the task of Maudslay some twenty years earlier. The surface is now much weather-stained, displaying streaks and blotches of dark color, probably due to the weathering-out of ferruginous matter contained in the stone. The master sculptor appears to have utilized in a measure the original irregularities of the great block, the flattish base of which rests at the ground level on a floor composed of three hewn stone slabs.

· · · · · ·

"Approaching the stone from the east it is observed that the entire surface is elaborately sculptured, now in high, now in low relief, and in graceful arrangements of strange forms so diversified and intricate that analysis of the maze-like complex seems at first quite out of the question. There is a compounding and confusion of nattural elements—human, reptilian, avian, and grotesque—in all degrees of convention intermingled with formal patterns, scrolls, cartouches, and glyphic inscriptions, altogether amazing, yet distinctly attractive and highly decorative. Notwithstanding our failure at first to comprehend a single feature of the work, the touch of the master was recognized in every form and line. The western side is nearly identical in treatment and proved to be equally incomprehensible; and the reason for this, as was afterward learned, is the fact that the figures on these faces are incomplete in themselves, being continuations and appendages from the sculptured figures of the upper surface, which, to be traced and understood, must be approached by the student from that surface.

"Proceeding to examine the work in detail, we pass to the north front, where the attention is at once directed to an elaborately and elegantly costumed human figure, strongly yet delicately carved, which occupies a central position in the broad face of the block. The figure is seated, Buddha fashion, and presents a placid and dignified mien. Including the headdress, it is about seven feet in height. Although the features are somewhat mutilated, they distinctly suggest a young and comely person, possibly a female, although there appears to be some difference of opinion among students on this point.

. . . . . .

"The costume is of superb design, testifying to the advanced state of culture and refinement attained by the people of Quirigua. The details are so elaborate as to defy adequate description, hence the drawings and photographs must be relied upon mainly to tell the story. The headdress embodies a crown-like band over the forehead, surmounted by a complex of grotesque masks with deep-set eyes and vicious fangs, and a maze of scrolls, plumes, and symbols—all sculptured with a vigor and delicacy suggesting the master work of the Orient. Connecting with the top of the headdress are two pairs of strange appendages which extend to the right and left over the upper margin of the stone; they are ornamented with incised checkerwork and various devices in relief. A graceful necklace spreads over the shoulders of the figure and expands across the chest into a broad gorget, in the center of which is set a grotesque mask. The mask is repeated at the waist, and from this the garb extends down over the crossed legs in an apron-like arrangement embodying various serpentine elements and symbols, and terminating in radiating plumes. The wristlets and ear ornaments are of usual Mayan types, the latter extending out over the shoulders.

"Seeking to determine the exact relation of the sculptured figure to the strange forms which surround it, we discover that it sits in the mouth of a great reptilian monster whose upper jaw is arched above, passing behind the headdress, while closing in on the figure at the sides the tusk-like fangs of the reptile are to be seen. The outer surfaces of the jaws are embellished with scale-like

Monument No. 11, The Great Turtle or The American Dragon—front, Quirigua, Guatemala

Monument No. 11—back, Quirigua, Guatemala

Monument No. 11—side, Quirigua, Guatemala

Monument No. 11—top, Quirigua, Guatemala

groups of glyphs and cartouches, and to the right
and left in the curves of the upturned jaw are the
deep-set eyes of the monster, the pupils of which
are embellished with glyph-like figures in relief.
Beneath the figure the lower jaw of the reptile appears with great rounded fangs at the sides. At
the right and left near the base, and connecting
back over the sides, are sculptured panels in which
grotesque and distorted demons appear, each holding tightly against his form a device having the
appearance of a glyph. The possible significance
of the human figure and its relation to the reptilian
monster will be referred to later.

"Passing to the south face of the stone, we discover, occupying a central place in the surface, a
great mask-like visage of forbidding aspect, of the
type characteristic of the 'Long-nosed God.' Although this deity is given varying attributes in the
different Mayan centers of culture, it is thought
probable that in the present connection it may represent the god of the underworld and possibly also
of death. The great staring eyes are set in features
of strange conformation, and the wide mouth displays fangs with molars at the right and left and
the usual tusk-coils springing from the outer corners. At the sides are the ears, embellished with
squarish loops and pendants, while above rises the
headdress of unique and striking design. Enclosing
the face and extending in terraced form across the
headdress is a glyphic inscription neatly carved
and tastefully arranged. Above the forehead and
surrounded by the inscription is a beautifully designed scroll-enclosed panel from which looks out
a human face, the hands also appearing at the lower margin, while above and extending to the upper
surface of the stone is a superbly chiseled device set
against the crown of plumes which expands widely
to right and left. Medallion-like embellishments
are overlaid upon the plumes, which terminate on

the shoulders of the image in an ornamental beaded appendage.

"To the right and left of the inscription, richly embellished, rounded, column-like forms or shoulders are encountered, which connect backward at the base with flattish scaled plates suggesting the flippers of the great sea-turtle, and it is doubtless these features that gave the original name, the 'Great Turtle,' to the monument. Observing their termination in what appears to be a claw, it is suggested that they were not intended as representations of the flippers of any particular natural form, but rather of a mythical reptilian divinity of nondescript characters. Their presence, recalling the open jaws at the northern end, make it apparent that the sculpture as a whole was intended to represent the mythical bicephalous reptilian monster sometimes referred to as the Earth Monster or God, a frequently recurring conception in the native pantheon. We may well assume that the sculpture embodies the Quiriguan conception of this deity, the forms of which are elaborated in various ways and in endless combinations according to the attributes assigned to it in the mythology of the different peoples. . . .

"Climbing to the back of the strange monster the imagination of the observer is profoundly stirred. Although representing no known form in any kingdom of nature—a pure work of the imagination—a strange compounding and overlapping of human, reptilian, and avian elements, it conveys vividly the impression of a living thing—a dragon out-dragoning all the composite monsters of the Orient. So virile are the forms, so tense the coiling, so strong the impression of life, that a thrill almost of apprehension steals over one, for there is a distinct suggestion that the bulging imprisoned inner monster might break its bonds, uncoil its length, and slide away into the deep shadows of the forest immediately at hand. . . .

"Standing thus in the center of the domed surface, one does not at once realize that his feet rest on the flattish, highly conventionalized nose of a gigantic visage the body of which, probably conceived of as possessed in common with that of the two-headed monster beneath, is partly obscured by rococo-like overlays of serpentine forms spreading out to right and left and extending down over the sides of the stone to the base. The great eyes of the creature, deeply sunk in squarish sockets, are nearly two feet in diameter and are embellished with ornamental lashes in the form of vertical bands terminating in beads which possibly symbolize tears or rain. The place of the pupils is occupied by a figure resembling a glyph. A second pair of eyes smaller but similarly treated occur one on the right and the other on the left near the margin of the stone. The broad wonderfully embellished nose or snout extends downward, as seen in the illustration, to the lower margin of the stone and on either side appears a group of three incisor teeth. The cheeks are embellished with scroll-work which extends to the right and left connecting with artistically sculptured groups of space-filling figures of usual types. Over the strongly modeled eyebrow scrolls is a wide panel occupied by boldly sculptured features not readily explained but which suggest highly conventionalized facial elements. Bordering this panel above are the wiggling serpentine forms that spring from the headdress of the seated figure on the north side and which connect directly with the reptilian heads draped over the sides of the stone.

. . . . . .

"While the great Dragon of Quirigua may be regarded as representing the culminating stage of

religious art in aboriginal America, it serves also
to mark the highest level reached in esthetic refinement. The religious motive was the strong dynamic
force which, more than all other agencies combined,
carried culture forward through the prolonged
stages of savagery and barbarism to the borderland
of civilization. Due to a highly centralized religio-
political form of government, the people and their
resources were readily available in carrying out
great undertakings, and rapid strides in the development of institutions and arts were possible.
The esthetic faculty dependent largely on non-
esthetic activities for its manifestations was thus
afforded its greatest opportunity.

"The arts of taste had their origin, as had those
of religion, in the state of savagery; and with some
very ancient peoples, as the Trolodytes of western
Europe, decided advance was made in both graphic
and plastic representation of life forms, and this
quite independently, so far as evidence is available, of any religious association or influence. The
Maya in the beginning may have passed through
a corresponding stage of non-symbolic art but,
howsoever this may be, it was not until religious
symbolism gave special significance to the sub-
ject-matter of representative art, that particular
advance was made toward the higher esthetic expression. With this great group, as with the American peoples generally, the esthetic in its higher
manifestations grew as a vine upon the strong stem
of religious symbolism. Religion furnished the conception and the energy and skill necessary to its
realization; it prepared the design, supervised its
application to the stone, and drove the chisel that
carved it. It demanded results in form, finish, and
embellishment of the highest order, for in view of
their devotees the gods appreciated the beautiful
as well as the essential. We do not lose sight of
the fact, however, that appreciation of the quali-

ties regarded as pleasing to the gods had its origin
in that which was pleasing to the man. Certain
qualities of form, line, color, and arrangement gave
pleasure to the eye; certain qualities of finish gave
pleasure to the touch, while certain sounds were
grateful to the ear, and this appreciation of the
qualities called esthetic was a thing of slow growth
in the human mind, but of great moment in the
history of culture. To the pleasure afforded by
qualities of the works themselves were added the
incentive of religious fervor, the ambition to excel
and the fascination of creating.

"The importance of the esthetic element in Maya
art can hardly be over-estimated. It is doubtful
if any people at a corresponding stage of cultural
evolution was more highly gifted with artistic
genius and appreciation and gave more attention
to its application to all forms of art than the
Mayan race. Every plastic form and every line of
the Dragon bear testimony to this fact. It was not
religion that stipulated that no straight line and
no right angle should appear in the image of the
Dragon; it was not religious restriction that provided that no curve should be the arc of a circle,
that every curve should be subtile, and that all outlines of glyphs and cartouches should take the
roundish, calculiform character. Every feature of
design had complete esthetic supervision and plastic freehand methods prevailed at all times over
the mechanical. In the creation of this monument
the great motor force was religion, but the ever-
watchful esthetic impulse joined hands with that
force in making it a masterpiece of art.

"Dependence of art on religion is amply shown
in what has been said, but the fact may be further
illustrated. If in the course of progressive decadence of a primitive culture the religious impulse
should lose its hold on the people, it appears that
although the artistic sense might survive in large

measure, no block would be hewn from the quarry, no great stone would be carried to sacred precinct, no glyphic inscription or mythic conception would be applied to the stone, and no hand would be available to undertake the task of esthetic realization."

This description of a great masterpiece by a master critic may well serve to bring to a close the study of ancient American art that we have here attempted to present.

III. Religion in the Cultural Evolution

To MAN of the Old Stone Age, the world was pretty much of a chaos. Nevertheless, as he looked upon it with wonderment, he strove to understand it, and to man's credit be it said that whenever and wherever he has tried he has in a measure succeeded. Everything about him has engaged this thought: everything on earth—rocks, plants, animals, the ocean, streams, and rain; everything above the earth—sky, sun, moon, stars, rainbow, clouds, and winds. These things he could observe and form conclusions about—weird beliefs for long, but ever a-questing from known to better known, from error to truth, until in possession of a vast body of beliefs about the phenomena of nature around him.

In his long contact with his world, man sensed something behind all these phenomena that was greater than they were, and that they all obeyed. He could see the action of the thunderbolt in the riven tree or the man lying dead at his feet, and this might arouse acute fear, but back of the thunderbolt he would sense a mighty Power, vast, unknowable, beside which all else was puny and insignificant. Back of all was the mysterious Power which all obeyed, which inspired more than fear. If it could do these tremendous things, man must be dependent upon it; must be helpless in himself; must therefore implore its mercy and appease it with praise and sacrifice and adoration. This constituted worship. Since this mighty Power manifested itself in many forms, its tendency was always to disintegrate into a pantheon—an invisible world peopled by spirit beings of vast power, both beneficent and malevolent. Christianity has been the most successful of all religions in holding the idea of deity together, maintaining the concept of one Almighty Power in the universe. Where the Christian conception of one divine power and of man's relation thereto had its origin, may never be fully agreed upon, but certain it is that in the form that was to carry it around the world it came from the Man of Galilee. Next most exalted idea of deific power is found among the Plains Indians and the Pueblos of northern America. If this was the original pattern of the religious belief of the race, it broke down as it moved toward the tropics. The spiritual culture of the Middle Americans was on a far lower plane than that of the desert communities of the Southwest or of the nomadic Plains people.

In trying to understand the place of religion in the cultural evolution of tropical America, we must face certain facts. The aboriginal ceremonial life there was interpreted through ecclesiastical eyes. A Christian priesthood, zealous for the destruction of idolatry, fired with the idea of converting a race to the only, to them, true faith, could not be the most reliable source of information on this subject. I have myself seen Indian religion so pathetically misunderstood, its ceremonies so completely misconstrued, by the perfectly well intentioned, that I am dubious about anything except personal, first-hand observation, uninfluenced by religious bias. Therefore, while we must accept Father Bernardino de Sahagun for Mexico, and Bishop Diego de Landa for Yucatan, as eminent authorities on the religion of Aztec and Maya, we must not sidestep the historian's obligation to apply critical tests to the testimony, even of eyewitnesses. The history of ancient Mexico by the Franciscan monk, Father Sahagun, is certainly the best contemporary authority on the

Aztecs. Historians and anthropologists are alike indebted to him for a mine of source material, also to Mrs. Fannie Bandelier for her excellent translation. It must be remembered that the information was gathered a generation after the coming of the Spaniards to Mexico, the writing not finished until more than half a century after the Conquest. It contained many erroneous observations to begin with. It comes to us through the Nahuatl and Spanish translations. Sahagun enumerates many gods, which he says were adored by the ancient Mexicans. There can be little doubt that the Aztec pantheon came directly to them from the Toltec. There were deities, male or female, to preside over about all imaginable phenomena; war, rain, water, food, medicine, fire, occupations, etc. The attributes and functions of these gods are described in great detail, and the descriptions afford much valuable information, but the informants had been for years under Christian influence—many of them "converted." The Indian "confessional," as described by Sahagun, ideas of sin, hell, repentance, etc., suggest Christian acculturation, unmistakably. Where he says, "All prominent mountain peaks, especially such around which rain clouds will gather, they imagined to be gods," we recall the various "Sacred Mountains" of the Pueblos—not gods in any sense, but in some cases the seat of deific powers, especially in the clouds that gather over them, or of shrines consecrated to such phenomena as war, hunting, fertility, and the spirit world.

Hundreds of cultural conceptions, described by Sahagun, are paralleled in the Pueblo—that is, if the same method of interpreting information is used. The origin of the calendar, the meaning of calendar-festivals, is in the information given Sahagun by his informants, but it has to be worked out by discriminating examination. There is actually little difference in function and method between an Aztec priest and a Navaho medicine man—each a necromancer, a dealer in magic, a master of flim-flam. But with it all was earnest striving for spiritual truth. Not all priests were fakers. Many, as with the Pueblos, were devoted ministers to the spiritual needs of their people.

For the Maya, we have Bishop Diego de Landa's *Relación de las Cosas de Yucatan,* another priceless mine of information. As evidence, it must be subjected to the same critical examination that is necessary with the works of Sahagun. He was not the historian and ethnologist that Father Sahagun was, but he blazed some valuable trails in the study of Maya religion and daily life. Among the Maya, religion was in about the same condition in Landa's time that it was among the Aztecs. This would be expected, for by the early part of the sixteenth century Yucatan was thoroughly Aztecized. It was more degenerate, and this too would be expected, for the Old Maya culture had broken down centuries before; the renaissance in Yucatan was built upon degenerate cultural survivals to which were added the intrusive elements from without, producing for Landa's study a melange of religion in which magic, superstition, astrology overwhelmed about every impulse to a truly spiritual life. There was the same multiplicity of gods, even greater devotion to idol making and calendar making; more complete breaking down of once significant rituals; terror of demons and evil spirits of every kind. Landa says that they observed idolatrous practices to such an extent that in times of public misfortune all, even the women and children, burned incense and prayed to their gods to deliver them and check the demon who caused the harm. He says that they had many idols and sumptuous temples, and in the houses of priests and headmen were shrines for private sacrifices. It is told that on journeys many carried incense and plates on which to burn it, setting up, every night, stone shrines for incense burning and for invocation to their gods for safe return. They made pilgrimages to ancestral shrines, to holy places, such as the sacred *cenote* at Chichen Itza, to make sacrifices and offerings. They stopped at ruined temples by the way to burn copal and offer invocations. All this seems like echoes from Pueblo land, where ancestral shrines are still visited, where invocation and offerings of sacred meal are still made; where the prayer plumes are still placed by the wayside, and the spirit powers recognized in the old spiritual way. I am of the opinion that in the time of Landa and Sahagun there was much of the uncorrupted spiritual culture surviving, but unnoticed because of the barbarous ceremonial life that was so conspicuous. In fact, there is to this day much practice of fine ancestral ceremonial that passes unnoticed except to the inquisitive eye of the anthropologist. I am convinced that a wealth of ceremonial and ritual survives in remote districts of Mexico and Guatemala, to make life worth while to the living Aztec, Zapotec, Maya, Quiché, and Cakchiquel. I have seen many vestiges of it myself, and am going to hold that brief for the modern Indians of Middle America until young anthropologists, looking for the hard job, prove me right or wrong.

As you see the survival of religion in the cultural life of tropical America, it all smacks of degeneracy, but with vestiges there to take one back to the fine spiritual culture of the plains and desert peoples of northern America. The conviction grows upon one that up there is where the great mother-culture germed and matured and survives, and that here in tropical America it decayed under environmental conditions that tended always to becloud the spiritual vision. Then too, the Spaniards came to unsettle it still further. The priests saw and described only this decadent religious life, and added to the confusion of it with their new ceremonies and saints and images. One wonders that there is left a spark of pure autochthonous spiritual life in the descendants of the ancient Americans. Fortunately there is, and we hope and pray that it can again be fired into living flame, for to the Indians it was "the good way."

It was the worst in religious practice that came in for description and condemnation at the hands of the zealous *conquistadores* and priests. They played up to the limit, honestly, I concede, the idolatry that they witnessed, and when it came to viewing such practices as human sacrifice, they were appalled. Make due allowance for the natural exaggeration engendered by these loathsome sights, and there is plenty left that may be acknowledged. At the same time, it must be pointed out that human sacrifice was practiced not at all by the northern sedentary Indians, sparingly, if at all, by the early Maya-Quiché and Toltecs. The Aztecs all but had a monopoly on the custom, and it has not been proved that they practiced it extensively in pre-Spanish times. Remember too that it was a religious custom of an intensely superstitious people who reposed fanatic faith in their gods. The Spaniards came upon them suddenly, with incomprehensible powers. They possessed unheard-of engines of destruction. They were beyond the human plane. The generation of the Conquest saw Aztec dependence upon their gods fanned into a frenzy of supplication. Sacrifice without stint or limit was conceived to be the thing that would appease them. That time brought forth an epidemic of human sacrifice never before known in America. It was a perfectly natural expression of their terror of the new enemy, and their feeling that only the gods could save them, in the belief that these demoniac beings must be appeased before they would function again in their behalf. It is not a matter for especial wonder that the Aztecs of the Conquest generation lost their heads through terror, and tried to get right by murdering a few thousand friends and foes alike for the satisfaction of their gods. The civilized world in our generation lost its head and sacrificed some millions of manhood in battle, and millions of its women and children by starvation, to a spector not so bad as that which frightened the Aztecs out of their senses.

Summing up my own conclusions, I may say that I see in the religion of Aztec and Maya a vast confusion of ideas about deity, a degenerate system of beliefs derived from an ancient mother-culture, possibly the Pueblo, exalted in its original form, decaying in the adverse environment of the tropics, yet holding to certain fundamental ideas which even yet are discernible. There is, to be sure, obvious multiplicity of gods, and it might be thought that there was never the conception of an all-pervading deific power, comparable to the Wakanda of the great North American plains, or the Awanyu of the Southwestern desert. Examining every phase of their culture, one is convinced to the contrary. Their art was a complete expression of their religion. One motive, the feathered serpent, prevails throughout their esthetic world. In their painting, ceramics, sculp-

ture, architecture, it holds the commanding place. I
can see in it no other significance than that of a mighty,
all-pervading, spirit being.

The being pictured as a flying serpent was the most
potent and most widespread of all conceptions of deity
of the Indian race. Union of the major powers of earth,
symbolized by the serpent, and sky, symbolized by the
bird, it prevailed among all the higher cultures of ancient America. Awanyu of the Pueblos, the serpent
that lives in the sky; Quetzalcoatl of the Toltecs and
Aztecs (*Quetzal,* sacred bird, *coatl,* reptile); Kukulcan of the Yucatecans (*Kukul,* the quetzal bird, *can,*
serpent), are identical conceptions beyond question.
The feathered serpent runs as the dominant motive
through all Pueblo, Toltec, Aztec, and Maya art. The
plumed serpent of the Indian symbolized pure, deific
power, the union of male and female elements, earth
and sky, in one mighty being. The many conceptions
and explanations by white interpreters of this stupendous idea give us a melange of different kinds of god—
creator god, wind god, rain god, fair god, ugly god,
etc.—with numerous varieties of culture hero and of
superman. He is made into a discoverer of corn, teacher
of agriculture, astronomer, inventor of the calendar,
promoter of arts and crafts, law-giver, maker of
religious rituals, all-round scientist—in fact about
everything that the Indian never conceived of. This
confusion reflects the condition of mind of the Indians of
post-Conquest time, from which most of the ideas
about Quetzalcoatl have been derived and still further
corrupted. In the American Southwest, the term,
"Montezuma" now covers a multitude of confused ideas
—creator, god, warrior, founder, priest, leader of migration—even the ruin-mounds in places being called

"Montezumas." So the once clear concept of mighty power, the all-pervading Quetzalcoatl, has come to be a complex of degenerated myths upon which writers of another race have exercised a colossal amount of invention.

The Pueblos along with their Awanyu concept had their war gods and rain gods and other minor deities, but the whole religious structure was built around the one major conception of Deity. So in all probability, Huitzilopochtli, the war god, and Tlaloc, the rain deity, with all the minor figures that came to be represented in the Aztec pantheon, were subordinate to Quetzalcoatl. At any rate, that is the only explanation which makes sense that I can get out of that vast confusion. So I am going to let it go at that.

IV. Daily Life

From what has gone before, it should not be difficult to picture the daily life of the Indians who faced the Spanish Conquest. With all the reservations and cautions concerning the testimony of the time on the religious practices, we may recommend that Father Sahagun, Bishop Diego de Landa, and the soldier, Bernal Diaz, be read as authorities.

There is every reason to think that rural life was then much as it is today. That comes in for description later. It can be seen in the remote villages of Mexico and Guatemala in its pristine simplicity. But the great religious centers must be restored to the picture. That has been in part accomplished already through the study of their ruins. No better description exists of an important living temple precinct than that of Aztec Tenochtitlan, by Bernal Diaz, comrade in arms of Cortéz. The following account, recording his first impressions of a great Indian community and the life therein, should be read by everyone. It depicts first a great market. There we witness the life of the masses. The market is still a large factor in the life of the Indians of the tropics, the best place of all for the study of their material and social culture. Second is a temple scene which may be considered typical of the priestly life of every great sacred place, a life in which the masses had little part, but which dominated their thinking. It must be remembered that Bernal Diaz is not free from the exaggerations of the time, and that in describing phenomena he is compelled to use a vocabulary that was not devised for what he is here witnessing and telling about:

".... When we arrived there at the great square, we were astonished at the crowds of people, and the regularity which prevailed, as well as at the vast quantities of merchandise, which those who attended us were assiduous in pointing out. Each kind had its particular place, which was distinguished by a sign. The articles consisted of gold, silver, jewels, feathers, mantles, chocolate, skins dressed and undressed, sandals, and other manufactures of the roots and fibres of nequen, and great numbers of male and female slaves, some of whom were fastened by the neck, in collars, to long poles. The meat market was flocked with fowls, game, and dogs. Vegetables, fruits, articles of food ready dressed, salt, bread, honey, and sweet pastry made in various ways, were also sold here. Other places in the square were appointed to the sale of earthenware, wooden household furniture such as tables and benches, firewood, paper, sweet canes filled with tobacco mixed with liquid amber, copper axes and working tools, and wooden vessels highly painted. Numbers of women sold fish, and little loaves made of certain mud which they find in the lake, and which resembles cheese. The makers of stone blades were busily employed shaping them out of the rough material, and the merchants who dealt in gold, had the metal in grains as it came from the mines, in transparent tubes, so that they could be reckoned, and the gold was valued at so many mantles, or so many xiquipils of cocoa to the size of the quills. The entire square was inclosed in piazzas, under which great quantities of grain were stored, and where were also shops for various kinds of goods. . . .

"From the square we proceeded to the great temple, but before we entered it we made a circuit through a number of large courts, the smallest of which appeared to me to contain more ground than the great square in Salamanca, with double inclos-

ures built of lime and stone, and the courts paved
with large white cut stone, very clean; or where
not paved, they were plaistered and polished.
When we approached the gate of the great temple,
to the flat summit of which the ascent was by a
hundred and fourteen steps, and before we had
mounted one of them, Montezuma sent down to us
six priests, and two of his noblemen, to carry Cortes up, as they had done their sovereign, which he
politely declined. When we had ascended to the
summit of the temple, we observed on the platform
as we passed, the large stones whereon were placed
the victims who were to be sacrificed. Here was a
great figure which resembled a dragon, and much
blood fresh spilt. Montezuma came out from an
adoratory in which his accursed idols were placed,
attended by two priests, and addressing himself to
Cortes, expressed his apprehension that he was fa-
tigued; to which Cortes replied, that fatigue was
unknown to us.

"Montezuma then took him by the hand, and
pointed out to him the different parts of the city,
and its vicinity, all of which were commanded from
that place. Here we had a clear prospect of the
three causeways by which Mexico communicated
with the land, and of the aqueduct of Chapulte-
peque, which supplied the city with the finest water.
We were struck with the numbers of canoes, passing to and from the main land, loaded with provisions and merchandise, and we could now pre-
ceive, that in this great city, and all the others of
that neighborhood which were built in the water,
the houses stood separate from each other, com-
municating only by small drawbridges, and by
boats, and that they were built with terraced tops.
We observed also the temples and adoratories of
the adjacent cities, built in the form of towers and
fortresses, and others on the causeway, all white-
washed, and wonderfully brilliant. The noise and

bustle of the market-place below us could be heard almost a league off, and those who had been at Rome and at Constantinople said, that for convenience, regularity, and population, they had never seen the like. Cortes now proposed to Fra. Bartholome to apply to Montezuma for permission to construct our church here, to which the father for the present objected, thinking it ill-timed. Cortes then addressing himself to Montezuma, requested that he would do him the favour to shew us his gods. Montezuma having first consulted his priests, led us into a tower where was a kind of saloon. Here were two altars highly adorned, with richly wrought timbers on the roof, and over the altars, gigantic figures resembling very fat men. The one on the right was Huitzilopochtli their war god, with a great face and terrible eyes; this figure was entirely covered with gold and jewels, and his body bound with golden serpents; in his right hand he held a bow, and in his left a bunch of arrows. The little idol which stood by him represented his page, and bore a lance and target richly ornamented with gold and jewels. The great idol had round his neck the figures of human heads and hearts, made of pure gold and silver, ornamented with precious stones of a blue colour. Before the idol was a pan of incense, with three hearts of human victims which were then burning, mixed with copal. The whole of that apartment, both walls and floor, was stained with human blood in such quantity as to give a very offensive smell. On the left was the other great figure, with a countenance like a bear, and great shining eyes, of the polished substance whereof their mirrors are made. The body of this idol was also covered with jewels. These two deities, it was said, were brothers; the name of this last was Tezcatepuca, and he was the god of the infernal regions. He presided, according to their notions, over the souls of men. His

body was covered with figures representing little
devils with tails of serpents, and the walls and
pavement of this temple were so besmeared with
blood that they stunk worse than all the slaughter-
houses of Castille. An offering lay before him of
five human hearts. In the summit of the temple,
and in a recess the timber of which was most highly ornamented, we saw a figure half human and the
other half resembling an alligator, inlaid with
jewels, and partly covered with a mantle. This
idol was said to contain the germ, and origin of all
created things, and was the god of harvest, and
fruits. The walls and altars were bestained like the
rest, and so offensive, that we thought we never
could get out soon enough.

"In this place they had a drum of most enormous
size, the head of which was made of the skins of
large serpents: this instrument when struck re-
sounded with a noise that could be heard to the
distance of two leagues, and so doleful that it deserved to be named the music of the infernal regions; and with their horrible sounding horns and
trumpets, their great knives for sacrifice, their
human victims, and their blood besprinkled altars,
I devoted them, and all their wickedness to God's
vengeance, and thought that the time would never
arrive, that I should escape from this scene of
human butchery, horrible smells, and more detest-
able sights."

By going through the entire work of Father Sahagun, one will get light on almost every phase of the
life of the ancient Mexicans. It is buried in the ex-
haustive details of religious practices, calendrical festivals, etc., and there is nowhere a summary that affords
a succinct picture of the daily domestic life. His *His-
toria General de las Cosas de Nueva España* is an inexhaustible source, but it requires long and patient

sifting to get out the material for a connected picture. His informants were exclusively Indians. The great value of his work is in that it reflects so accurately the native thought in the Indian's own mode of expression.

Education was mainly a training for priestly service. With such a great part of life devoted to religious practices, many young men had to be prepared for the numerous priesthoods. Here are a few samples from the Sahagun account, of how boys were prepared to become "ministers to the idols." It was a pretty strenuous kind of education. These regulations are quoted from Sahagun's *History of Ancient Mexico,* Fannie Bandelier's translation, Fiske University Press:

"The first custom was that all those ministers of the idols who were called Tlamacazque were to sleep in the house of the Calmecac. The second rule was that they all swept and cleaned that house at four o'clock in the morning. The third one was that the already bigger boys had to go to look for and gather maguey-points; the fourth rule was for still older boys to bring in fire-wood on their backs from the forest; this wood was needed for the fires which were lighted every night; and when any construction work in clay was to be done, be it building walls, ditches, watering canals, or field work, they all went to work together at daybreak, only those who had to watch the house and those who had to carry the food to the workers, remaining; no one ever lagged behind, and they all worked with great discipline and good order. The fifth rule was to stop work somewhat early; they then went at once to their monastery to be in charge of the services of their gods and to perform penance exercises and, first of all, to bathe. At sunset they began to get all the necessary things ready, then, at eleven o'clock at night, they went on their way, each one alone by himself, carrying the points of maguey, a shell on which to play a tune on the road, an incensory of clay, a pouch or bag in which to carry the incense, torches and the points of maguey. Thus each one went out naked to deposit the maguey thorns at his particular place of devotion, and those who wanted to do very severe penance went far towards the forests, mountains and rivers. The older boys would go as far as half a league to a determined place; there they would deposit the points of maguey, inserting them in a ball made of hay, and then would return, each one alone, playing on his shell. . . . The eighth rule was that every midnight all had to get up to pray, and he who did not awake and rise was punished by pricking him with points of maguey leaves in the ears, the chest, thighs and legs, in short, sticking maguey thorns into his whole body in presence of all the ministers of the idols, so that he might take warning. The ninth rule was that no one should be overbearing, or offend one another, nor should anyone be disobedient to the order and customs they observed, and if at one time or another one of them appeared intoxicated, or should live in concubinage or commit some criminal act, they killed him outright, executed him with garrote, roasted him alive, or shot arrows at him. If anyone committed a venial sin they pierced his ears and sides with maguey thorns or awl. The tenth rule was that the boys were to be punished by piercing their ears or by whipping them with nettles."

The Maya of Yucatan, according to Diego de Landa, lived in towns, the land well cleared and weeded and set out with trees, the homes of the common people being upon the outskirts. The houses were covered with straw or palm leaves, the roofs having a steep pitch so that they shed rain. They were fine-looking people, he says, but usually bowlegged from the way the women carried the children, astride their hips. The men, not the women, used mirrors. They bound a board on the forehead to make it flat, and pierced their ears for pendants. They had no beard, claiming that their mothers singed their faces in childhood with hot cloths. They painted the body and face red and practiced tattooing. They wore a wide sash wound around the waist and hanging down in front and behind, the ends being decorated with embroidery and feather work. A square mantle was worn about the shoulders. They wore sandals of hemp or deer skin. The principal food was corn, prepared in many different ways. They made stew of vegetables and game, keeping fowls in large numbers. Evidently they lived rather well when .they had food, but were able to get along with little when necessary. They took their meals on the floor, the men not eating with the women.

They played ball and games like dice, and enacted dramas, being fond of comedy, taking off the Spaniards and priests, as the Pueblos do the *conquistadores* and archæologists. They had a drum to beat with the hand, and one of hollow wood played upon with a stick with a ball on the end. They had trumpets of conch shell and wood, and an instrument made of turtle shell played with the palm of the hand. They made whistles of bamboo and deer bones, and flutes of cane. Their dances, as described, clearly resembled those of the Pueblos.

Their industries, in addition to agriculture, were pottery making and woodwork, and arts for trade in the market or on their long trading journeys. They exchanged work in farming, owned the land in common, but held what they produced individually. The land was worked mainly in January, February, and March, using the planting stick and stone hoe, as did the northern Indians. They had community hunts and roasted their game to keep it from spoiling. They had bows of wood strung with hemp cord, and arrows of cane tipped with obsidian and fish teeth (shark?) points, and were good marksmen. They also had spears with flint points, and metal axes—copper hardened by beating with stone. They had round shields of cane framework covered with deer hide.

Like all Indians, they loved to make presents to neighbors, friends, and strangers, were hospitable to visitors, always offering food and drink, sharing what they had, however little, and, if caught with nothing in the larder, going out to get something in some way. The women were discreetly silent as a rule, but nevertheless had their part in domestic affairs. "Medicine men" were numerous—priests dressed in jaguar skins. They had two war captains in each community, were for the most part peaceable, and when going to war went silently, evidently depending upon surprise attack. They were relentless in punishment when the accepted customs were violated. The young people, like all other Indians, were respectful to the old. They married early, the women were uniformly chaste, good housekeepers and mothers, helped to sow and cultivate the crops and raise the poultry and domestic animals.

The subjects which were taught to the young, but not all, were computation of the years, months, days, festivals, and ceremonies, and of natal days and periods; the art of divination, forecasting coming events; remedies for sickness, the numerical system, writing and reading the characters with which they wrote, genealogy in which they took much pride.

Paralleling this picture of daily life of fifteenth-century Aztec and Maya with that of all the sedentary

Indians, from New Mexico to Peru, we find the common factors amazing, if we leave out the abnormally developed religious part, or tone it down to what were probably the original elements. The unified pattern for the race, for the continent, is unmistakable. To this race, the Old World did not exist. Their world was this isolated continent, its boundaries the sky and the seas which, so far as they were concerned, were equally limitless. It was their continent, their world, by right of discovery, occupation, long possession, by virtue of the culture which they had derived from its soil and winds and natural life. But the uniqueness of this race was not destined to prevail in the land that nurtured it, because of an idea that was evolving in a restless brain across the sea. A disaster such as, in no other instance in human history, has so completely overwhelmed a race was ready to break over them. The spacious land was to be theirs no longer. Their very lives were to come under a hand unknown to them. The juggernaut of destiny was moving silently to their destruction.

PART SIX

THE CATACLYSM THAT BROKE OVER AMERICA

"Beware when the great God lets loose
a thinker on this planet."
—RALPH WALDO EMERSON.

PART SIX

THE CATACLYSM THAT BROKE OVER AMERICA

I. Where Destiny was Forged

It is the year 1487. Let us pay a visit to Tenochtitlan, the island stronghold of the Aztecs. The Great
Chief now is Ahuitzotl, eighth to rule over the Aztecs,
now the unchallenged masters of Anahuac. The
wretched little band of stragglers of 1324 has become
a powerful tribe. The little sanctuary of mud and grass
of 1427, built on piles in the swamp, has grown into
the Great Teocalli, vastest religious establishment on
the continent.

The sun is setting upon the most fervent celebration
ever known in ancient America. The hosts that have
come from distant valleys and mountains to participate
in the dedication of the temple of Huitzilopochtli, all-
potent Aztec divinity, the mighty god of war, number
many thousands—some said millions. They have been
treated to a spectable to put them in lifelong awe of
the deity and his priesthood, the sacrifice of enemy cap-
tives—some say four thousand, some one hundred
thousand. The lowest guess will do. It is probably too
high. A much smaller number would stupefy the people, for human sacrifice is a new rite in Anahuac.

Lingering for a few years in this land of the supernatural, we sense a pall of terror over these simple
folk. A pagan priesthood has attained its goal—the
enslavement of mind and spirit of an entire people.

The power of free, wholesome thought is gone. The mass mind is looking for disaster in appalling form.

A great eclipse of the sun occurs at midday. For five hours there is darkness, with the stars shining in the afternoon. This can mean but one thing—great sky monsters are coming to devour men, women, and children. So say the "medicine men" who have the power of looking into the future and foretelling coming events. That they are known to be colossal liars is of no importance. Aztecs like other people like to be humbugged.

Suppose we find one honest diviner who actually is endowed with the power to pierce the unknown. Our old diviner looks across the sea to the east, expecting to see terrific forces gathering, but, strangely enough, no world-shaking powers are in action. The scene is anything but portentous. In a bare little cell in a poor Franciscan monastery, La Rabida, near the southern point of Spain, two men sit at a table, poring over charts and projections and astronomical calculations. One is a sailor of obviously more than ordinary knowledge of navigation, and a fanatical certainty of statement; the other, a priest of mind unfettered by dogma. The sailor is said to have come from Genoa, his name, Cristóbal Colón; the priest is Fray Juan Perez de Marchena who, in times past, has been father confessor to his Queen, Isabella of Castille.

What could an Aztec seer see in this commonplace scene to cast the faintest shadow over Anahuac or disturb a world? Who could imagine that these are the most momentous discussions ever held on this planet; that because of them the veil will be raised from an unknown world; Spain be the greatest colonial Empire under the sun—exalted by untold wealth and destroyed

298

by prosperity; Christendom flung around the globe; the evolution of a race of men interrupted for centuries, perhaps for all time? A race's destiny is being forged there in the barren cell of La Rabida.

What would it have meant to our Aztec seer could his vision have followed the Genoese sailor as he trudged to the field capital of his sovereigns, the holy city of Santa Fe, facing Granada; seen him unfold his mysterious maps before his Queen and expound his unbelievable theory; then trudge away, disconsolate, to give another country the opportunity of the ages; but, overtaken by the Queen's messenger at the bridge over the little *arroyo,* and summoned back for another audience, convincing at last that wisest of queens of the unbelievable; and there see signed the most momentous decree that ever sovereign was permitted to put seal upon?

The Aztec seer, following this hardly noticeable succession of events, would have seen, in the humble chapel of Saint George in the little port of Palos, the sailor on his knees all night before his Deity, then the solemn march down the hill in the early morning to board the little caravel, one of three that were to make world history. Even as this series of world-shaping events draws toward the close, the Aztec seer can see little in it to cause anxiety in Anahuac. Compare the shabby sailor-adventurer, even though now admiral of a diminutive fleet, with the splendor of Ahuitzotl. But follow the vision through:

> "Behind him lay the gray Azores,
>   Behind the Gates of Hercules;
> Before him not the ghost of shores;
>   Before him only shoreless seas.
> The good mate said: 'Now must we pray,
>   For lo! the very stars are gone,

Brave Adm'r'l speak; what shall I say?'
  'Why, say: "Sail on! sail on! and on!"

" 'My men grow mutinous day by day;
  My men grow ghastly, wan and weak.'
The stout mate thought of home; a spray
  Of salt wave washed his swarthy cheek.
'What shall I say, brave Adm'r'l, say,
  If we sight naught but seas at dawn?'
'Why, you shall say at break of day:
  "Sail on! sail on! and on!" '

"They sailed and sailed, as winds might blow,
  Until at last the blanched mate said:
'Why, now not even God would know
  Should I and all my men fall dead.
These very winds forget their way,
  For God from these dread seas is gone.
Now speak, brave Adm'r'l, speak and say—'
  He said: 'Sail on! sail on! and on!'

"Then pale and worn, he paced his deck,
  And peered through darkness.
    Ah, that night
Of all dark nights! And then a speck—
  A light! A light! At last a light!
It grew, a starlit flag unfurled!
  It grew to be Time's burst of dawn.
He gained a world; he gave that world
  Its grandest lesson: 'On! sail on!' "

—JOAQUIN MILLER.

Still the Aztec diviner could see in this closing vision nothing to alarm his people. But the cataclysm will break soon enough. Rumors will fly up and down Mexico and Central America, of supermen, white, bearded, mounted on strange beasts, and armed with weapons that emit fire and thunder.

II. A Continent Unveiled: A Race's Tragedy

One cannot avoid a feeling of regret that Columbus never knew the full purport of his achievement, and that he had to suffer such outrageous defeats in the end. But that is not the way to look at it. No greater victory ever came to mortal man. The moment he set foot on New World soil his place in history was won; in fact, his work was finished. Subsequent honors and struggles and degradation were of no consequence. He had unveiled an unknown world, perhaps unwittingly. He had carried a mighty thought to fruition, by his indomitable courage and strength of will. Puny by comparison are Alexander the Great, Julius Cæsar, Genghis Khan, Tamerlane, Napoleon, and loud-mouthed modern dictators. Not even in the dauntless voyage was the greatest glory of a heroic soul. In the poor cell of La Rabida the world was enlarged, the history of all mankind turned into new channels, and a new destiny for an entire race of men forged in the brain of the sailor of Genoa. Adventurers without number, later, played their part on the stage, but Columbus was the thinker "let loose on this planet," near the end of the fifteenth century A. D.

The great discovery came at a propitious time. The ten years devoted to driving the Moors from the land where they had no business to be, but to which they clung for nearly eight centuries, developed the manhood of Spain. That mighty struggle brought the flower of Spanish chivalry to the banner of Ferdinand and Isabella. Courage, loyalty, endurance, sportsmanship, ambition, were fruits of the ten-year combat. With the siege of Granada, there culminated a vast formative influence upon the Spanish character. Adventure had become a necessity. What outlet was there for that terrific energy, after the fall of Granada? Columbus furnished the answer. Fighting the Moors gave no such opportunity for high adventure as did the call of a New World. Fighting and fortune, a grand combination, beckoned the manhood of Spain. The conflict with the Moors was ideal preparation for this wider field of action. Only incredible daring, superhuman endurance, had any chance in this game. Cortéz, Alvarado, Pizarro, and Coronado, with their small rabbles of gentlemen and roughnecks, were the ones called of destiny.

They carried to the Indians a mode of warfare that was entirely new to them. The Indian, as a hand-to-hand fighter, always gave a good account of himself. Battle-axes, spears, bows and arrows constituted his equipment. As a strategist, knowing how to take advantage of bush and rock, he was incomparable on his own ground and fighting in his own way. He has never been found lacking in courage or efficiency. But arms spouting fire and thunder, warriors on strange beasts, which seemed at first a part of themselves, put an element of terror into the business that offset disparity in numbers. These psychological factors might have been overcome in time, but Cortéz used the old strategic principle of warfare, "divide and conquer," with deadly success. He discovered the hereditary tribal feuds and, by enlisting Indians by the thousands to fight their own relatives, was able to bring his army up to equality with the Aztecs in numbers.

Four major factors entered into the defeat of the Aztecs, first, the calamitous predictions of their own priests, that had been going on for a generation or two; second, the new mode of warfare, bearing out the predictions of their soothsayers; third, the Spanish tactics—arraying Indians against Indians; and, fourth, the indomitable courage and ability of the small Spanish army.

Number three was, no doubt, the deciding factor. The pall of superstition spread over the people by their priests went far. Psychology is a potent factor in war, but this could have been dispelled by a few brave spirits, such as the eleventh great chief, Cuauhtémoc. The illusion of immortal beings, even gods, waned as they saw dead horses and dead Spaniards. Morale could have been restored. But in war, deities have nearly always been "on the side of the heaviest battalions." One wishes, purely as a sporting proposition, for in the long run the result would have been the same, that the Tlaxcalans might have kept out of it. Without so many odds against them, the Aztecs might have modified the course of New World history considerably. They were a courageous tribe, and the Indians a courageous race, which has always raised up valiant leaders in times of struggle. Fighting Spaniards on something like equal terms would have brought out new resources, allayed their superstitions, unified rival communities, perhaps integrated Mexicans, Tarascans, Zapotecs, Mixtecs, Maya, Quiché, into a nation.

War as a factor of culture evolution has not been discussed in this work. A word on that subject will be in order here. That physical combat has been a powerful stimulus to culture growth cannot be denied. That it developed the manly attributes of courage, chivalry, respect for opponents, sportsmanship, physical power, and endurance, is certain. But I would draw a line between primitive combat and "civilized" war. There is no use trying to compare the struggles between Moor and Christian, Norman and Anglo-Saxon, Spaniard and Aztec—pre-machine age battle—and what is now called war. The former was to the brave and the strong; the latter is to the coward and the bully. There is no basis for comparison. Making war by modern methods is simply amplified crime. I believe in boxing and football and Homer for youth. Trained fists and muscles are the basis of a manly art, that of self-defense. The gun and knife are the resort of the criminal and the degenerate. Your up-to-date army sent against an alleged "uncivilized" foe, however decrepit and defenseless, doesn't even march. Its soldiers are hauled to the scene in motor trucks with a service of supply to insure three square meals a day; with machine guns, artillery, airplanes, tons of bombs, and, just as a precaution against the helpless "enemy," stores of poison gas. Such is the equipment for a modern war of even the jackrabbit class. Pretty safe and pretty dirty business, calling for little courage, no exceptional endurance, little brains, and for an objective, brutal, cowardly murder in which men, women, and children are slaughtered indiscriminately. Warfare in this year of our Lord 1936 is a display of cowardice and crime on a colossal scale. But it is thus in this age of progress that "civilization" is brought to the "backward" peoples. If this be *civilization,* give me the stone ax and the plumed serpent.

However bitterly we may think of the treatment of the Indians after they were subdued; whatever we may be compelled to say about the after results of the Spanish Conquest, we can unhesitatingly hold that the Conquest itself was one of the great adventures of all time, and that it was carried out in no more brutal fashion than was the custom in the wars of the time. Invading an unknown land of enormous and effective population,

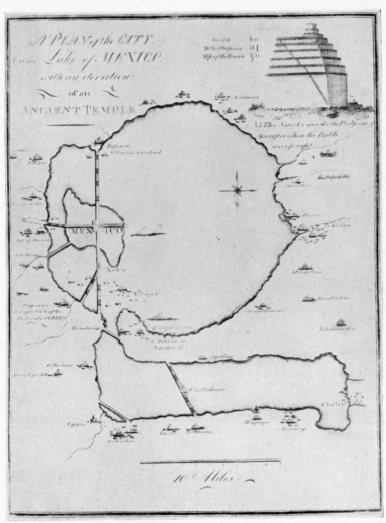

From Bernal Diaz' True History of the Conquest of Mexico

Plan of the City and Lake of Mexico

Tarascan Boy, Michoacan

supposedly savage, with a mere handful of soldiers, even though with the advantage of firearms, was an enterprise that called for sustained courage and a resourcefulness in meeting emergencies that has rarely been equaled.

It is not within the scope of this work to write a history of the Spanish Conquest of America. There are many works available on that subject. If only one is read, it should be *The True History of the Conquest of Mexico,* by Captain Bernal Diaz del Castillo, written in Guatemala City nearly a half-century after the Conquest (finished, he devoutly says, on the twenty-sixth day of February, 1572), to be had in various translations and editions. This blunt old warrior, participant, according to his count, in one hundred and nineteen battles (while Julius Cæsar had only fifty-three to his credit), makes no bones of the fact that they were scared as they penetrated the unknown land. "We had enough to do to protect ourselves, for I vow to God and say amen thereto, that we were every day repeating our prayers and supplicating to be delivered from the perils that surrounded us."

Cortéz commenced his march to the conquest of Tenochtitlan from Cempoalan near the gulf coast, not far from the present city of Vera Cruz, in August, 1519. Bernal Diaz says with emphasis, "We never much exceeded four hundred men." Fighting Indians was not the whole of Cortéz's job. As with every efficient leader, he had jealous rivalry from within and treachery from without to deal with. In the face of all this, he coolly dismantled and sunk his ships; there was to be no turning back. Another case of "sail on." There was soon fighting enough to satisfy the most ambitious of Spanish cavaliers. At Tehuacingo they were engaged by a host (Bernal's guess—commensurate with his acknowledged fright, being forty thousand). In this succession of battles we get a picture of the mode of warfare on both sides:

"Their first discharges of arrows, stones, and two-headed darts which pierced any armor, and through the body where unprotected, covered the ground and they continued to advance until they closed upon and attacked us with their lances and two-handed swords, fighting foot to foot and encouraging each other by their cries and shouts. Our artillery, musketry, and cross-bows played on them, and the home thrusts our infantry made with their swords prevented their closing upon us as much as they had done on the former occasion. Our cavalry also charged with such effect that, next to God, it was to them we owed the victory. At one period I saw our battalion completely broken, nor could all the exertions of Cortez for a time rally it, such was the pressure of the enemy upon us."

Reaching the Tlaxcalan country, there were some pitched battles and then, as a consequence of the old salt feud, the alliance against Montezuma, destined to be the decisive factor in the war, was concluded. At Cholula, site of the great Toltec Temple of the Sun, treachery was tried by the Indians but foiled, thanks to the concubine of Cortéz, Marina, and as a lesson, some six thousand Cholulans (another Bernal Diaz guess) put to death. "We executed their punishment on them in a manner that they will ever remember; for a number of them were killed by us instantly, and many afterward burned alive, very contrary to the expectations they had formed from the promise of their gods." An early demonstration of frightfulness as a civilizing agency!

On the eighth day of November, 1519, Cortéz made his "adventurous and magnanimous entry" into Tenochtitlan. Montezuma II, great chief since 1502, offered every possible inducement to keep him away, but no military resistance. It was strictly a peaceful mission, according to Cortéz, to acquaint them with the greatness of his sovereign and to enlighten them concerning the Christian faith. There was much exchange of presents, of compliments, of protestations of everlasting love and friendship, such as modern enemies indulge in while watching for the safe chance at homicide. The Spaniards settled down for a protracted visit; the Aztec chief indicating from time to time that it might be pleasantly terminated. Something has been told in a previous chapter of what was to be seen in the pueblo.

Eight days after the *entrada* it seemed expedient to seize the person of Montezuma, the excuse being the killing of a Spanish captain and six soldiers on a pillaging expedition down near the gulf coast. Montezuma was also charged with responsibility for the Cholula affair. So a "visit" was paid to the chief and, with every assurance of respect and honor, speedily demonstrated by putting him in irons, he was conducted to the quarters of Cortéz and, from that time on, held a prisoner in his own stronghold.

Reports of the remarkable success of Cortéz's invasion of Mexico engendered bitter rivalry at home. He was compelled to take time out from his main objective to meet an expedition sent out by his enemy, Velasquez, under the command of Narvaez, which had landed on the gulf coast. He accomplished this speedily and satisfactorily, and, leaving his principal enemies in jail and attaching to his own person a part of the army of Narvaez, he returned to the main issue, the conquest of Mexico.

The news that reached Cortéz from Tenochtitlan was extremely disturbing. Pedro Alvarado, who had been left in command, was beseiged by the Indians, a number of his men killed and his quarters set on fire. No better excuse could have been asked by Cortéz for now taking up with all possible severity the conquest of the Indian capital. The Aztecs had apparently lost much of their superstitious dread of the Spaniards, and were infuriated by the continued imprisonment of their chief. They were now prepared to give a proper account of themselves. Bernal Diaz says, "Our quarters had been attacked by multitudes at the same moment; they poured in such discharges of missile weapons upon us there that they immediately wounded upwards of forty-six, twelve of whom afterwards died. Neither our firearms nor our good fighting could prevent the enemy from closing in upon us for a length of time. The enemy still continued their attacks, but all we had hitherto suffered was nothing to that which succeeded. They set fire to various parts of buildings which we occupied, thinking to burn us alive or stifle us with the smoke, and we were obliged to stop it by tearing down the building or by throwing earth upon it. All the courts and open spaces of our quarters were covered with their arrows and missile weapons. The Mexicans came to meet us with their whole force and both parties fought desperately, but as the numbers of our opponents were so immense, and as they constantly brought up fresh troops, even if we had been ten thousand Hectors of Troy we could not have beaten them off, nor could we by our cannon or firearms make any impression on them. Some of our soldiers who had been in Italy swore that neither among Christians or Turks nor the artillery of the King of France, had they ever seen such desperation as was manifested in the attacks of those Indians." The description of the battle as it continued certainly gives us the impression that the Spaniards now had an enemy to deal with that would demand their utmost resources. As the situation became more and more desperate, Cortéz conceived the idea of bringing the imprisoned Montezuma to his aid. The great chief was, accordingly, brought out to address from the roof his attacking legions. Historians may never agree as to just what happened on this momentous occasion. The Spanish account is that a shower of arrows and stones fell about the unhappy chief, and that from this attack the chief was mortally wounded, killed by his own people. The story of the Indians ascribed the death of Montezuma to Cortéz himself.

So, this unhappy chief passes out of the picture of the conquest of Mexico. There is a world of literature to be read concerning him, much of which is unreliable, but out of it all, each one interested in finding his permanent place in history will be able to form some rational opinion. There will never be any approach to agreement concerning the character of Montezuma II. By some writers he has been made out a vacillating, weak, even cowardly monarch. On the contrary, he was a sane, thoughtful, courageous leader, facing, as he well knew, inevitable doom. He could not stand against an earthquake. The story of his death by a stone in the hands of his own people comes through the Spaniards. He was probably killed by Cortéz, as the Indians claimed. The larger consequence of that tragic episode was that an entire race was made conscious of its helplessness. That so much of its spirit survived the wreckage, that it still produced strong, independent individuals, is high testimony to its moral and spiritual reserves. By way of personal description we have the statement of Bernal Diaz: "The great Montezuma was at this time aged about forty years, of good stature, well proportioned, and thin: his complexion was much fairer than that of the Indians; he wore his hair short, just covering his ears, with very little beard, well arranged, thin, and black. His face was rather long, with a pleasant countenance, and good eyes; gravity and good humour were blended together when he spoke. He was very delicate and clean in his person, bathing himself every evening. . . ."

As a final word concerning this unique character in American history, I must point out again that he was priest, as well as military chieftain, and that this fact is of great assistance in arriving at a just estimate of his career.

The culmination of the desperate struggle in Tenochtitlan came with the battle of the Great *Teocalli*. It was doubtless a Homeric combat, but with the advantages of the Spaniards in the way of firearms and cavalry now so greatly worn down, with the numbers of the Aztecs swelling to where the Spaniards, even with the assistance of their Tlaxcalan allies had become one to many, there could be but one result. The retreat of the Spaniards over the causeways and across the lagoon back to the mainland was a rout. This was the bitterest night in the career of Cortéz, and for his army one of utter discouragement. There was nothing to comfort them, save that some had escaped with their lives. This was the famous *Noche Triste,* at the end of which we see Cortéz seated under a great tree (still

visited by thousands of sightseers in modern Mexico),
contemplating the pitiable remnant of his army—more
than one-half his Spanish soldiers, two-thirds of his
Indian allies dead—artillery, ammunition, stores, and
a vast quantity of the loot of gold in the bottom of the
lake.

A famous episode in the struggle was the unbelievable leap of Pedro Alvarado in making his retreat
along the broken Tlacopan causeway bridge. Bernal
Diaz is not accountable for that romantic story. He
gives it scant credence and naïvely says:

"As to that fatal bridge which is called the leap
of Alvarado, I say that no soldier thought of looking whether he leaped, much or little, for we had
enough to do to save our own lives. It must however have been as he stated when he met Cortes,
that he passed it upon the dead bodies and baggage, for if he had attempted to sustain himself
upon his lance, the water would have been too deep
for him to have reached the bottom of it; and the
aperture was too wide, and the sides too high for
him to have leaped, let him have been ever so active. For my part I aver that he could not have
leaped it in any manner, for in about a year after,
when we invested Mexico, I was engaged with the
enemy on that which is now called the bridge of the
leap of Alvarado, for they had there made breast-
works and barricades; and we many times conversed
upon the subject at the spot, and all of us agreed
that it could not have happened. But as some will
insist upon the reality of it I repeat it again, it
could not have been done, and let those who wish
to ascertain it view the place; the bridge is there,
and the depth of the water will prove no lance could
reach to the bottom. . . ."

The flight of the Spaniards from Tenochtitlan was early in July, 1520. It was followed, four days later, by the battle of Otumba, not far from the great pyramid of Teotihuacan, the most decisive battle of the war. This was a fair fight, with the victory to the Spaniards, in many ways a personal victory for Cortéz whose deeds of valor reached the zenith on that day. Of this battle, Prescott, in his *History of the Conquest of Mexico,* says:

"It was undoubtedly one of the most remarkable victories ever achieved in the New World. And this not merely on account of the disparity of the forces but of their unequal condition. For the Indians were in all their strength while the Christians were wasted by disease, famine, and long-protracted sufferings; without cannon or firearms, and deficient in the military apparatus which had so often struck terror into their barbarian foe; deficient even in the terrors of a victorious name. But they had discipline on their side, desperate resolve and implicit confidence in their commander."

And Bancroft, in his *Annals of Early Mexico,* gives it a still higher place in history:

"Obviously this battle was the most important so far in the New World; and it must ever be regarded as one of the most remarkable in history. The natives were probably much less numerous than the estimates of the boastful victors (20,000), still they were immensely superior in number and condition to the Spaniards, enfeebled by recent defeat, by wounds, and want. Further, the latter had no firearms wherewith to terrify the natives, only swords and pikes. Their main advantage lay in their horses, their discipline, and the genius of their leader, all strengthened by the enthusiasm born of a national pride and a certain knowledge that failure meant utter destruction."

The army of Cortéz now withdrew to Tlaxcala, where, among the allies who had likewise suffered terribly at Tenochtitlan and Otumba, they settled down to recuperate from their frightful experiences. But there was no breaking the spirit of Cortéz. In a few months he was to fight his way back to the shores of Texcoco, to conquer again the surrounding towns, to launch the brigantines brought, "knocked down," over the desert and mountains of Tlaxcala and put together at Texcoco; to occupy and destroy the Aztec capital. The difficulties of this campaign can hardly be overestimated. While Cortéz had rebuilt his army and greatly increased the number of his allies, replenished his artillery, ammunition and stores, he now faced an enemy no longer deluded by belief in the superhuman character of the white men, an enemy thoroughly infuriated by its past experiences and fighting with its back to the wall. Moreover, the leadership was no longer in the hands of Montezuma II. That post had passed to the young and indomitable Cuauhtémoc. Here was a captain worthy of leadership in any army of any race, from Trojan to the present day. He was at this time only about twenty-three years of age, had been given a priestly education in his youth, but, as his subsequent career showed, was under no religious handicaps, was in fact one hundred per cent a warrior. He was said to be a nephew and son-in-law of Montezuma, and had passed through all of the previous scenes of the Conquest, from the earliest landing of the Spaniards upon the Mexican shore. In physical courage, in warlike accomplishments, and as a strategist, Cuauhtémoc was the equal of any captain that was brought out by the Conquest of the Americas.

Some historians of the Conquest have been impressed with the extreme ferocity of Cuauhtémoc, and have made this the excuse for the brutal treatment meted out to him and his followers by the conquerors. Those who go to the extreme in the defense of the Spaniards, speak of all who exalt the character of Cuauhtémoc as sentimentalists, and ascribe to him every form of inhuman cruelty that has ever been thought of for the detraction of the Indian race. I imagine that the Aztecs became rather bloodthirsty in the course of their conflict with the Spaniards. I think so because they were human beings, of a race that did not always take its punishment lying down. Perhaps Cuauhtémoc went pretty far in meeting the Spanish policy of frightfulness in kind. But, from the day of his first prominent appearance in history, the day of the killing of Montezuma on the roof of the temple, by somebody, whether it was Indian or Spaniard, through all the events of the war, including the driving of the Spaniards from their island stronghold on the *Noche Triste;* through his accession to the chieftaincy and his heroic defense of his tribe on the return of Cortéz to the attack; through his final defeat and surrender, and the torture that he is said to have undergone in resisting the conquerors' quest for gold, in which he simply displayed the typical Indian stoicism; and to his final murder by Cortéz at some place in southern Mexico, during the march to Honduras, Cuauhtémoc was an ideal captain, an ideal man, a true Indian. Among the heroes of the "red" race, I place him at the top, and this without diminishing in any respect my estimate of Atahualpa of the Peruvians, Geronimo of the Apaches, or Tecumseh of the Shawnees.

With the events above described, the career of Hernando Cortéz may be said to have been finished. True, he attained to distinction as Marquis of the Valley, but from here on his star was clearly on the decline. He was on the way to join the Great Admiral. As with Columbus, the meeting of jealousy and rivalry in every virulent form, was now to be the principal occupation of Cortéz. There could have been, in his last years, little satisfaction or enjoyment of what he was able to retain of the possessions that he had gained. As to recollections of the Conquest in which he took the leading part, I should say they would be just about those of any leader whose place in history was gained through war. He was certainly one of the most remarkable captains of all time. Much could be truthfully said of him by way of detraction, but the other side of the picture should not be overlooked. As before suggested, the truth will be found between the extremes. What Bernal Diaz had to say of his chief must receive great consideration. He gives us a striking picture of both the personal appearance and character of Cortéz:

"I will now proceed to describe the person and disposition of the Marquis. He was of a good stature and strong build, of a rather pale complexion, and serious countenance. His features were, if faulty, rather too small; his eyes mild and grave. His beard was black, thin, and scanty; his hair in the same manner. He was very well limbed, and his legs rather bowed; an excellent horseman, and dexterous in the use of arms. He also possessed the heart and mind, which is the principal part of the business. . . . In his appearance, manners, transactions, conversation, table, and dress, every thing bore the appearance of a great lord. . . .

". . . He was very affable with all his captains

315

and soldiers, especially those who accompanied him in his first expedition from Cuba. He was a Latinist, and as I have been told, a bachelor in laws. He was also something of a poet, and a very good rhetorician. . . . He was very patient under insults or injuries. . . . He was very determined and headstrong in all business of war, not attending to any remonstrances on account of danger. . . . Where he had to erect a fortress, Cortes was the hardest labourer in the trenches; when we were going into battle, he was as forward as any.

". . . In military service he practiced the most strict attention to discipline, constantly going the rounds in person during the night, visiting the quarters of the soldiers, and severely reprehending those whom he found without their armour and appointments. . . . In his early life he was very liberal, but grew close, latterly; some of his servants complaining that he did not pay them as he ought, and I have also to observe that in his latter undertakings he never succeeded. Perhaps such was the will of heaven, his reward being reserved for another place; for he was a good cavalier, and very devout to the Holy Virgin. . . . God pardon him his sins; and me mine; and give me a good end which is better than all conquests and victories over Indians."

Next on the program in the subjugation of the Indians of Middle America was the conquest of Guatemala. This enterprise fell to the ablest and most spectacular of Cortéz's captains, Pedro de Alvarado. He was the right hand man of Cortéz during all the Aztec campaigns, and if he had personal ambition to shine as a conqueror in Mexico, it does not appear throughout his part in that great enterprise. Always he appears as the loyal soldier supporter and protector of his chief. When the time came for the conquest of

Guatemala it was inevitable that Alvarado should be chosen to head that expedition. It was not quite the blind undertaking that the Spaniards had entered upon in 1519, for by this time a good deal was known concerning Central America and its inhabitants. But it required the invasion of a still rougher country and the conquest of a more capable enemy.

As noted heretofore, the highlands of Guatemala, including the present Honduras, produced and maintained a population of the highest quality known in the Indian race. The environmental conditions were unequaled for the development of both physical and cultural pre-eminence. In their splendid isolation, the Maya-Quiché and their relatives the Cakchiquels and Zutuhils had matured a culture that had contributed vastly to that of the Maya, which, in the fertile and temporarily favorable low country of the Motagua and Usamacinta Valleys and of Yucatan, had reached the zenith of cultural evolution in the Indian race.

Alvarado's task was the destruction of two great strongholds heretofore described, namely Utatlan of the Quiché, and Iximche of the Cakchiquel. The conflict over these strongholds rivaled that of the battles around Tenochtitlan. The story is best told in the reports of Alvarado to Cortéz to whom he still rendered a soldier's loyalty, though he had now stepped into the position of a *conquistador* in his own right. There was much repetition of the experience in Mexico. The invasion was preceded by predictions of calamity on the part of native priests: there would come, speedily, an enemy that would be invincible and cruel beyond description. Utatlan would be completely destroyed and the glory of the Quiché would pass in a terrific whirlwind of destruction. Furthermore, as in Mexico, local discord between tribes and chiefs would play a decisive part. Quiché and Cakchiquel had been bitter enemies during the years preceding the invasion. It was easy to play them off, one against the other, and this Alvarado had learned from his old leader. It was a shorter campaign than that of Mexico, partly because of the more brilliant leadership of Alvarado, and party because of the even more acute enmity between the native tribes.

In describing the capture of Utatlan, Alvarado tells how the hospitality of the city was extended to them, the Indians "thinking that they would lodge me there and that when thus encamped they would set fire to the town some night and burn us all in it without the possibility of resistance. And in truth their evil plan would have come to pass but that God our lord did not see good that these infidels should be victorious over us, for this city is very strong and there are only two ways of entering it." He relates how they politely retired from the city, concealing his plans through presents and protestations of friendship, until he could, by fire and sword, bring these people to the service of His Majesty, the King of Spain. The upshot of this strategy was that, instead of being burned in the Indian town, he successfully carried out the capture and burning of the principal chiefs. To shorten the story, what by strategy and what by the usual brilliant attack of the Spaniards, the subjugation of Guatemala was soon accomplished. Alvarado proceeded to make his conquest permanent by the founding of his capital, first near Iximche, the present town of Tecpan, but later, because of the bitter cold of that plateau, in the beautiful vale of Almalonga at the foot of the extinct Volcan de Agua. But Alvarado was not cut out to be the administrator of a civil state. Although he gained the title of Captain General

and *Adelantado,* he soon turned over the administration
of the capital to his brother Jorge, and was off on further expeditions of conquest. Of all the soldiers who
gained renown in the New World, during this period
of adventure, Alvarado was the most restless. It would
seem that the urge to die with his boots on possessed
him from the beginning to the end of his career. He
burned to share in the spoils of Peru, of which lurid
stories were flying up and down the continent, and did
not rest until he had invaded the domain of Pizarro and
actually won a share, though as it turned out a not very
important one, in the loot that Pizarro was wresting
from the Incas. His dream of an expedition to the
Spice Islands occupied his turbulent mind for some
time, but was never consummated.

It was only a side issue that led him back to Mexico,
not to the old battle ground of the Valley of Anahuac,
but to assist in an invasion of Jalisco to the northwest.
It was in this Quixotic enterprise that the meteoric
career of Alvarado came to an end. He was accident-
ally killed, in the latter part of June, 1541, by the fall
of a horse, not his own, upon him on a rocky, mountain
trail, in the course of one of his most savage battles with
the Indians. His remains rest, almost certainly, under
the pavement, probably below the high altar, of that
most beautiful ruin in America, the cathedral in Guatemala Antigua, destroyed by the great earthquake of
1773.

Alvarado was the most brilliant of a numerous family of soldiers. His brother, Hernando, was a favorite
captain in the army of Coronado in his far-flung expedition to the banks of the Rio Grande, in what is now
New Mexico. Hernando possessed some of the qualities, at least, of his more illustrious brother, among

319

them being an impetuosity that sometimes made trouble for his commander. Jorge Alvarado was the brother left in command as governor of Guatemala City, while Pedro pursued his campaigns in distant lands. Other Alvarados mentioned were Juan, Gomez, Gonzalo, Diego, all soldiers bearing some responsibilities in the Conquest. But all were pretty completely overshadowed by the Captain General and *Adelantado*.

Pedro Alvarado, *"Tonatiuh*—the Child of the Sun," so named by the Aztecs, was the typical *conquistador* of romance. His Indian name reflects the impression that he made upon the simple "red" folk in the days of their first naïve superstitions concerning the Spaniards. He was physically the ideal Spanish cavalier, and there can be no doubt that in courageous deeds he earned his reputation. His superhuman "leap" may be apocryphal; however, I can swallow even that story. A steel-muscled soldier, only a jump or two ahead of a furious rush of Indian spears would have been capable of a quite unbelievable athletic feat. In the circumstances, I concede that Alvarado may have done a pole vault across that bloody chasm on the Tlacopan causeway, the like of which has never been seen in the Olympic games.

Alvarado, as a character in history, will never have an assured place. Described by many historians as utterly brutal, unscrupulous, heartless in his treatment of the Indians, his name will always be anathema to those who see him through the eyes of his detractors. On the other hand, to his admirers, he will always be the paragon of chivalry, or a demigod, at the very least another Bayard "without fear and without reproach." It is safe to accept again in these matters of bitter contention the dictum of Immanuel Kant, "Between the extremes we usually find the truth." Alvarado was the right hand of Cortéz in the conquest of Mexico, and was unswerving in his loyalty. He was more impetuous than his chief, lacked the poise of Cortéz, and was probably less humane. He was the favorite among the captains and probably deserved to be. Beside the personal qualities which endeared him to his leader, he was the unrivaled soldier of the Conquest. He never lost the affection of the great Captain General, however much he might get him into trouble. He is pictured by his detractors as overweeningly ambitious. This may be true, but all the more credit to him that his reputation as a loyal subordinate remained untarnished.

Alongside this, everyone should place the estimate of the historian, Bancroft: "First there was the fiery and impetuous Pedro de Alvarado, hero of the Achilles or Sir Lancelot school, strong and symmetrical as a goddess-born; haughty, choleric, sometimes staunch and generous, passionate in his loves and hates, with the mixtures of license, loyalty and zeal for the church. He had not eyes to see from where he stood in the warfare of his day, at once the decline of the fiercer barbarism and the dawn of a truer and gentler heroism. Already we have discovered flashes of temper and tendencies to treachery that display his character by too sulphurous a flame; but we shall find in him much to admire as a conquistador and governor." This probably touches upon about every quality, good and bad, possessed by this most dramatic figure in Spanish-American history.

The subjugation of the Indians of Mexico and Central America was the work of Cortéz and Alvarado with their numerically insignificant armies. Their part was simply that of soldiers in a most daring undertaking, and it must be said that as soldiers their part was carried out. They are not to be held responsible for what followed the Conquest. The real tragedy of the race is to be laid at the door of those who took over the business of exploiting the Indian through the succeeding years. In this sorry chapter of history, one need not attempt to find wherein lay the greatest blame. The military, the ecclesiastics, the *hacendados,* all had their part in the destruction of the native American cultures. To arrive at a just judgment concerning what befell the hapless Indians of Middle America, during the sixteenth and seventeenth centuries, one must sift an interminable mass of evidence. Since what we have generally been taught came through Spanish sources, it seems only fair to present the Indian side of the picture through their most valiant friend. This was the Dominican priest, Father Bartolome de Las Casas. "Father of the Indians," he was called, a title which he earned through more than a half-century of incessant combat. It meant nothing to Las Casas whether he struck at fellow priests or military leaders, or governors of provinces, or officials of highest rank in the home government, he was out to protect the under dog. We may concede that he became too vehement in his procedure, that he exaggerated greatly in describing the atrocities that he witnessed, but we must also agree that he saw enough with his own eyes to warrant almost any conceivable line of attack. It may be doubted if in all history a wronged people ever had a more effective champion. Whatever may have been his faults of exaggeration, one can feel only admiration for a valiant soul who, from the days of young manhood to the age of ninety-three years, never relaxed in his denunciation of the evils that he saw, never lowered his arm in the attack upon authority that was destroying the defenseless. He had no means of taking a census of the Indians slaughtered or starved or burned, but he could bring eminent corroboration in asserting that the Indian population of Cuba was destroyed to the last individual by massacre and famine. He could testify from personal knowledge, and with at least some eyewitness support, to the heartless burning of *caciques* at the stake, to barbaric executions that imagination is hardly capable of grasping. To his everlasting credit be it said that he never minced matters in his revelations concerning the acts of those in high places. In his idealization of such characters as the Inca, Atahualpa, he had the example of one of the most courageous souls in all history, to set over against the unparalleled savagery of Francisco Pizarro, extorting the maximum ransom that he could obtain, then burning his prisoner at the stake for not being favorably disposed toward the Christian faith.

Las Casas was right in his thesis that the Indians of the tropics, especially of the Antilles, were physically incapable of the heavy labor imposed upon them by the planters. The introduction of negro slavery to the New World, for which Las Casas has been blamed, was an expedient, at least in part justifiable, to which he resorted in the hope of saving his Indians from extinction. It was certainly true, and is true to this day, that the negro race carry easily the heavy work that civilization brought to the tropics, to which the Indians are totally inadequate. Those who can see in Las Casas only the emotional bigot, must at least concede to him the qualities of dauntless courage and of intellectual acumen which enabled him to meet and put to rout, year after year and decade after decade, the forces marshaled against him by his enemies. Here again is one of those characters whose place in history can never be satisfactorily adjusted. The strategy of "smear" is not a recent device of American politics. It is an old game, worked with considerable success by the detractors of Columbus, of Cortéz, Cuauhtémoc, Alvarado, and of Las Casas. Unfortunately, the "smearing" of great characters does not end with their lives. There is still an incredible bitterness manifested by historians in the "smearing" of these great figures in early American history. Las Casas had more than his share of it and, unhappily, it is still going on. But out of it all, certain undeniable facts emerge. He was more than an emotional enthusiast in a great cause. He was an intellectual giant. His five-day debate with the historian, Sepulveda, before the council in Valladolid, ranks in cold logic with the plea of Burke in the trial of Warren Hastings. His *Account of the Destruction of the Indies*, presented to the emperor in 1542, printed in Spain in 1552, was a devastating revelation of massacres and cruelty of every sort, which brought upon Las Casas a storm of accusations and insults, but which, because of the impression made by it upon the King, got substantial results.

Nevertheless, the Europeans (not the Spaniards only) left little undone during the decades following the discovery, to bring to a tragic conclusion the cultural evolution of the native American race.

III. Modern Life in Mexico and Central America

Every reader will want to know something of the present state of the land that witnessed such a splendid cultural evolution for a thousand years or more, and which was overtaken by such a tragic fate. A brief account of the modern Indian life in that ancient land will be in order. Some account of the Otomi, Aztec, Tarascan, Zapotec-Mixtec, and Maya-Quiché, of today will serve the purpose.

The populations of Mexico and Central America are still predominately Indian. Gamio found, in his census of the Valley of Teotihuacan, published in 1922, that racially the population numbered about two-thirds Indian, the remaining one-third being largely mestizo; this in a valley that has since the Conquest been in close contact with the capital city. Outside of the large modern cities of Mexico and Central America the pure white population is negligible.

1. The Otomi

The Otomi are a numerous people scattered over the states of Queretaro, Guanajuato, San Luis Potosi, Michoacan, Mexico, Tlaxcala, Puebla, and Vera Cruz. They are thought by some ethnologists to be among the most ancient of tribes in Mexico, and there is much to support this view. I am disposed to regard the Otomi as an ancient mother-culture out of whose virile, barbaric communities bands flowed to the Valley of Mexico, and perhaps to the lands farther south. Their culture is still primarily agricultural, poor in esthetic products. They are conservative, not of the highest order of intelligence among the tribes of Mexico. They produce and consume much *pulque,* and raise a fair supply of corn for their own use. Their arts and crafts are mainly those necessary for their own domestic use, though in their markets and at the railway stations some native products of fair quality can be bought.

2. *The Aztecs*

The Aztecs still occupy the Valley of Mexico, the ancient Anahuac, and overflow into the adjacent states. They are naturally the most mixed in blood and. most acculturated of all Mexican Indian breeds. The purest Aztec culture, including language, is found in the state of Morelos, notably in such villages as Tepoztlan and Yautepec, where the pure pre-Conquest Nahuatl speech is still habitually used.

The modern Aztecs are an industrious people, frightfully poor in some localities, such as the Valley of Teotihuacan, where only a small number of the population have land of their own. Gamio, in his *Population of the Valley of Teotihuacan,* 1922, pointed out that in this area, with a population of 8,330, ninety per cent of the acreage belonged to seven large property owners, the remaining ten per cent to 416 small owners. This left 7,914 totally landless people, the result being that the great majority were on the lowest possible subsistence level, both as to food and housing. He describes a time, 1912 and 1915, when, owing to the failure of rain, the people subsisted on a little corn mixed with the woody shavings of the maguey plant. Mortality from influenza reached twenty-five per cent of the population in some villages. It is sincerely hoped that the Mexican Government has been able to remedy this desperate situation, a condition which was not confined to this one valley.

The Aztecs in some communities add substantially to their living by the practice of their native arts and crafts, especially the weaving of *sarapes,* the making of pottery, and the manufacture of "antiquities" for the tourist trade. Their gardens near the City of Mexico especially Xochimilco, Chalco, and other lagoon villages, display a competence in agriculture comparable with that of the olden times, the archaic methods being little changed.

Closely related to the Aztecs in language and culture, the Tlaxcalans of the state of that name, are a superior type of Indian, physically and intellectually. They still have the habit of building small villages clustered about larger towns, as in the ancient times. They are good farmers and industrious in the practice of their native arts and crafts, pottery making, weaving, and some wood carving. They were never friendly to their relatives, the Aztecs, in fact, contributed largely to their downfall by joining with Cortéz against them, as we have seen.

3. *The Tarascans*

Little modified by modern contacts, the Tarascan people inhabiting the mountainous region of Michoacan, extending south beyond the Balsas River and north into Jalisco, are characteristically a lake and forest people. Their most flourishing settlements are about the Lakes Chapala and Patzcuaro. Their linguistic relationships are not fully established. Somatologically they are quite distinct. They are conservative, reserved with strangers, but once acquainted are hospitable, genial, with a keen sense of humor. They are agricultural, but derive also a good supply of food from the lakes. Their arts and crafts are not numerous, but in the making of platters of beaten and carved wood, decorated with lacquer work, which seems to have been indigenous, they have a unique art. They have preserved well their independence, both in government and culture.

The Tarascans are seen to best advantage on and about Lake Patzcuaro. They are extremely primitive in many villages; shy, gentle people, dependable within the range of their abilities. Your guides among them can safely feed you off the country, while exploring their own range. They may serve up to you for dinner a small monkey in an attractive stew, under pretense that it is a squirrel, not "with intent to deceive," but simply that the *patron* must not be allowed to go hungry, and they have discovered that some white men have an unaccountable prejudice against eating one of their favorite articles of food. True, a young monkey served whole in a stew, on one of their wooden platters, does suggest cannibalism; I never could get used to it. They know every footpath in their own forests, but will not go far from home. It is on the water that their special abilities are manifested. In their flat-bottomed boats, "dugouts" made from a single tree, they negotiate the lakes in expert fashion, and so accurate is their knowledge of their waters that you may depend upon your Tarascan boatman never to set out across the lake with you if there is danger of squalls coming up. It is sometimes difficult to understand why your boatman, in the early morning, refuses to put off with you to the islands or farther side. By ten o'clock, you know. In the middle of Lake Chapala or Patzcuaro, is no place to be in a flat-bottomed dugout in a high wind.

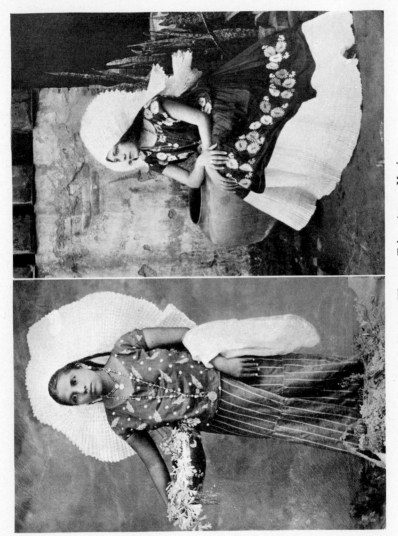

Tehuana Indian Women, Tehuantepec, Mexico

Zapotec Dancers—Note Similarity to the Great Headdresses of Quirigua Statues

The above description applies to the primitive communities of Tarascans who are still living the life of centuries ago. Many have risen to the level of the best citizenship of Mexico in recent times, the result of favorable cross-breeding. Some of modern Mexico's foremost scholars and statesmen have been justly proud of their Tarascan blood. The state of Michoacan is well represented in the roster of strong men of Mexico. The Tarascan stock has made a worthy contribution to the life of modern Mexico.

In the little chapel at Tsintsuntsan, on the shore of Lake Patzcuaro, is the priceless *Entombment* of Titian, presented to the Tarascans by the Emperor of Spain, in recognition of their loyalty. No money consideration can get it away from them. They have had what must seem to them fabulous offers. A woman caretaker sits before it, knitting or embroidering, whenever the chapel is open.

4. *The Zapotec-Mixtecs*

The Zapotecs and Mixtecs, as before stated, may be treated as one stock. They occupy the state of Oaxaca and portions of Puebla and Guerrero. Southern Mexico is one of the most fertile sections of the republic. It is seldom that the Indians there are without fair crops of corn, wheat, and oats, though I have been in places, particularly on the barren Pacific coast strip that lies within their territory, where food was so extremely scarce that I was reduced to a diet of turtles' eggs, dug out of the sand for me by Indian children. Likewise, in a section of the hill country, east of Oaxaca, I counted myself lucky when I could get the shy bush people to produce one or two *tortillas*. Not only was there real scarcity of food, but there was great difficulty in finding anyone at home. Men, women, and children took to the bush like rabbits on the approach of a white person, and it required much coaxing by a Mixtec guide to get a few old people back to the huts.

But on the whole the Zapotecs and Mixtecs are among the best Indians of Mexico. They are physically superior to the Aztecs at the present time, probably not so degenerated as a result of the Conquest. Intellectually, they are also above the ordinary. A stock that could produce a Benito Juarez, the George Washington of the Indian race, and a Porfirio Diaz, the strong man of modern Mexico, has something to be proud of. I look for this stock to take an important place in the making of modern Mexico.

These people still practice some of their primitive arts with great success. They are among the best weavers of Mexico. Their fine *sarapes,* always recognized by their unique designs, abound in the markets, museums, and private collections of the United States, as well as in their native land. They weave many useful articles such as hammocks, carrying baskets, etc., out of the abundant native fiber. The art of pottery making survives, but in this they are not pre-eminent.

The most interesting branch of the Zapotec stock is the Tehuana of the Isthmus. The women of Tehuantepec are famous for their natural beauty, faultless complexion, Juno-like figures, and unique costumes. They are larger than the men, more energetic, more intelligent. The costume that makes them so conspicuous, wherever seen, consists of a skirt, usually of velvet, often embroidered, a broad white band around the bottom; a waist as brilliant as the velvet jacket of a Navaho, and, most spectacular of all, a combination of headdress

and cape. It is snowy white, always clean and starched.
The cape-like part of it, sometimes of lace, may be
worn over the shoulders, falling to the waist, with the
upper part serving as a collar; again, the cape, stiffly
starched, may be worn as a headdress, framing the face.
The photographs show the different methods of wearing it. The sight of a bevy of fifty Tehuantepec women
so arrayed, moving in their dignified way down the
street to market or to church will not be forgotten. A
more picturesque costume is not to be seen among the
peasants of Switzerland, the Balkan countries, or in
Oriental lands. They are rarely seen farther from home
than the port of Salina Cruz, occasionally in the market
at Oaxaca. I know of no other people who make such
constant use of the water. They literally live in the
tropical rivers. I have noticed among the Zapotecs
many vestiges of ancient religious practices. Evidently,
much could be recovered by patient work among them
that would throw light upon the ancient culture.

5. The Modern Maya

The present inhabitants of this ancient land, extending from Tabasco and Chiapas in Mexico to British
Honduras, could hardly be credited with such a virile
ancestry as that indicated by the ancient ruins that have
been heretofore described. With the exception of the
warlike Sublevados of the eastern coast of Yucatan,
they are a docile, peace-loving people, living for the
most part in the bush, and showing no inclination toward the practice of the arts, such as architecture and
sculpture, in which their ancestors excelled. If they
have any knowledge of a calendrical system they keep
it to themselves. There is little to indicate any deep-

seated religion other than a mixture of the more sordid superstitions of the past with such elements of Christianity as they can, in a limited way, appreciate.

The old arts and industries are practiced very much as in pre-Conquest times, though with some modern improvements, especially in Yucatan. Here there grew up a great industry, that of the cultivation of the native *sisal* plant for the manufacture of hemp so extensively used in the harvest fields of the United States. This industry for many years enriched the *hacendados* of Yucatan, and gave labor and wages to many natives. After the breaking of the Mexican Revolution, it waned to a small fraction of its former output.

There is considerable weaving of articles for domestic use, pottery making is not extensively practiced, and the art of wood carving, once so skillfully practiced in certain centers, has declined to mediocre level.

Family life is on a low plane, except as in such favored localities as northern Yucatan, and the health of the people of the lowlands is lamentably poor. We found our Indians of the Motagua Valley to be excellent *machete* men, within the limits of their strength, but they were of little service when it came to chopping. For work of that character it is necessary to use the Caribs of the coast and highlands.

There is nothing picturesque in the costume of the modern Maya, save in a few favored towns where the women may practice embroidery in colors to some extent. The jungle still abounds in the indigenous plants, and the Indian families supplement their principal crop, the corn, with the growing of yams, *papayas,* breadfruit, *aguacates,* squashes, and beans. They secure game and fish in limited quantities, and eggs are a staple product.

332

On the whole, the modern Maya impress one as being at best a backwash from the more favored people of the highlands. The most reasonable supposition is that they are the least fit, the left-behind descendants of the old inhabitants, those who were too much reduced by disease and adversity to muster the necessary strength and ambition for an exodus into the highlands. The population is nowhere dense, the villages are small with many families scattered about in isolated places. One would like to hope that the old virility and ambition that carried the ancient Maya to such astonishing cultural levels could be revived, but for this quite numerous branch of the Indian race in Central America I can foresee only further decline.

6. Quiché and Cakchiquel

It is in the highlands of Guatemala that we see Central American Indian life in something very near the pre-Conquest state. Nowhere else in Middle America is to be found such unadulterated material culture; such perfectly preserved esthetic activities; such clear vestiges of the ancient religious life.

It would be difficult to conceive of a more favored country for the maintenance of indigenous culture at its best. The climate is ideal, the high altitude offsetting all enervating tropical effect, resulting in conditions almost as favorable as those of the temperate zones. Most of the staple food plants are indigenous, and when they are lacking are attainable at near-by lower altitudes. In natural healthfulness the country is unsurpassed.

The strong Quiché and Cakchiquel tribes were never so immersed in subversive religious practices as were the Aztecs. The strongholds, Utatlan and Iximche, had their temples to be sure, but there was nothing that would have absorbed the energies of the people for generations in building, nor exhausted them in the fanatical practices connected therewith. In place of constant performances of calendrical ceremonies there were, and are, seasonal dramatic performances at proper intervals, much as among the Pueblos. Agriculture receives its needed attention. Material culture is kept at a high level of production through the frequent market days, in many places two a week. These markets have far more than an economic significance in Indian life. They serve the place of school, social center, news distribution. On great market occasions, thousands congregate and spread out their wares. They like to sell their stuff, but seem never unhappy or disappointed when they have to pack it up and carry it back home, or, in the case of their livestock, drive or lead it. Here they match wits in trade, calculation, judgment of quality of products and fabrics. Here they visit, swap yarns, play games, gamble, tell stories, listen to the admonitions of the "medicine men," burn their incense and go to prayers. It is the "County Fair" of the aborigines. It affords opportunity for travel and for picking up ideas from foreign parts. It is the great effective agency for the preservation of culture.

In the making of fine fabrics, the Quiché and Cakchiquel hold the top place. Only the ancient Peruvians approach them in fineness of weave, durability, color, and design. What the ancient Guatemaltecans could do in this line we do not know, for fabrics are not preserved when buried in that wet country, as in Peru. But there is no discounting their present work. They display in their textiles an artistic sense not at present matched in America, and hardly surpassed in Oriental lands.

These are simple folk, happy in the kind of life that their ancestors found good. May they never be disturbed in it. How wise the Christian priest who simply holds before their eyes the symbols of a great new faith, but protects their right to keep the venerated ways of old. I am thinking of Father Rossbach at Chichicastenango, for forty years a devout soldier of the cross in a remote land, and at the same time a valiant defender of the human right to remain human. It is safe to predict that in the highland communities of Guatemala, that republic will always have an industrious, contented, dependable citizenry.

IV.   A RACE'S FUTURE

THE Indian race in Middle America has in its favor
a cultural tradition that should insure to it a permanent
place among the peoples of the world. Its non-mechanical character is in its favor, for it is thereby spared a
problem in adjustment that is the despair of European
civilization. The "machine age" has brought a desperate time to European peoples, has, on the face of it, deprived the masses of mankind of just that which made
men and women. When they all shaped their own fist-
hammers, their own flint blades; their own shelter, when
by their wits they procured their food and clothing;
when they withstood the very elements in the fight for
survival, they had a part in creation. Not "every man
a king" (last word in demagogic drivel) but *Every
Man a Man* was the idea that made for the manhood
of humanity. Bear in mind that while no other creature
on this planet can do anything one whit better than his
remotest ancestor did, man, as long as he had a
chance, added steadily to his creative ability from age
to age.

If we let the anthropologist have his way and give
man a million years or so for the evolution of his culture, it may seem to have been a pretty tedious business,
but think of the clammy cave at the beginning of the
road and "hundred gated Thebes" or hundred storied
Empire State building at the other end! Call it "progress" or "creation" as you like. Then think of the mud-
dauber's nest in the cave man's cave and the same
creature's nest under the eve of your house! Reason
permits of only one conclusion: humankind is a sharer
in creative power and no other being is.

336

Going back to the idea of man and machine, or man and anything else that deprives him of responsibility and toil: it is difficult to see how he is going to hold his own. Functioning is the only thing I know of that will keep an organ, or man, normal. Relieve him of walking, working, striving, planning; supply his wants regardless of his own efforts or initiative; guarantee his security with government dole or old-age pension, or other incentive to idleness or thriftlessness, and you have man on the way to the level of the mud-dauber. But the advocates of the millennium of leisure hasten to explain how man is going to use that leisure in pursuit of the more abundant life. Perhaps he will; but a good many years spent in the study of humanity has not disclosed to me any benefits that have ever accrued to the human species through leisure that are in any way comparable to those attained through hard, incessant work. Cessation of function in man points to imminent senility. He functions best under the spur of necessity. Not more leisure but more work is my prayer for humanity.

So these calm unhurried Indians that have been able to survive the blasting of European conquest through inherent, cultural resistance, going serenely on with the creation of their lovely fabrics, utensils, ornaments; exercising their fingers and brains and resisting the machine that promises quantity production and leisure, may yet have a notable part to play in the civilization of America. At any rate they are not dropping dead with heart failure nor congesting sanatoriums with psychopathic wreckage, nor demanding of society dole or bonus or security. The resourcefulness of the race that is still able to wrest subsistence from scarcity, to woo happiness in creating beauty out of raw elements, to hold esthetic above animal satisfaction, is something of which the western world is in dire need. The white man seems to have lost confidence in himself and in his kind. The widespread hysteria of the present time is, at bottom, a panic of uncertainty about three or four square meals a day. The Indian calmly takes up the slack of his stomach with a belt woven with his own hands. The making of lovely things makes life worth living, regardless. He likes to eat but that isn't the chief end of life. He is capable of happiness though hungry. The fear of a pinch in his pocketbook or in his stomach throws the white man into a depression. The Indian, down to his last meal, goes to sleep in serene confidence in himself and the beneficence of nature. White men, down to their last automobile, are prone to begin to think about embezzlement, or larceny with violence, or, as a last resort, self-destruction.

The Indian has much to his discredit, it is true, but he isn't a cry-baby. There is every reason to think that the Indian blood and brain cells and protoplasm can be vastly beneficial in the world. The resourcefulness of the race that gave to America Cuauhtémoc, Atahualpa, Nezahualcóyotl, Benito Juarez, Porfirio Diaz, Tecumseh, Geronimo, and Sitting Bull, grades well against the inability of present-day white peoples to get themselves out of a tight place. Low material culture is not all disadvantageous. Ability of nations to blast one another off the earth, and that's what material culture has arrived at, does not make for survival, and, after all, survival is the first consideration of humanity.

The spiritual culture of the Indian race is strongly in its favor. In this I include its esthetics, religion, and morality; in the great culture centers—the Southwest, Aztec Mexico, Central America, Peru—the practice of sculpture, painting, architecture, drama of religious ceremonials, mythic rites, virtually every form of creative art, constituted the life of the people. Providing for the physical wants of life was accomplished through ritual. The making of war and the preservation of peace were effected through symbolic ceremony. It is no exaggeration to say that, among the higher cultures of America, life was spiritualized to a degree not attained by any other race.

But many are saying that this sort of culture is the most vulnerable of all; that it cannot withstand the onslaught of force; that armed barbarism (or civilization) tramples it down, and that survival, the first consideration of humanity, is therefore impossible. Let us not be too sure. May it not be that this is exactly what has enabled the Indian race to survive? Its physical subjugation complete, the race has marvelously retained its culture traits. The ancients produced no more beautiful pottery, painting, design, ceremonies, than do the Pueblo Indian artists of the Southwest, nor more lovely fabrics than those made in Mexico and Guatemala and Peru today. Through it all the race has not declined numerically. It may be that what has seemed to be its weakness in comparison with its conquerors is exactly what made for its survival. The deep, calm, spiritual life of the Indian race might conceivably be brought to influence the turbulent, destructive, hysterical tendencies of the white. It is possible that what appeared to be its destiny in its templed past may, in the long run, be achieved. At any rate, I have long since dropped the idea of "The Vanishing Race."

Working against the Indian, however, are factors that may prevail over his inherent cultural virility. The great white scourges, whisky, tuberculosis, influenza, venereal disease, have, from lack of the partial immunity that comes from long contact, been more deadly than have the white man's arms. In the United States the old spirit of independence and resourcefulness can hardly withstand the forces that constantly tend to destroy those traits. The Indian can never escape the fact that he is the ward of a well-meaning government, and, whether he is ruled by the stern hand of the War Department as in times past, or by the emotionalism of a present-day Indian Office that thinks it is preparing him for independence by spending ever-increasing millions in depriving him of his self-reliance, the result is the same. The inherent manhood of the Indian has been the admiration of all who had the intelligence to recognize it, and manhood is built in no other way than by self-help. That goes for white, black, or yellow as well as for red humanity.

So my final judgment as to the future of the Indian race is that, if given a chance, it may still realize a great place among the peoples of the world; that the destructive forces working against it *may* prevail, to the world's great loss, but that, at any rate, the Indian may rest "secure that the future will be worthy of the past." My hope is that America may have in store for the now dominant race some of the beneficent gifts with which it endowed its aboriginal children—traits that I devoutly hope may not perish from our spacious land. As to the color of those in whom these traits are enshrined, I am not concerned. As to the countries that will have the honor, and the good fortune, fully to utilize the gifts of the Indian race in forging the national character and life, I am of the opinion that we must look to the south of the Rio Grande.

To rebuild a shattered culture is the problem of every

country in Middle America. It certainly is paramount in Mexico, Guatemala, Honduras, Ecuador, Peru, and Bolivia. In such countries as Chile and Argentina there is no longer any Indian problem, that element in the population having been "liquidated" long ago; but there is one of race mixture.

The so called Latin-American countries are Indian countries by predominance of blood, and in several of those mentioned above, the numerical preponderance is from two-thirds to four-fifths Indian. The welfare of such a population is a racial problem in addition to being all other kinds of problems that peoples are to their governments, and government based on scientific ethnological principles does not exist.

Bearing in mind that the population of these Middle American countries are predominantly Indian—a race with a great culture history that has been wrecked by ruthless conquest—a race that normally is strangely inarticulate—and you have the problem of Middle American government. It calls for more wisdom than exists in any nation that I know anything about. An inarticulate minority means perennial unrest; an inarticulate majority is a smothered fire and means endemic rebellion—unless some new and wise system is devised. No ruling class ever seems to understand its subjects of another race. The psychological chasm between races and peoples is never bridged. It calls for profound ethnological knowledge, which politicians do not have, and sympathetic interest which does not get far unless possessed by those in authority.

These populations had unknown centuries for their own autochthonous growth, three centuries of tutelage under the European mother, and have had one century of independent, nominally democratic government.

With high admiration for the great characters in Middle American history, Juarez, Bolívar, San Martín, and sincere personal regard for the statesmen, scholars, thinkers of my own time and acquaintance who have given their best for Hispanic-America, I must believe that the successful forging of a nation has not yet been achieved in any Middle American country. That our success in the United States of America has not been over brilliant I cheerfully concede, and when we think of the vast problem of Indian population with which they have contended, and the mess we have made with our small Indian affairs, we grow humble by comparison.

A fundamental mistake was made in laying the foundations of the modern Middle American countries. When they achieved their independence and did not quite know what to do about it, except that they did not want anything more to do with kings, they naturally looked about for models of republican government. This meant France and the United States of America. Their constitutions, then, were almost ready-made. A principle vital to democracy had to be overlooked, namely, that, when governments are instituted among men, they derive their just powers from the consent of the governed. "The governed," in this case, were mainly the millions of inarticulate Indians who naturally could not give their consent because of not knowing what to consent to. So it became government by a small ruling class, an imitation of democracy, and the nations were off to a century or two of revolutions and civil wars.

In the sincere endeavor to make democracy work, another major mistake has been made by some of the countries, notably Mexico, in allowing, even inviting, outsiders, mostly emotional North Americans, to take a hand in their affairs, even to the extent of asking their aid in writing new constitutions. No Middle American country was ever helped one iota by these officious foreigners who, ineffective at home, have been able to butt in south of the Rio Grande. In a quarter of a century of acquaintance with Mexico, the only persons encountered by me who knew anything worthwhile about Mexican population problems were Mexicans. Anyway, it is best to let people make their own muddle and work themselves out of their muddles. Going to Middle America, or to other foreign countries, with the sole purpose of learning from them, one is never disappointed—and the foreigners are not misguided. In fact, there is great mutual helpfulness in this. It is time we were discovering America and understanding our American neighbors; incidentally, giving them a chance to understand us. The psychology of our neighbors to the south is predominantly the old peace-loving disposition of ancient America, ready to meet confidence with confidence, respect with respect, good will with gifts that we find it hard to match. Is it not possible that in the spiritual unity that once pervaded the people of an entire continent there may be found the *American spirit* that is capable of binding the countries of the New World into an association of nations that will work?

AFTERWORD

LOOKING back over the writing of this volume and the years of preparation for it, I am impressed with the very small advance that has been made in a quarter of a century in knowledge of man in ancient America. It would be discouraging were it not that in the whole vast field of anthropology indisputable knowledge of man remains pathetically small, with little appreciable gain in many years. The subject invites theorizing. Joyce states the obvious truth where he says: "It is sad to note how large a proportion of the literature dealing with American archæology serves only as a monument to wasted energy and misplaced zeal." However, the study has not been fruitless, though there has been much digging in barren soil and too much play of imagination in lieu of real work. By critical study of documentary sources, excavation and interpretation of ruins by exacting methods, and study of culture traits of the people who are still living the old community life in or near the old places, we are gradually restoring the picture. We have three roads by which to approach the subject, history, archæology, ethnology. Checking one against the other, having the testimony of each with which to square, to verify, supplement or disprove, we are at last arriving at a stronger position from which to study ancient life in America.

The question of the antiquity of man in America is where it was in the days of the "Trenton Gravels" and "Calaveras Skull" controversies. The additions are an equally nebulous lot of "finds" of more or less fossilized fragments of man and of vaguely related cultural objects. Kansas, Nebraska, New Mexico, Nevada, California, Minnesota, Florida, Mexico, Argentina, all have made their contributions of evidence that has had front page in science with enthusiastic adherents for a time, passing soon into doubtful category, and then dropping out entirely. It must be admitted that at the present time no "evidence" of Quaternary or earlier man in America is out of the controversial realm.

On the subject of the origin of the native American peoples, libraries have been filled with books. Writers, in sober earnest, but with scant reason, have derived them from the Egyptians, Phœnicians, Hebrews, Hindus, Mongols, Polynesians. Some would give them a multiple origin, finding in them contributions from about all the continents and races. The question remains where it has been for many years, with indications that the purely fantastic ideas about it are slowly losing ground. There is reason to hope that somatic, linguistic, and cultural data, acquired by methods that meet the requirements of science, correlated with facts of human geography that are being established, will eventually account for early population movements on the American continent. I should not expect the problem of the origin of the Indian race ever to be solved. It has not been for any race.

The study of the cultural life of ancient America has been fairly satisfactory though there have been few new contributions to the racial history in a quarter of a century. More ruins have been uncovered, more cultural material has been retrieved for museums and laboratory purposes. This has widened our view of what the race accomplished when it had a chance, and should increase our respect for it. There have never been any "epoch making discoveries" in American archæology, but there is, I believe, a growing appreciation of the Indian's kind of culture. If so, then there is a growing appreciation of fine esthetic achievement, of high morality, of steadfast spiritual poise, for those are attributes of the Indian race. More than forty years ago, Adolph Bandelier said, "The valuable discoveries that the mode of life of the American aborigines was primitively framed after one sociological principle on the whole American continent, and that consequently the culture of the American Indian has varied locally only in *degree,* not in *kind;* that the religious principles were fundamentally the same among the Sioux and the Brazilians, and that physical causes more than anything else have lain at the bottom of local differences in culture, have not until lately been recognized as *facts.*" The most convincing subsequent studies of the race have served to confirm that declaration, to an extent that places it beyond dispute. The Indian's *kind* of culture being what it is, its continent-wide unification is of utmost consequence to humanity.

It is an especial pleasure to affirm that in long study of ancient life in the American Southwest, and in Middle America, I have found no reason to dissent from Bandelier's generalization. No single fact concerning any race has been more firmly established than that of *unity* in the American. That the racial life and character became unified along such exalted lines is something for every Indian to be proud of and strive to uphold. That America has been capable of implanting such traits in the human species should be to every American, aboriginal or intrusive, a matter of pride and hope.

My own picture of ancient life in America—the great Southwest, Mexico, Guatemala, Peru—is fairly clear. That I have been able to make it somewhat clear to others is an earnest hope. It has become fully integrated in my own mind. Pueblo, Aztec, Maya, Inca, with all the related peoples, contemporary and antecedent, are one. Was one of these, perhaps the ancient Pueblo, a great mother-culture, from which all derived? *Sabe Dios.* There are countless questions to be asked, few that will be answered, about these amazing people. Of this I am certain, that of the races of men brought forth by this earth, none has lived to higher purpose, none has carried the torch of existence more valorously, none has more undauntedly "lived the heroic life." Looking back over the long road it has traveled; gathering up the fragments of the beauty it has created and weaving them into the fabric of modern life; contemplating the spiritual heights to which it rose and the depths into which it was cast and the smoldering spirit that still occasionally flames out, one must say to the Indian race, "No matter how often defeated, you are born to victory."

THE END

INDEX

INDEX

INDEX

INDEX

INDEX